BRITISH CARAVANS
VOLUME 1
MAKES FOUNDED BEFORE WORLD WAR II

BRITISH CARAVANS
VOLUME 1
MAKES FOUNDED BEFORE WORLD WAR

By Roger Ellesmere

Herridge & Sons
In association with The Caravan Club

Published in 2012 by
Herridge & Sons Ltd
Lower Forda, Shebbear
Devon EX21 5SY

Design by Ray Leaning, MUSE Fine Art & Design

ISBN 978-1-906133-46-7
Printed in Singapore

Acknowledgments
Particular thanks are due to Angela Cox, Caravan Club Collection Curator at
The National Motor Museum, Beaulieu, for making material from the Club
Archive available and for researching illustrations. The Caravan Club is thanked
for its support of and contribution to this publication.The author and the
publisher are also grateful to the Editors of *The Caravan* for providing illustra-
tions from the magazine's archive. The author expresses his appreciation of
Michael Ware's part in helping him find a publisher for this work.
Others who kindly gave permission for the reproduction of illustrations are
Bradley Doublelock Ltd, Carlight Trailers Ltd, CSC (Specialised Vehicles) Ltd,
Davan Caravans Ltd, Mr & Mrs Gardner, Getty Images, LAT Photographic,
Mortons Archive, Motoring Picture LIbrary, National Motor Museum Trust,
Rollalong Ltd, Swift Group.

The illustrations in this volume have been drawn from many sources, including
those listed above and the author's own collection. Others are of unknown or
uncertain origin, or are sales material or otherwise in the public domain. While
every effort has been made to identify sources, if anyone's copyright has been
breached in respect of any illustrations, or if no credit or incorrect credit has
been given, then both the author and the publisher apologise unreservedly and
undertake to correct errors and omissions upon these being brought to their
attention in any future editions.

CONTENTS

INTRODUCTION

A 1913 38hp Lanchester Landaulet with the 1914 trailer caravan built for his own use by Frederick Alcock. The production of trailer caravans for sale did not commence until 1919.

In the early years of the twenty-first century the building of British trailer caravans is primarily in the hands of relatively few manufacturers producing large numbers of vans. It was not always so – in *The History of the Caravan*, W M Whiteman, former editor of *The Caravan*, notes that in 1939 there were 92 known makers of trailer caravans with more than 100 others having gone out of business since 1919. These figures exclude makers building only showmen's vans or tent trailers. Outputs varied from about 300 a year down to six and it is doubtful if 20 makers were producing the 50 vans a year needed to qualify for membership of the Caravan Manufacturer's Association. Research for this book has turned up a number of makes which would not qualify for inclusion in

Whiteman's figures and some (e.g. Bowser and Weathershields) which are neither caravans nor tent trailers, but they have been included out of interest. In any case tent trailers are something of a grey area – Whiteman classes the Rice as a folding caravan although nowadays it would probably be regarded as a tent trailer. It has not been possible however to identify all of the near 200 makers suggested by the above figures and inevitably a number of the most obscure are long forgotten. After the Second World War the number of manufacturers increased dramatically, many of them ill-qualified and over-optimistic. Between 1948 and 1950 the number of self-styled caravan manufacturers known to *The Caravan* reached 400 although by 1955 this had reduced to about 120 plus 'backyard builders'. Even early in 1962 the Index of Prices in *Modern Caravan* still listed 82 makes.

Although an early motorist, Frederick Alcock, built a trailer caravan for his own use in 1914, the production of trailer caravans for sale did not commence until 1919. Several early makers started by building a caravan for their own use, and after loaning or hiring this built more vans for hire before progressing to building for sale. Because customers often preferred spending four or five guineas a week on hiring a van rather than £125 to £250 on buying, hiring was an important part of the business for early makers and as late as 1932 at least 14 manufacturers were still running hire fleets. The practice, before the Second World War, of selling new vans with full domestic equipment including china, cooking utensils and cutlery, probably had its origins in the necessity of providing these items for hire vans. Piggott Bros of Bishopsgate, London, were old-established makers of camping equipment who produced some innovative designs from 1920 and had far greater resources than the general run of new makers, but gave up the caravan business after about five years. Eccles, whose origins lay in a moribund haulage business, grew into a substantial concern far ahead of other manufacturers in industrial methods, factory organisation and national publicity. When most other makers, even those producing very good vans, such as

Car Cruiser, Raven and Winchester, were operating in unsuitable premises, the works into which Eccles moved at Stirchley, Birmingham, in 1927 were the first in the world purpose built for caravan manufacture. However even they devoted a substantial part of their production capacity to specials since the market was too small to ignore any sector of it for the sake of , and not until the late 1930s did Bill Riley, the Eccles boss, come to realise that having the largest and best organised factory in the industry logically led to producing popular price models in quantity – the National of 1939 being built in then unprecedented batches of 50.

Early makers and the first dealers spent a lot of time travelling around the country attracting attention by driving along popular streets, handing out leaflets, inviting inspection by the public and being harried by the police. There was widespread ignorance of what was being offered – they were sometimes thought to be advanced publicity men for a circus or to be selling some new kind of bathing hut.

The caravan industry has produced some colourful characters including W E C Knott, J C Beckett and P Escott North. Knott was a controversial figure who produced first Midland and then Bluebird caravans in large numbers, but for many years he remained firmly outside the organised industry and in conflict with it.

R McCombie Metcalfe towed the 8½cwt Stirling Ten up the 1 in 7 Sutton Bank with this 295cc Isetta bubblecar.

Beckett was associated with Jubilee, Eccles and the dealer A S Jenkinson before setting up the dealers Beckett's of Bromsgrove, and in the late 1940s/early 1950s conducted an advertising competition with Jenkinson based on mutual sniping. Beckett's advertising often featured a drawing of him wearing a halo and he attended the 1952 Caravan Club National Rally with a neon halo mounted on the roof of his caravan. Escott North of the dealers Midland Counties Caravan Co attended the 1947 National Rally in a 'Wild West outfit, guns and all'.

A dominant style of the 1920s was the square-ended lantern roof van with bowed sides, most often associated with Eccles although similar vans were produced by several makers. Whilst C Fleming-Williams, the founder of Car Cruiser, had championed streamlining from 1920, the style really came into fashion with the Winchester of 1930 and, with the addition of a lantern roof, was the accepted style for a connoisseur's van for the rest of the 1930s – even being continued by makers such as Avondale after the Second World War. There were numerous extending models including the ATC, Atlas Bishop, Bampton, Fairway, Fohlo and Shadow, as well as the Laycock single-wheel camping trailer and three-wheeled vans by Ensor, Spowart and Sunray. Various makers have produced trailers intended for towing by motorcycle combinations – the Rudge of 1927 was built by a motorcycle manufacturer, the Dinky and Penguin (Universal) of the 1950s were aimed at this market and the makers of the Bond Minicar three-wheeler introduced a trailer tent in 1962. The 7ft 6in Hutchings Tom Thumb of the late 1920s was aimed at owners of the small cars which were expanding the motoring community – the Jowett being a popular make with caravanners – and in the late 1940s Norris Bridgens tackled some formidable gradients towing a Thomson camping trailer with a two-cylinder Jowett Bradford van. In the 1950s R McCombie Metcalfe, a garage owner from Wensydel, towed an 8½cwt Stirling Ten up the 1 in 7 Sutton Bank with a 295cc Isetta bubblecar. The Austin 12/4 was a popular towing car in the mid-1930s and when David Thomson had wind tunnel tests carried out at the Royal Technical College, Glasgow, this was the chosen car in conjunction with various models of caravan bodies. In 1949 the secretary of Essex County Cricket Club towed his Eccles Active with a 1927 Rolls-Royce, and the owner of the Dinky Midi Special of 1960 towed his van with a Bentley. Whilst a number of dealers had makers build models specially for them, some, such as Harrington (Harco), moved to dealing after producing vans themselves and some makers, such as Burlingham, Pilot and Thomson, also dealt in the products of other makers.

In 1927 the police at Honiton, Devon, prosecuted a number of caravanners in connection with the use of overrun brakes, the legality of which was uncertain. Bill Riley drove down with one of his vans and gave a demonstration of the braking to the police on Honiton Hill. After this and a lengthy hearing the Bench dismissed the charges, and as a result of widespread newspaper reports other police forces were deterred from bringing similar prosecutions. It is hard to credit now but until the mid-1950s, apart from the number plate light, trailers were only obliged to display a single rear light, with no requirement for brake lights or direction indicators – a 1951 test report mentions the caravan being supplied as standard with a bicycle type dry battery rear lamp. Road traffic law with regard to caravans could be confusing – the 22ft maximum overall length of trailer which could be towed was illogically defined not as length overall but length excluding drawbar; no definition was given of the unladen weight, which had to be marked on the nearside of the van; caravans towed by a motorcycle combination (limited by law to an overall width of 5ft and an unladen weight not exceeding 5cwt) had to display a T sign to the rear but other caravans did not.

For many years the basic suspension system remained a beam or cranked axle with half-elliptic springs and it seems astonishing with hindsight that it was 1959 before independent suspension became a talking point for buyers but, with the speed limit for caravans only increasing from 30 to 40mph in 1963 (40mph on motorways only from 1958), there was little incentive for makers to give serious attention to stability on tow. The limit for close coupled four-wheeled trailers did not increase from 20 to 30mph until 1954. However by 1962 almost half the touring caravan makers had some or all of their models on independent suspension, albeit with nine different systems in use. When the British Caravan Road Rally started in 1954, for the first couple of years before trade entries came to dominate, amateur competitors adopted a happy-go-lucky spirit where a competing car might be occupied by a man and his wife with two or three children asleep in the back.

Some early vans had a primitive brake operating on only one wheel, a type used on belt-driven motorcycles having a fibre block which engaged with a bolted-on V section rim. Better braking was obtained with the external contracting band brake before the general adoption of the internal expanding brake. Actuation was initially either by Bowden cable manually controlled from the towing car or by automatic actuation making use of the thrust which occurs when the car is braked and the trailer tries to overrun it. Eccles and Piggotts had automatic braking in 1920 but initially this was operated by a lever pivoting on the drawbar with no control of the rearward thrust. This was achieved by mounting the coupling on a sliding shaft with a coil spring in compression enclosed in a protective steel box controlling the thrust, and had been adopted by most makers by 1934, with a secondary spring or hard rubber collar to cushion the take-up of pull from the car. Cheltenham used friction damping rather than a coil spring from 1933 and there was also a Rice design which had the sliding shaft housing made as two chambers filled with oil which, passing under pressure from one to the other, produced progressive damping, but this was generally not taken up due to the cost and it was not until the introduction of the B & B long thrust hydraulically damped coupling in 1959 that a really satisfactory system became available. Some heavy vans were fitted with vacuum-servo braking. The first couplings were of the pin and eye type, with a steel rod projecting from the towpole ending in a flat with a hole in it. This was inserted into a yoke attached to the back of the car and a pin passed between the two. The hole had to be a loose fit around the pin to allow articulation, resulting in an unsatisfactory, noisy arrangement of questionable safety. By 1934 the cup and ball universal joint was in use by nearly all makers – as well as the products of specialist chassis manufacturers, several makers had their own exclusive design – and in some cases the ball was mounted on the caravan rather than the car. A Wilkinson-Cox invention was the corner leg operated by a wheel brace. He had previously used DWS lazy tongs car jacks as legs on some Raven models and the new leg was probably derived from this. By 1934 this type of leg was in general use though apparently more people pirated the design than took a licence to use the patent. A technical cul-de-sac in the late 1940s/early 1950s was the dolly, a wheeled device of American origin designed to relieve the rear springs of the towing car by taking the load of an excessively nose-heavy caravan. R McCombie Metcalfe produced two designs – the first, the Wensleydale Caratow, with two wheels connected between car and caravan with two ball couplings in series, which was prone to , and the second, the Aidatow which bolted rigidly to the rear of the car and had a single non-castoring sprung wheel which was prone to tyre scrubbing on corners. Another maker, J B Allen, produced the Allenbrook and as the illustrations above indicate, both were most ungainly affairs. Both makes attracted the attention of the police and under legal and practical handicaps the device was soon obsolete. The Caratow

1949 Wensydel Caratow and 1951 Allenbook were dollies supposed to be an aid to towing!

illustration also indicates a common fault on many vans – the very short drawbar – since one factor required for good stability is that, relative to the length of the van, the distance between the wheels and the coupling should be the maximum practically possible.

Initially most caravans had no chassis as such, the springs being attached to the longitudinal wooden floor joists with a central joist extended forward as a towpole, but gradually the steel chassis was adopted – often bought in from a specialist maker. Gradually various methods of obtaining a lower ride were adopted, including underslung springs, cranked axles, bumped chassis and floors mounted below the main joists. Flooring was either tongued and grooved boards or plywood. Exterior panelling was experimental up to about 1934, with doped canvas, sheet steel, plywood/waterproof fabric and armoured plywood (plywood faced with sheet steel or aluminium) all being used, as well as thin solid mahogany panels (mainly used on collapsible vans) but from 1930 there was a general switch to hardboard (oil bound Tempered Masonite on the best vans). Roofs were insulation board or plywood covered with canvas bedded down on white lead. From the 1920s it was common to offer single or double panelling – the latter costing £15-£25 extra – but by 1938 some makers had realised double panelling might actually be cheaper as the framing did not need to be carefully planed and polished. Various insulating materials were used – Alfol reflecting aluminium foil by Car Cruiser and latex blanket by Airlite in 1936, with cork sheet by Cheltenham, glass silk by Supremus and Tropal (kapok blanket) by Raven in 1938. Framing was mostly ash, with steamed bends on the better quality makes and bends sawn from solid wood on cheaper vans. After the war, at a time of huge demand, the availability of the materials and components needed for building caravans was severely restricted, and whilst aluminium exterior panelling is taken as the norm nowadays it only came into general use in 1947 when hardboard, the preferred pre-war material, became virtually unobtainable.

Before the Second World War there were some vans such as Bertram Hutchings' Concords and J L Balmforth's Cara-Bungalows which were intended for static use, and by the late 1930s some users were living all the year round in large but readily towable vans. The 15ft Raven Yeoman of 1937 was designed as a living van, and caravans were much in demand during the war as temporary living accommodation. Concern about the poor sanitary arrangements and unsightly appearance of holiday and weekend sites springing up in places such as the Cheshire and North Wales coasts and Severn Valley had led to legislation to control camping and caravanning in the form of the Public Health Act of 1936 which introduced a system of site licensing. After the war the demand for caravans quickly reached unprecedented levels, with the desperate housing shortage leading to slum colonies of caravans and shacks at places such as Box Hill, Chertsey, Staines and Weybridge which had been weekending centres before the war, and around cities such as Coventry. Many second hand vans with thinly disguised serious faults were supplied at exorbitant prices by unscrupulous dealers and, with a few

notable exceptions such as Balmforth, Country Life, International and Kinninmont, vans intended for residential use were essentially based on touring van design – the 1946 14ft 9in Eccles Enterprise was supplied in quantity for housing at the US base at Burtonwood, Lancashire. At the same time, whilst touring caravan holidays were restricted until the final end of petrol rationing in 1950, holidays in static caravans around the coast were in demand due to the great increase in the number of workers benefitting from holidays with pay. Most of the caravans were small or medium size tourers, many of which were elderly, but also labelled as caravans were colonies of old bus bodies in the Isle of Sheppey and elsewhere, and on the Lincolnshire coast sections of glider fuselages had been fitted up for occupation. At one coastal resort in North Wales accommodation was provided in converted chicken houses. The pre-war legislation was wholly inadequate to cope with the scale of expansion. A distinction needed to be made between static and mobile caravanning, which were leading in different directions, but, because the residential caravans of the period could not hope to comply with building by-laws, manufacturers were wary of discarding the caravan connection. There were sound reasons for this reluctance – in some cases local authority officers did not consider whether or not a caravan was in law a building but assumed the building by-laws applied to anything lived in and therefore that a residential caravan must be illegal. The bad conditions on sites were also perpetuated by planning policies. It was common practice to give planning permission for only a few years at a time, typically five years but occasionally only one year, with a routine final condition that at the end of the period the licensee must clear the land of all development and restore it to its former condition. Under these constraints, spending a large amount on roads, sanitary blocks, water and electricity supplies in the hope that further permission would be granted was a risky undertaking, even assuming that a loan could be obtained for a venture where security was patently absent. At the very least such policies provided site operators with a perfect excuse for inaction. The negative connotations arising from bad conditions on residential sites also affected attitudes to touring caravanners who resented this. The situation did not materially improve until the passing of the Caravan Sites Act of 1960.

A-Z OF MAKES

ABBEY *See* AVALON

ABC

An 8ft long x 4ft 6in wide rigid-bodied 2 berth sleeping trailer which cost £37 in 1939

ABURNS

Based at Culver Road, North Road, Lancing, Sussex, Aburns claimed that their vans were made by coachbuilders of wide caravan experience. Steel or timber framed vans, furnished or unfurnished, were offered at prices from £100 in 1939.

ACE

ACE CARAVANS

£98 10s. ex Works

£10 DEPOSIT. BALANCE SPREAD OVER MONTHLY PAYMENTS

Start paying your deposit now and secure delivery for next EASTER.

ACE CARAVANS

ACE WORKS, MOOR LANE, STAINES

Telephone: Staines 2040   Telegrams: Travace, Staines

The 1938 Ace was referred to by unfriendly competitors as 'the packing case' on account of its square lines and rough finish.

L Pellatt, of Staines, Middlesex, was a rather mysterious figure, believed to have had a somewhat chequered career in caravans, who started manufacture of the Ace in February 1938. His intention was to create a big market with a family caravan costing under £100. Pellatt publicised his new make very effectively. Having announced a production plan of 300 vans a year – a very large number at that time – he started Ace with a ceremonial opening of the works, took a stand at the *Daily Mail* Ideal Home Exhibition and invited many trade personalities to an evening dress dinner at Pinewood film studios. Dramatic effect was achieved at the dinner when W J Riley of Eccles made a staged entry at a well-chosen moment. Eccles were one of the leading makers and here was their prestige being lent to a van which unfriendly competitors called 'the packing case', from its square lines and rough finish. At £98 10s the 12ft 4 berth was certainly cheap, but established dealers were reluctant to take it up and it was mostly sold through garages and other new retailers.

Later in the year there was also a 6 berth 18ft Trailer Bungalow costing £145 but nothing more is known of this van and the three models on offer in 1939 were the Popular 4 at £98 10s, the Lightweight 4 at £105 and the 2 berth Runnymede at £65. There was also an Ace camping trailer in 1939, 6ft long x 4ft wide, sleeping two under a canvas hood and costing 16 guineas. Production ceased during the Second World War and whilst new models were reported to be at prototype stage in 1946 these do not appear to have gone into production.

ADAMS

Adams Caravans Ltd, Copt Elm Road, Cheltenham, started production in 1937 with three 14ft models, the single panelled Prince at £145, double panelled Charlton at £160 and de luxe double panelled Majestic at £225. The vans were built on Brockhouse chassis, sides were panelled with ⅛in thick 'A' quality Sundeala, with Sundeala hardboard for the ends, and the roofs were covered with Perfecto material. Although earlier models had been fitted with half-drop windows, for 1938 all the vans had top-hinged windows. It was reported in October 1938 that W A Adams had resigned his directorship of the company and he started Cotswold Caravans later in the year. Models at the end of 1938 were the Prince, Charlton, £198 10s 15ft Majestic, 10ft 6in Junior in £85 2 and £92 10s 3 berth versions, £125 14ft Comet, £185 14ft 6in Crusader and £295 17ft 6in Courier. The Crusader and Courier were double panelled but this cost £7 10s extra on the Junior and £15 on the Comet. Specials were also built to meet the

requirements of individual customers. The company lasted only a short time, a winding-up order being made at Cheltenham County Court on 8th February 1939 on the petition of the chassis manufacturers J Brockhouse & Co Ltd, when it was stated that the amount owing to July 1938 was £479

1937 Adams Charlton – elsewhere the Majestic is described as a 14ft van.

AIREDALE

Airedale caravans were built by G Harrison of Sandbeds, Bingley, Yorkshire from 1933 although no details are known of vans produced before 1938. An advertisement in July of that year refers to £140 14ft 4 berth lantern roof and £97 11ft 6in 3 berth models. Later in the year several 1938 vans said to have been used for a few weeks only were offered 'at greatly reduced prices' – presumably these were ex hire vans. Caravans were also built to special requirements. There was a £100 4 berth 13ft 3in lantern roof model in 1939, by which time the firm had moved to Crossflatts, Bingley.

1939 Airedale. This Yorkshire maker had been in production since 1933.

AIRLITE

Clifford R Dawtrey had worked for the Swallow Coachbuilding Company of Coventry (later to become Jaguar Cars Ltd) before setting up the Airlite Trailer Co in 1935 at Old Meteor Works, Coventry, with financial assistance from William Warmsley of Swallow. The original model was a 9½cwt lantern roof 4 berth costing 85 guineas which featured independent suspension, each wheel being mounted between two semi-elliptic leaf springs and dispensing with the need for an axle. Night-time division of the caravan into two compartments was by means of a curtain – at the time generally regarded as extremely

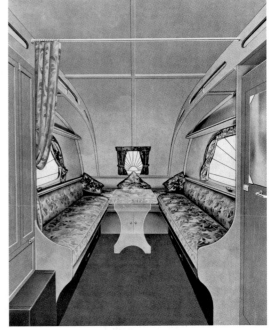

*The Art Deco styled 1936
Airlite and a Singer Nine
Sports Coupe.*

primitive. In 1936 the firm moved to Clay Lane, Coventry, and produced a 12ft 4 berth van costing 100 guineas. The lantern roofed body had one-piece side panels of Sundeala hardboard with Lloyd hardboard roof panelling, and was in the Art Deco style with bold, sweeping side mouldings. The metal-framed windows had a sunray design in gold lining with a patent spring catch providing variable adjustment. The van was fitted with a chromium-plated rear bumper, and double panelling to the walls and roof

was available at an additional cost of £18. Two Rippingilles oil stoves were provided for cooking, and a wardrobe was built on the inside of the caravan door. Independent suspension had been discontinued and the chassis was fitted with a tubular dropped axle and long flat springs which were found to give good stability.

New models in 1937 were the £220 16ft 6in Coronation, £150 12ft 10in Popular and £100 10ft 6in Minx folding caravan. The Sundeala panels on these vans stopped short of the ends and the corners were rounded with no visible joints. This was achieved using a patented method by which Bakelite plastic paste was pressed cold onto a strip of steel mesh, hot ironed into shape and faced with fine canvas embedded in the Bakelite to give a perfectly smooth finish. The technique was tricky and proved unreliable, the plastic sometimes crazing. Airlite were the only popular price maker to fit Bottogas LPG equipment as standard in 1937. Parts manufactured in the Airlite works rather than being bought-in from outside suppliers included axles, ball hitches, brake units, chassis, door hinges, jockey wheel mountings, stoves and metal window frames and catches.

The 16ft 6in Royal of 1938, intended for carrying passengers, had above average brakes, safety glass windows, a rear bumper and towed superbly. The interior had a soft ceiling of buttoned plastic and the front end kitchen was fitted with twin draining boards and oven cooker. In the middle of the van were facing settees and a freestanding table. Selling points included a metal lined and drained wet coat

A 1937 Airlite Minx folding caravan at the 1947 Caravan Club National Rally. Note the somewhat unequal division of labour!

cupboard, a gas fire with fume extractor, dressing table, and shaving and cocktail cabinets, but night-time division was again by curtain. The possibility of Airlite also building cars was reported in 1937, a model with a chassis specially designed for towing being mentioned, but the company failed in 1938 although Clifford Dawtrey formed Coventry Steel Caravans Ltd in the same year.

ALBAN

An Alban entered by F K Little won first prize in the Camping Trailer class at the Caravan Rally that was organised by *The Autocar* at Minehead in Somerset in August 1932.

Alban Camping Trailer at The Autocar Rally, Minehead 1932: more tent than trailer! (LAT Photographic)

ANGELA

Angela with family group around 1930.

1923 Angela – the make was named after the maker's daughter.

THE NEW ANGELA

This old firm—the PIONEERS of the LANTERN ROOF STEAMLINE CARAVAN—offer you a new model bristling with new ideas

Absolutely the LIGHTEST in weight—the LEAST WIND-RESISTING—the MOST LUXURIOUSLY FITTED (Vi-spring type beds, etc.,)—and WITHOUT DOUBT the BEST BUILT

We are enlarging our works, and fitting them out with the latest machinery to give the finest fittings and finish in the trade.

REMEMBER— ANGELA CARAVANS are GUARANTEED for TWO YEARS —a FACT which SPEAKS for ITSELF

15 ft. 2-compartment, 4-berth Angela, £160

This 15 ft. two-compartment four-berth model at **£160** fully equipped is the best value the trade offers.

Other models from **£85** fully equipped.

Deferred Terms.

CARAVANS for HIRE

Send for new season's catalogue.

ANGELA CARAVANS LTD.
Main London-Coventry Road
FLAMSTEAD, Near ST. ALBANS
Phone: MARKYATE 31

ANGELA LEADS THE CARAVAN WORLD IN BEAUTY

The date when Wallace R Purdey began manufacturing trailer caravans is not known. He was an established builder of horse drawn caravans for travelling showmen before turning his attention to trailers. Originally working at Higher Poynton, near Stockport, he is thought to have moved to Flamstead, Hertfordshire, in the late 1920s. The works were situated on the main London-Coventry road and the caravans, which had the square ends, bowed sides and lantern roofs typical of several 1920s makes, were named after his daughter. The range in 1933 included a £55 8ft 2 berth, £58 3 berth, £70 4 berth and 12ft, 13ft and 14ft models priced at £100, £110 and £120 respectively but, in common with other old-established manufacturers, a streamlined model was introduced, albeit still with leaded light windows. There were no agents, the vans being sold direct to the customer, and the factory also operated a hire fleet.

In August 1939 a budget model priced at £120 was being advertised under the slogan 'Your best ARP [Air Raid Precautions] is a Caravan in some quiet spot'. At around the same time Mr Purdey was apparently making wardrobes for army officers but nothing is known about the make after this date.

A 1934 Angela advertisement. The first streamlined model had been introduced in the previous year.

ARAB (1)

The £69 Arab camping trailer was described in 1933 as 'sufficiently ambitious to be classed as a folding caravan'. Equipped with spring beds and cooking equipment, the Arab was manufactured by The Auriol Engineering Works Ltd, Goldhawk Road, London W6, who also made a range of luggage trailers costing from £12 10s. By 1934, when Auriol had moved to Hammersmith Road, London W14, they were reported to be concentrating on building the luggage trailers, and production of the camping trailer had been discontinued.

A 1933 Arab advertisement. Luggage trailers were also produced by the firm.

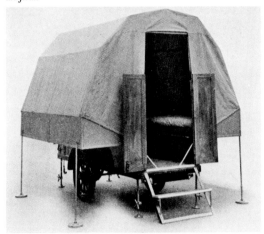

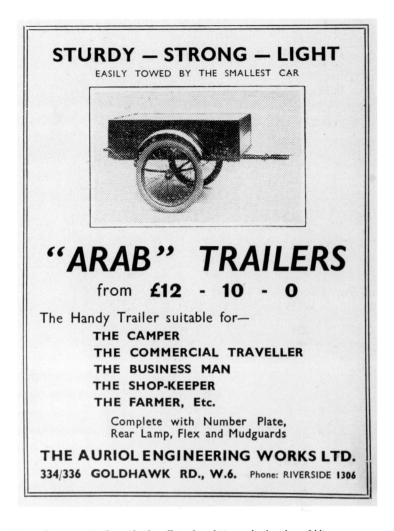

The 1933 Arab Camping Trailer, said to be sufficiently ambitious to be classed as a folding caravan.

ARAB (2)

Although the manufacturers of Arab caravans, Cattell's of Crawley, Sussex, were established in 1921, they may not have started caravan building until some time later. In 1935 they were producing the £45 9 ft 2 berth Vixen, £53 10ft 2 berth Special and a £78 11ft 3-4 berth van, but by 1936 the 11ft van had been replaced by an £86 12ft 3-4 berth model later named the Commander. These three models continued for 1937 and were joined by the £140 15ft 4 berth Verden. Advertising included slogans such as 'Ring Crawley 449 for the Morris of the caravan world' and 'The number of people Arabvanning is increasing'. 1939 models were the Vixen, Special and Commander, priced at £55, £65 and £90 respectively. Showman's and special types were also built.

1936 Arab. The makers advertised their products as 'The Morris of the caravan world'.

ASCOT

1938 Ascot. The maker's previous experience related to building gliders.

W R Scott of Ascot Caravans, Albion Street, Dunstable, Bedfordshire, introduced a 13ft 6in 4 berth model costing £165 in 1938. The van was advertised as 'manufactured by aircraft constructor' – referring to Scott's previous experience in building gliders, Dunstable being a leading gliding centre. Caravans were also built to customer's designs.

ATC

1930 ATC telescopic caravan. 84 turns of a handle lifted the upper half of the body to provide full headroom inside.

Alfred Thomas Skinner of Maidstone produced the A T Unique telescopic caravan under a patent granted to him in 1927, but by 1930 manufacture had been taken over by Thomas Cook & Son, also of Maidstone, with the name changed to ATC (automatic telescopic caravan). A handle engaged with the end of a shaft located beside the rear step. The shaft ran the length of the chassis and had a screw thread device which pulled four wires running over a series of pulleys to each corner, up inside the corner to the top of the lower half of the body and down to fix to the base of the top half. 84 turns of the handle lifted the top half so that its base came up to the level of the top of the lower half, thus providing full headroom. Four turnbuckles locked the top in its raised position. The lantern roofed, single panelled body was constructed of varnished mahogany plywood on an ash frame and the steel framed windows were diamond leaded with glass only 2mm thick. A single glazed and leaded door was fitted to the top half of the body with double doors below. Artillery wheels were fitted and cable operated brakes were actuated by a simple spring-controlled over-run mechanism. Since the closed height was 5ft it was possible to enter the van and lie on the berths even with the top lowered.

The vans were sold in 7ft 6in, 9ft and 12ft lengths, priced in 1933 at 60 guineas, 100 guineas and £140 respectively. Entering the 5ft wide two berth 7ft 6in model at the rear, on the offside was a lift out enamel bowl set under a folding draining board/work surface, with a storage cupboard below and a corner cupboard above. A slatted berth on the nearside folded up against the van side when not in use, with a folding table attached to the underside. Lift up doors gave access to storage space beneath a fixed berth on the offside and a railway carriage style storage net was fitted above this berth. Cook's appear to have built the ATC as well as camping trailers for around three to four years.

1931 ATC 7ft 6in van. 9ft and 12ft models were also available.

ATLAS (BISHOP)

Atlas Trailers and Caravans, London Road, Chelmsford, were reported to be making a streamline caravan and utility trailers in 1933. By early 1934, trading as Atlas Caravan Co, the firm had moved to High Street, Ponders End, Enfield, and were producing a new £75 2 berth caravan. The caravan weighed 6cwt and had Insulite panelling, genuine leaded-light pattern windows, Villiers stove and Moseley Float-on-Air mattresses. This model was quickly followed by a 9½cwt 4 berth 13ft 6in van costing £105.

Taking the contemporary fashion for streamlining to extremes, the design of the 2 berth Aerovan introduced later in the year was said to be inspired by airship practice. Costing £120 in single panelled form, with double panelling adding a further £20, and finished in light blue and silver, the 10ft long x 6ft 4in wide van had an overall height of 5ft 4in with internal headroom of only 4ft 4in. The makers were said to have found that a market existed among sports car owners for a model with very low, clean and rakish lines, and felt that owners of a super-streamlined van of this kind would be prepared to sacrifice headroom in order to obtain the advantages of easy towing and garaging gained by the low overall height, but this does not appear to have been the case and the Aerovan was only in production for a short period.

The proprietor of Atlas was said to be a Mr Pellar at the beginning of 1935, when it was reported that the firm had moved to new works at Napier Road, Enfield, following a fire at the previous factory in December 1934. By April of 1935 the firm was known as Atlas Coachbuilding Co Ltd and was located at Willow Tree Lane, Yeading Lane, Hayes, Middlesex. The range at this time comprised the £152 10s 15ft 4 berth Jubilee, Standard 2, 3 and 4 berth vans costing £80, £90 and £110 respectively, £75 2 berth Featherweight and £150 Special Hire model with lantern roof, as well as trailers costing between £9 9s and £30 and a caravan chassis costing £19. The Jubilee was available with oak lining at an additional cost of £15, or walnut lining for an extra £20, and the windows were fitted with roller blinds – a feature largely ignored by other makers. There also appears to have been a £210 4 berth Atlas de luxe in 1935. This was another extreme example of streamlining, with a side profile reminiscent of a rugby football leaving full headroom only in the centre of the van.

The 16ft Atlas-Bishop, displayed at The Camping Club Exhibition in April 1935, featured a rotating bay

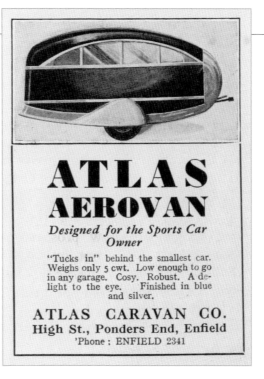

1934 Atlas Aerovan. The internal headroom was only 4ft 4in but the makers felt that owners of a super-streamlined van of this kind would be prepared to sacrifice headroom in order to obtain the advantages of easy towing and garaging gained by the low overall height!

The 1934 2 berth Atlas, whose excessive streamlining severely restricted internal space.

The Atlas Bishop · The Atlas Trailers · The Jubilee Atlas

Atlas vans at the 1935 Camping Club Exhibition.

1935 Atlas-Bishop. After a damp spell it was impossible to get the rotating bays to retract.

in each side wall which extended the width at waist height from 6ft on tow to around 10ft on site. Each bay contained a double bed which could be arranged

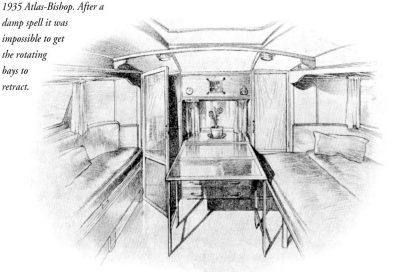

as a settee for daytime use and there was also a single bed with a full size bath underneath. In standard form, double panelled to waist height in hand french polished walnut, the cost was £175. A de luxe version, fully double panelled, with parquet flooring and chromium plated window frames, cost £250. A wireless was a £12 10s extra. This was another model which only remained in production for a short time – apparently after a damp spell it was impossible to get the bays to retract – but in 1936 The Lion Coach-building Corporation, The Green, Southall, Middlesex, advertised the £195 Supa Bishop which appears to have been the same design, having Bishop patent revolving bays and a bath under the single bed. There was also a £260 Supa de luxe. A report on a meet of the Midland Centre of the Caravan Club appearing in the December 1948 issue of *The Caravan* mentions two Bishop vans in attendance, one owned by Mr and Mrs J H Bishop of Shirley. It seems likely that these were pre-war vans and that Mr Bishop was the patentee of the revolving bays.

AT UNIQUE *See* ATC

AVALON (ABBEY)

This make is known to have been in production before the Second World War but no details of the vans from this period are available. A & F Rix, Abbey Coachworks, Rainham Road South, Dagenham, Essex, who were also builders of caravans for travelling showmen, commenced post-war production around 1951, initially under the Abbey name, with a 22ft living van costing £695. The Avalon name was used from 1952 although the dealers A S Jenkinson Ltd of Taplow, Buckinghamshire, were still

advertising Abbey vans until as late as 1954. The 1952 Avalon had four single beds, two of which were in separate bedrooms with the other two folding down from the kitchen bulkhead.

Initial advertising for the 'New 22ft Avalon Everest' in 1954 appears to have been undertaken by the dealers The Essex Caravan Centre, of Leigh on Sea. The price was £550 with 'no delivery charges in Essex'. From December 1954 however Rix were running their own advertisements for the Everest in the caravan press. There was also an 18ft Everest and in 1955 a new 22ft van, the Spacemaster.

In 1957 The Essex Caravan Centre, who had been advertising the Citadel and Grandee models under their own brand name, also advertised the £435 Essex Alhambra 'formerly the Avalon Junior', although Rix appear to have been manufacturing 22ft Everest and 18ft Everest Junior models into 1958. Rix also produced the Pedigree range for the distributor D A Davey of Boxhill.

The 1954 Avalon Everest was offered with 'No delivery charges in Essex'.

AVONDALE

A H Fisk started work with the family joinery manufacturing business of H Fisk & Son, Wakefield, at the age of fourteen in 1929. Having previously been a keen camper he built his first caravan in 1937 and commenced commercial production in 1938, although this appears to have been a sideline to the joinery business and was described as a hobby. No details are known of these early vans and production ceased in August 1941. In 1945, with E B Quibell, Fisk formed the Wakefield dealers Pennine Caravan Co Ltd – an associate company of the national dealer network United British Caravan Co Ltd – and in the same year recommenced caravan production with the 16ft x 6ft 9in Avondale Swan, a streamlined lantern roof model costing £664 7s 6d in 1946, styled along the lines of vans fashionable in the 1930s and 'Designed by practical caravanners and proved and tested under searching conditions'.

A brochure, undated but c.1946, gives details of the Swan, mounted on either Brockhouse or Worth undergear with 3/4in tongued and grooved flooring overlaid with double ply linoleum and a carpet strip. The triple panelled walls had a double air cavity and were panelled externally with hardboard and internally with plywood finished insulation board. Aluminium exterior panelling was available at extra cost. The lantern roof incorporated eight opening lights, cooking and lighting was by Calor gas, and a choice of 3 or 4 berth layouts was offered. A Pither's anthracite stove was fitted but a dressing table could be supplied in place of this. Extras available were a 12 gallon water tank with electric pump and a geyser type gas water heater. An indication of the difficulties faced by caravan manufacturers at that time is a note that 'Specification and drawings are adhered to as far as possible, but no guarantee can be given that they will not be modified from time to time, until the limited supplies of material become more readily available'.

The same brochure featured the 14ft x 6ft 6in V-roofed Swallow, although an errata note stated that this van was not in production, and when a new 14ft van was introduced in mid-1947 this was the Swift, styled on the same lines as the Swan, as was another new model in 1947 – the 18ft Cock o' the North.

A H Fisk resigned his directorships of Pennine and United British in November 1947 when he took over the running of H Fisk & Son from his father. Fisk's also assembled International vans for Northern Coachbuilders of Newcastle-upon-Tyne. The author spent a holiday with his parents at Bridlington in the late 1950s in a hired 18ft streamlined lantern roofed Avondale said to date from the late 1940s, but this cannot be identified with any of the above vans and a 1949 dealer's advertisement refers to a 1948 18ft Avondale Trailer Coach which implies a coach shaped van, but no details of such a model are known.

Swift. Swan and Cock o' the North models continued for 1949 together with a new van, the Tourist, a £375 13ft 4 berth end kitchen model with plain curved roof, aluminium exterior panelling and painted hardboard interior panelling enclosing an air cavity. Fisk's also became site operators in 1949 when they purchased a caravan site at Green Acre farm, Chapel St Leonard's. Models at the beginning of 1951

The 1946 Avondale Swan was styled along the lines of vans fashionable in the 1930s.

were the £650 Swan De Luxe and £399 Swallow. Both were 16ft 6in x 6ft 9in 4 berth end kitchen vans but the Swan was in the streamlined lantern roof style with oak-lined interior, whilst the Swallow had a plain curved roof and painted insulation board interior panelling, The 1952 Queen of the North was an elegant 21ft lantern roofed model aimed at the travelling showman rather than the ordinary caravanner. In October 1954 it was reported that the range for 1955

would consist of six models which included the £350 14ft 3in 4 berth Tourist, £425 16ft 5 berth Quintette, £525 18ft 6in 4 berth Avondale 19, and the Avondale 22, available in 4 or 5 berth versions at £725. The £375 14ft 4 berth Avondale Cruiser introduced late in 1954 was a model made exclusively for the dealers Stafford & Co, Kirkheaton, Huddersfield. At least one dealer was still advertising the make in 1956, but nothing is known of Avondale after this time.

AWB

A 1938 advertisement by Spensers (London) Ltd, notes AWB Caravans among makes fitted with Spensers Bottogas LPG equipment.

BALMFORTH

J L Balmforth started business in 1908. He was a wood carver at Brighouse, Yorkshire, specialising in work for travelling showmen such as horses for round-abouts and elaborate barge-boards and door panelling for caravans. The first Balmforth caravan was built for a showman in 1912 and the first two-wheeled van was produced in 1923. George W Sanderson was J L Balmforth's nephew and as a schoolboy spent his weekends and holidays learning the trade and helping

his uncle to build both horse drawn caravans and those designed for motor towing. Solidity rather than speed was the design keynote even on the trailer caravans, and solid tyres were not unknown. In 1936, as the business flourished, a move was made to more spacious premises, a hangar type building beside the main York-Scarborough Road, a few miles from Malton.

18ft 6in long Cara-Bungalows recognisably designed for static use were introduced in 1935. The box-shaped bodies suited assembly from jig-built sections, a method of construction first used by Balmforth in 1924. In 1937, when the Cara-Bungalow cost £95, Ideal models were available in 2, 3 and 4 berth versions at prices from £87. A 1937 advertisement refers to a new Aero model but no details are known and there also appears to have been a 22ft Cara-Bungalow costing £178. Both Balmforth and Sanderson lived in Cara-Bungalows for several years during the Second World War and in 1946 the type was re-introduced. 22ft long and priced at £535 with dining/sitting room, kitchen with serving hatch, toilet room and separate bedroom with fixed bed, these vans had what was to prove the predominant layout for residential caravans in the next few years, but at the time Balmforth's ideas were ignored by competitors and his small output meant he was unable to exploit the new market created by the post-war housing shortage. The lantern roofed 18ft 6in Queen priced at £558 was also introduced in 1946 and there was an 18ft 6in Cara-Bungalow model priced at £630 in 1948.

George Sanderson left his uncle after the war and

1937 Balmforth advertisement. The Cara-Bungalows were designed for static use.

became a woodwork instructor in Scunthorpe but returned to the firm in 1947 and was taken into partnership. At that time there were five employees and the works still consisted of the single pre-war hangar. A much more advanced residential model was the 22ft Empress, one of which, before being exported to India, was shown at 'The Caravan in Modern Life' exhibition held in the grounds of Chelsea Hospital in 1948. Costing £1,050, the Empress had a lantern roof, deep casement windows, bath and electrically operated water system. The Queen and the Empress did not display the elegance which was to distinguish Balmforth vans in later years. This was first suggested in the curved ends of the 17ft Albatross in 1949 and streamlined versions of the Queen and the Empress, now without lantern roofs, which appeared in 1951, and was further developed in the 16ft 6in Consort introduced in 1952. The final Balmforth body shape with stylish ogee curves to front and rear ends first appeared on the 16ft Albatross in 1955, to which a V front was added in 1961.

Later models were a 14ft 6in version of the Consort in 1953, the 12ft 6in Tern in 1956, 16ft 3in Dalesman in 1958, 14ft 3in Rosedale in 1961 and 14ft 6in Wharfdale in 1963. Custom built vans were made for showmen in the traditional ornate style, still on four-wheeled steerable chassis, until the early 1950s when aluminium panelling finally ousted the traditional wood construction. The firm also built many special purpose units such as trailers for the Dale mobile generator, which was exported to many parts of the world, and dental clinics which went into service in 23 countries. One of these clinics was also shown at the 1948 Chelsea exhibition and a heavily insulated version was built for the Shetland Islands. Other specials included libraries, a maternity centre, a police station, an exhibition unit for the North Eastern Gas Board and a soil testing laboratory for British Railways. By the 1960s there were 30 employees, while the works had been extended and modernised with a petrol station on the forecourt and showrooms for caravans and the Perkins powered boats which were a new venture for Balmforth. An anonymous outlet for the firm's craftsmanship was in motor caravans, two well-known conversions of the Volkswagen being fitted out with their caravan furniture and equipment.

J L Balmforth died, aged 69, in 1954. Balmforth & Co, which had a well-earned reputation for high quality, became Balmforth Caravans Ltd in 1954, Balmforth-Sanderson Ltd in 1961, and eventually ceased trading when the company was placed in voluntary liquidation in 1967 with a deficit of £21,694.

The 1951 Balmforth Empress was a move away from the boxy lines of the Cara-Bungalows.

The 1950 Balmforth Albatross displayed the first suggestion of the elegance which was to distinguish Balmforth vans in later years.

The 1956 Balmforth Albatross represented the final Balmforth body shape.

BAMPTON

Reg and Ted Bampton served their apprenticeship in coach building and the motor body repair trade in the 1920s. In 1932, when they were given the opportunity to purchase an acre of land in Swindon for £120, the brothers pooled their savings to buy it. They built their own workshops and sawmill using wood which their father had bought some years previously when army huts in the district were being demolished. A company was launched in May 1933, registered as an equal partnership with the name Bampton Bros, and soon attracted a limited amount of car bodywork business.

The Bamptons decided to set about designing and building expanding caravans, the first prototype being a 13ft 4 berth which extended from the rear making the van 15ft long on site. This was followed by a 10ft long x 4ft 9in wide 2 berth weighing 8½cwt which

A 1936 Bampton advertisement. The van had originally been named the Easitow.

extended to a width of 8ft 3in. Part of the offside wall was top-hinged and swung out to form a sloping roof, and a drawer section housing a double bed settee slid out on ball-bearing runners. Fittings included a full-length wardrobe, free-standing table, basin and two-burner paraffin stove. The van was very well made, with a finish much above its price class and had a V roof as well as V front and rear. A patent application was filed and in due course patent number 448,048 was issued in respect of the design. At first named the Easitow, the original price was £85, with a 4 berth model costing £120. One of the vans was parked outside Olympia during the 1934 Motor Show, resulting in its purchase by William Welford of the dealers Welfords Caravans of Warninglid, Sussex. It stood out on Welfords display ground for four months and having been suitably tested by foul weather and plenty of man-handling by customers the decision was taken to stock the Easitow, but after consultation the name was changed to the Bampton. Although sold mainly through Welfords, caravans were occasionally made for individual customers and a small hire fleet was also built.

The range at the end of 1938 comprised 10ft 2 and 3 berth expanding vans priced at £99/£115 single panelled, or £119/£135 double panelled, 10ft 2 and 3 berth vans costing £95/£105 or £110/£120, a 12ft 4 berth at £135/£152 10s and a 15ft 4 berth at £175/£195. Another model dating from before the Second World War had two side extensions, the larger for a double bed settee and the smaller for a toilet. Up to 1939 Welfords purchased vans regularly throughout each spring and summer, an arrangement which allowed Bamptons to build and stockpile caravans in the winter months when other work was scarce due to many car owners at that time only using their vehicles for six months in the year. The Bamptons always delivered vans to Sussex personally and no matter what time they arrived William Welford always paid on delivery. On one occasion when there was difficulty in meeting a delivery date the brothers worked all one day, all night and all the next day, setting off for Sussex in the evening. When they arrived at midnight Welford was already in bed but came down in pyjamas to write their cheque.

When the Second World War started there was initially a demand for caravans, principally for evacuation purposes, but by the early months of 1940 all caravan building and almost all private car repairs had ceased as the company applied its resources to work

on War Department and public service vehicles. For almost the entire period of the War the brothers slept in a caravan on the premises. When caravan building started again after the War, production of the extending vans was not resumed due to the amount of work involved in their manufacture. In 1951 Welfords were advertising seven Bampton models which ranged from the B102 10ft 2 berth at £369 16s to the C21 21ft 4 berth living van at £1,282, but as the decade advanced it became apparent that the building of high quality caravans was no longer financially viable and, as the Bamptons were not prepared to reduce the quality of workmanship, caravan building ceased in 1960 and the company concentrated on accident repairs, car conversions and commercial body-building.

This 1938 Bampton was still in use in 1958.

BANOVAN

Thomas H Waumsley of Banovan Caravans, Horncastle, Lincolnshire, started production in 1936. 1937 models were a £45 2 berth, £85 3 berth and 100 guinea 4 berth. Production continued after the Second World War, the make being advertised by the dealers Surrey Car Co Ltd, Richmond Road, Kingston-on-Thames in 1946-47. There was a 15ft 4

berth model in 1946 and the 1947 range comprised the £505 16ft Sherwood, £525 15ft Somersby and the 18ft Harrington. The advertised price of £95 for this last model was presumably a printing error!

The offside door was an unusual feature of the 1937 Banovan..

1947 Banovan – the price of £95 for the 18ft Harrington is presumably a printing error!

BAS

A £135 4 berth of 1935 built by Bartram & Sons of Sunderland.

1935 BAS. Perhaps unsurprisingly this rather unattractive van does not appear to have been long in production.

BEE AND DEE

A 15ft lantern roof van of 1937, made in Rochdale and costing £130.

1937 Bee and Dee, made in Rochdale.

BELWATT

T he only known model is a lantern roof van of 1934.

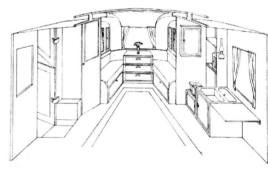

Interior of a 1934 lantern roof Belwatt.

BISHOP *See* ATLAS

BLUEBIRD (MIDLAND)

A lthough one of the dominant figures in caravan manufacturing for some twenty-five years, W E C (Bill) Knott of Parkstone, near Bournemouth, avoided personal publicity and the facts of his career are entangled in legend. He began caravan building around 1930, at the age of 16, scouring the area for old car axles which he converted for trailing. By the mid-1930s he was manufacturing in some quantity, with capital provided by his father, a prosperous Parkstone auctioneer, and by 1939 they were winning an appreciable share of the market. Knott's trading policy was unique, the caravans being made for sale 'as seen' and bearing no name plate or transfer. Through his father he supplied anyone who could resell, regardless of the ultimate use. The sellers often professed to be selling at much below list prices, but produced no catalogues and if pressed identified the makers as 'the well-known Midland Caravan Co', but were evasive about the company's location. The clue to the origins was to be found in newspaper advertisements inviting buyers to apply to Knott, auctioneer, Parkstone, or Knott, liquidator, Parkstone. The standard of workmanship was commensurate with the low prices and the vans were shunned by the established caravan dealers.

The success of Midlands made caravan building look easy, and over a long period a confusing sequence of ex-Knott employees and other imitators started up in the Bournemouth area, making low-grade caravans for short periods. During the Second World War some of the nameless caravans coming out of this area were of appallingly bad quality. In the caravan trade Bournemouth meant Midland's, and the reputation of these vans attached itself to the name. However a Bluebird Caravan Co had already been formed to carry on the business of E Knott and Son, and after the War a fresh start was made under the new name.

Little is known of the immediate post-war models although a 1947 advertisement refers to a Bluebird with lantern roof – a costly feature not usually found on low-price vans. Bluebirds were cheaper than other comparable makes and unlike the cut-price backyard makes were unmistakably factory products. Most importantly, in a time of shortage, they were available. Typical of Knott's aggressive pricing was the Bluebird Defiant of 1951, a 16ft van described as a 'mobile home', with solid fuel stove and insulated roof, selling at £325, or £299 without the stove – pricing which no other maker could match. Sales mounted rapidly, the range of models was enlarged and throughout the 1950s the whole caravan industry was on the watch for Knott's next move.

The early Bluebirds raised serious questions in the industry. Bluebirds were better than Midlands but, whilst Knott regarded himself as the Ford of caravan building, cutting costs by massive production and simplification, critics suggested that economy could go beyond a sacrifice of finish, comfort and convenience, and undermine fitness for purpose. In 1948 *The Caravan*, still using the Midland name, commented that the manufacturers had produced large numbers of caravans without a parking brake, pointing out that any buyer taking one of these vans on the road without modification was liable to prosecution for a

The 1952 Bluebird Bantam, 'suitable for 8hp car', and its interior.

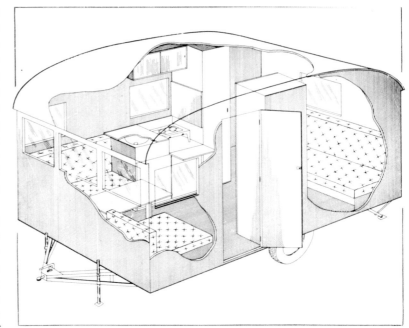

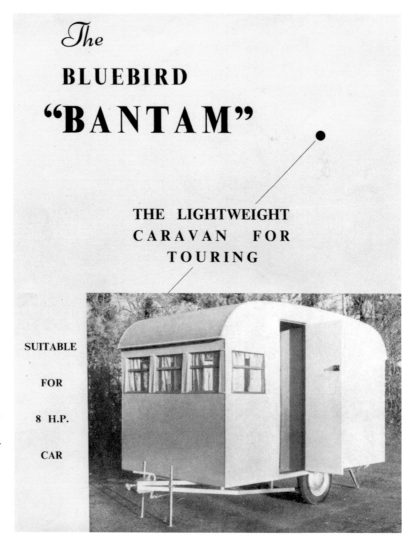

The

BLUEBIRD
"BANTAM"

THE LIGHTWEIGHT CARAVAN FOR TOURING

SUITABLE

FOR

8 H.P.

CAR

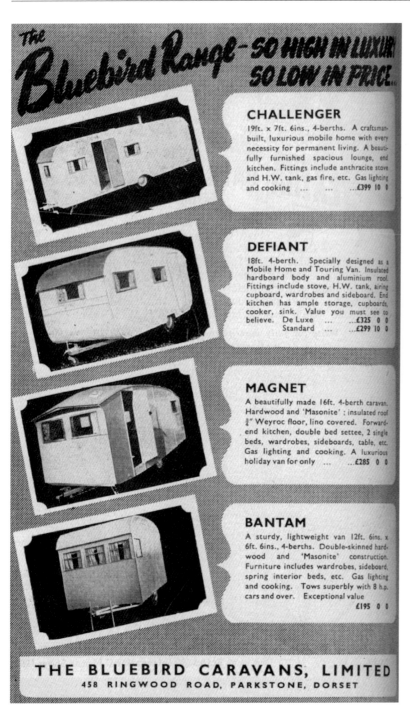

The Bluebird Range – SO HIGH IN LUXURY SO LOW IN PRICE...

CHALLENGER

19ft. x 7ft. 6ins., 4-berths. A craftsman-built, luxurious mobile home with every necessity for permanent living. A beautifully furnished spacious lounge, end kitchen. Fittings include anthracite stove and H.W. tank, gas fire, etc. Gas lighting and cooking £399 10 0

DEFIANT

18ft. 4-berth. Specially designed as a Mobile Home and Touring Van. Insulated hardboard body and aluminium roof. Fittings include stove, H.W. tank, airing cupboard, wardrobes and sideboard. End kitchen has ample storage, cupboards, cooker, sink. Value you must see to believe. De Luxe £325 0 0
Standard £299 10 0

MAGNET

A beautifully made 16ft. 4-berth caravan. Hardwood and 'Masonite' ; insulated roof ¾" Weyroc floor, lino covered. Forward-end kitchen, double bed settee, 2 single beds, wardrobes, sideboards, table, etc. Gas lighting and cooking. A luxurious holiday van for only £285 0 0

BANTAM

A sturdy, lightweight van 12ft. 6ins. x 6ft. 6ins., 4-berths. Double-skinned hardwood and 'Masonite' construction. Furniture includes wardrobes, sideboard, spring interior beds, etc. Gas lighting and cooking. Tows superbly with 8 h.p. cars and over. Exceptional value
£195 0 0

THE BLUEBIRD CARAVANS, LIMITED
458 RINGWOOD ROAD, PARKSTONE, DORSET

In 1952, when this Bluebird advertisement appeared, production was running at 120 vans per week.

considered necessary! Taken as some evidence of respect for implied warranty together with a distinct improvement in quality, this alleviated concerns and there was a tacit agreement in the industry to recognise the make, with many dealers rushing to obtain stocks of the vans. This was an important breakthrough for Knott who, with output in 1952 running at 120 vans per week and aiming for 175-200 per week in 1954, had reached the very front rank for output and needed the access to buyers which the big dealers could provide. This productivity was achieved in premises which whilst large, appeared disorganised when compared with the production line discipline seen in the Berkeley or Eccles factories. Gangs of men working like beavers built vans in various buildings and odd corners, from piles of materials lying within reach. A single design of body might be used for two or three models, so the shells were built first, to be drawn on and fitted inside as demand required. Painting came last, sometimes even while dealers' delivery vehicles stood waiting.

Knott had built up his power outside the organised caravan manufacturing industry, and when the National Caravan Council declared its intention to adopt a policy of Mutual Trading the scene was set for a major confrontation. The policy involved NCC Approved Manufacturers only appointing NCC Approved Traders as their agents and distributors, and NCC Approved Traders only selling the caravans of NCC Approved Manufacturers. In a letter published in *The Caravan* in June 1956 Knott, commenting on the decision to adopt Mutual Trading and on speculation about Bluebird's intentions in view of the fact that many NCC Trader members sold Bluebird caravans, said that the company had decided not to apply for membership of the NCC. He also said that Bluebird refused to be embraced in a system of restrictive practice and gave notice that, whilst the company would continue to manufacture a wide range of vans for purchasers of modest means, a new factory shortly to be opened at Parkstone would be devoted to the production of more expensive models – a clear challenge to the makers producing vans in a higher price range than the current Bluebird models.

The first of these new models was the 22ft Thunderbolt priced at £523 10s, quickly followed by the 20ft Fantasia at £459. Bluebird had no design department and, whilst some innovative designs were produced, tended to follow the designs of other manufacturers. The pre-war vans had looked very like Winchesters at a distance, and as the 1950s progressed Bluebird attracted complaints from other manufacturers that their designs were being copied. Reporting on the new 18ft Sabre in 1956, *The Caravan*

breach of the Motor Vehicles (Construction and Use) Regulations. However the September 1952 issue of *The Caravan* reported Knott as saying that all vans leaving the factory now carried a plate giving the manufacturer's name and address, that in future they would also have a 'Bluebird' transfer including the model name, and that the company was prepared at all times to co-operate with their agents if and when any complaints were received from purchasers, and would accept the return of a van for rectification – if commented that the appearance outside and in was very close to another make and that it seemed a pity that a firm with such great resources should be content to follow another's lead. More controversy was caused by the introduction of the 12ft 6in Cambrian in 1957. The body was styled in the contemporary Fairholme manner and the layout was a simplified version of a Raven design. This was seen by the NCC as a deliberate provocation – there was nothing Welsh about Bluebird or the Cambrian, but Fairholmes were made in Cardiff and their managing director J J Hennessy was a leading champion of the Mutual Trading policy.

When Mutual Trading came into force on 1st October 1956 the policy had been modified to allow Traders to sell one non-NCC make. This was described as a temporary measure, and matters came to a head at the AGM held during the NCC Trade Convention in March 1958 at the Majestic Hotel, Harrogate. Opposing each other during a four hour debate were the Manufacturers section, who threatened to enforce exclusive Mutual Trading piecemeal if it were not accepted by the whole Council, and some 40 Traders, who stood to lose a large part of their business if they were not allowed to sell Bluebirds. Knott was watching events from the Cairn Hydro Hotel just across the road, where he had a private bar for trade visitors and a marquee in which the latest models were displayed. The meeting was told that Eccles, with an output of 2,000 vans a year, had agreed to join the NCC if exclusive Mutual Trading was adopted, leaving Bluebird with an output of 10,000 vans in the previous year as the only important make outside. There was a three-to-one vote in favour of Mutual Trading and on the following day a meeting lasting about three and a half hours was held in a corner of the Majestic lounge between NCC leaders and the Bluebird directors. No agreement was reached and the talks nearly broke down several times. The problem was that a number of existing Bluebird dealers who were not NCC members were not considered suitable applicants for membership without improvement. Negotiations over several months eventually resolved this issue, and in August 1958 it was reported that Bluebird were to join the NCC in time for the introduction of Mutual Trading on 1st October of that year. After all this effort Mutual Trading was abandoned after a short life due to the likelihood of trouble with the Restrictive Trade Practices Court.

Examples of the enormous range of models produced over the years include the 20ft Heritage of 1954, 10ft Rambler of 1955, 22ft Paragon of 1956, and 8ft 6in Skylark of 1959. The Heritage was reported to have a notable quality of finish for the very

The 1957 Bluebird Cambrian, a controversial design seen by the National Caravan Council as a deliberate provocation in the confrontation over Mutual Trading.

moderate price of £419 10s and the 9½cwt Rambler, priced at £179 10s with Masonite exterior wall panelling and aluminium roof panelling or £189 10s with all aluminium panelling, was the cheapest 4 berth van on the market and remarkable value even by Bluebird standards. The Paragon featured a centre lounge with a double bed which by day slid away into the space below the beds in the two single end bedrooms, and the £209 10s 4 berth Skylark, the smallest van made by Bluebird, was claimed to weigh less than 8½cwt. Bluebird had produced the Nuhome end-to-end twin for the dealers Essby Caravans in 1952, and in 1958 introduced the 32ft 6 berth Sabrina Pullman comprising two 16ft vans joined end to end. The layout was designed by Noel Monks of the dealers Trailer Homes Company and was priced at £625.

Eye-catching models introduced at the first International Caravan Exhibition held at Earls Court, London, in 1959 were the 30ft x 8ft Pacific and the 14ft Dauphine. The £749 10s Pacific was the joint creation of Knott and the Wolverhampton dealer, Bill Allen, after both had visited the United States. American influence showed in the styling, which owed something to the covered wagon – the roof, whose edges were rounded into the side walls, extended to form a hood over the french windows which filled the whole front wall of the lounge. The roof sloped down from front to rear giving extra headroom in the

THE BLUEBIRD CARAVANS LIMITED
THE LARGEST CARAVAN ORGANISATION IN THE WORLD
PARKSTONE · POOLE · DORSET

lounge, and a fold down verandah outside the french windows was enclosed by metal railings. American influence was also seen in the layout, where the kitchen was treated as an extension of the lounge. To the rear of the kitchen were bathroom, fitted with a mixer tap with swivelling outlet to serve both the 4ft bath and the washbasin, children's bedroom with bunk beds, and a double bedroom. The solid fuel stove with back-boiler supplied hot water to kitchen and bathroom as well as a radiator in each bedroom.

The £289 10s Dauphine was novel in being virtually chassis-less. The only longitudinal member was a central tubular tow-pole forming a T with the independent suspension system comprising cranked wishbones pivoted from the central member and coil springs enclosing telescopic hydraulic dampers. First seen at the Bluebird trade show in September 1962 but not put into production until five months later, the £1,295 Swedish Cottage was a 26ft x 19ft side-by-side twin unit with a double and two single bedrooms, large kitchen, bathroom and lounge with french windows opening onto an integral patio. The lounge was carpeted but unfurnished and the price included Calor gas lighting, but electric wiring and a carport were extras available at £30 each.

The dealer, Doris Strowbridge, sold a range of modified Bluebirds under the Peoples brand name in the 1950-59 period. A new departure was the Highwayman motor caravan, first seen at the company's annual trade preview of new models in September 1958, which had a coachbuilt body mounted on the Austin 152 chassis and was priced at a very competitive £870. The Motovan Plus, a £795 conversion based on the Morris J4 van with elevating roof, followed in 1961 and there was also the £275 Rosette horsebox introduced in 1960. Another enterprise was site operation. Knott had bought the Northbourne golf course near Parkstone and turned part of it into the Fairway Caravan Park, where 350 Bluebird holiday vans were available for hire. Other Bluebird owned sites were at Mudeford, Hampshire and Looe, Cornwall.

Some idea of the scale of operations can be gained from caravan press reports during the late 1950s and early 1960s. In a 1959 report Bluebird claimed that in the early summer of 1958 their European distributor had placed an order for 800 vans, followed by an order for a further 1,000 in January 1959. Orders for 500

The 1959 Bluebird Pacific. American influence was evident in the joint creation of Bluebird's Bill Knott and dealer Bill Allen.

The Pacific also had an American-influenced layout with the kitchen treated as an extension of the lounge.

Pacifics and 400 Dauphines were said to have been taken during the 1959 International Caravan Exhibition and in 1961 Bluebird received an order for 200 special versions of the Pacific for the use of British Forces in Germany. In 1963 Knott was reported as saying that sixty vans were leaving the factory every day. Despite a tremendous workload Knott still found time for his hobbies of short wave amateur radio and cars, of which he normally had a fleet of six expensive models. Apparently when his doctors told him to get some relaxation he took up fishing – getting up an hour earlier to sea fish in his boat off Poole before starting work. Overheads were very low, Knott and his secretary Miss L P Proctor still being the only full-time office staff when output had reached around 5,000 vans a year.

The writer of an article in *Modern Caravan* in October 1963 recalled how, during a visit in the early 1950s, he had speculated on the likely size of the fire insurance premium in view of the vast quantities of highly combustible materials about the factory. Knott's response was that he didn't need insurance because the factory worked 24 hours a day and with all the workforce about a fire would be quickly spotted before it became dangerous. Timber was bought by the shipload, landed direct at Poole. Knott was the only caravan manufacturer with sufficient capital to buy on this scale and this capital, combined with a taste for risks, led him to help a number of new dealers to start business by supplying Bluebirds on credit.

In the year prior to Bluebird becoming a member of the NCC Knott had been joined by H Kirk and R C Yablon, new directors who had come from financial circles. Ron Smith, who had been works manager since the mid-1950s, also joined the board as works director. A private holding company was set up to acquire Bluebird Caravans Ltd and in 1959, under the name Bluebird Investments Ltd, was launched as a public company. Stock Exchange dealings in £507,010 issued capital began on 24th September with 700,000 ordinary 4-shilling shares offered. According to reports at the time Bluebird profits had risen from £189,000 to £670,000 in the previous six years. At the annual general meeting held on 15th August 1960, with net profit at £715,330 before taxation, a final dividend was declared which took the total for the year to 40%, a figure repeated in the following year. Late in 1962 Knott was reported to have bought two farms 'with an eye on the future', and in 1963 Bluebird merged with Sprite to become Caravans International Ltd in what was described as a reverse take over.

At an extraordinary general meeting held on 30th August of that year, shareholders of Bluebird Invest-

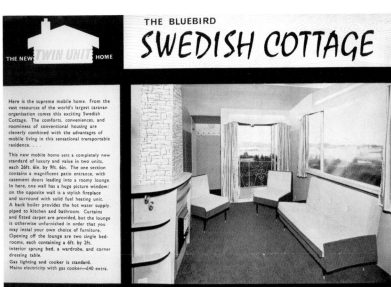

ments Ltd learned that Knott had sold his holding of 500,000 shares to R C Yablon for 19 shilings each. Ron Smith had left Bluebird in August and joined Astral of Hull as general manager. Interestingly the Bluebird Joie de Vivre introduced in 1963 was a 14ft 6in van with a 4ft overhang, housing a double bed, extending forward over the drawbar, and the 14ft 6in Astral Sunrise, also introduced in 1963, had a similar feature. Under the terms of the merger Sam Alper of Sprite became managing director of the new group and Knott was prevented from engaging in caravan manufacture for two years, though in 1965 he was back in production under the BK brand name.

1962 Bluebird Swedish Cottage – twin unit living, but electric wiring was still an optional extra.

BOWSER

A 1929 Bowser caravan sidecar ready for the road. (Courtesy of Mortons Archive)

The Bowser caravan sidecar also provided a garage for the motorcycle. (Courtesy of Mortons Archive)

Not strictly speaking a trailer caravan but worthy of a mention is the Bowser caravan sidecar of 1929. Made by Edward Bowser of Leeds, an established manufacturer of sidecars, the conventionally styled single seat open touring body could be converted in 20 minutes into a small caravan, the canvas walls even extending to provide a garage for the motorcycle. Equipment comprised two 6ft berths, toilet cabin with mirror, food cupboard, cutlery and folding windows. The cost was £39 10s.

BRANSBY *See* COVENTRY STEEL

BRISTOL

1947 Bristol De Luxe. Unusually the post-war van looks more streamlined than the 1939 model above.

THE NEW
BRISTOL 2/3 berth
PRICE ONLY £85

Do not hesitate to write for full particulars of this light-weight model. Also the **BRISTOL 4 berth £120**. OUR CARAVANS ARE BUILT BY CRAFTSMEN AND WILL LAST A LIFETIME
Hire purchase terms arranged—Hire fleet available

BRISTOL CARAVANS LTD.
WARMLEY TOWER, Nr. BRISTOL

The 1939 Bristol offered economy caravanning for £85.

Bristol Caravans Ltd, Warmley Tower, near Bristol, started manufacture towards the end of the 1930s. 1939 models were the 2/3 berth at £85 and the 4 berth at £120. A hire fleet was also operated. By 1946 the company had moved to Church Road, Kingswood, Bristol. The only model in 1947 appears to have been the Bristol De Luxe, a 16ft long x 6ft 4½in wide double panelled 4 berth with lantern roof and felt insulation. The £735 Kingswood was introduced in 1948 but by early 1949 the price had fallen to £650. Manufacture does not appear to have continued beyond 1949.

BROADLANDER (BROADWAY)

L G Blow, of Cardiff, was a furniture manufacturer who decided to build a caravan for his own use around 1937. He was persuaded to sell this van and then started to build others for sale. No details are known of the pre-war vans but in the late 1940s L G Blow & Co Ltd were producing vans under the Broadway name. In mid-1949 it was announced that production of the Overlander, an aluminium monocoque van designed by a London motor engineer, A R Hall, was to be taken over by Blows, with production of the Broadway ceasing and A R Hall being appointed a director. It was reported in August 1949 that the first Overlander model to be built at Cardiff was a 15ft 6in, 14cwt, 4 berth, centre kitchen van priced at £398, but the name adopted for the new van was the Broadlander. The design had been modified to incorporate a conventional chassis and drawbar, rather than the aluminium box floor and single bed lockers extended forward to make a tapered box, serving as drawbar and gas cylinder housing, which featured in the original Overlander.

Further modifications to the Overlander design were incorporated in a 20ft model introduced in 1952. A continuous band of 18 gauge aluminium formed the roof, end walls and outer floor section. This band was built on a temporary frame, the side walls and tongued and grooved floor being added

The 1952 Broadlander was developed from the aluminium monocoque Overlander.

before the whole unit was bolted to the channel steel chassis. Framing was hardwood, interior panelling hardboard with fibreglass insulation, and there was an air cavity between the outer aluminium and the lino covered tongued and grooved floor. The £798 van was advertised as having an unladen weight of 22cwt but a contemporary report speaks of an ex-works weight of 31cwt 2qtrs with a nose weight of 3cwt 1qtr! The Valor convector heater could be replaced by a solid fuel stove, and a drop-down double bed was offered as an alternative to the double bed settee in the centre lounge. Production does not appear to have continued beyond 1952.

BROADWAY *See* BROADLANDER

BURLINGHAM

Burlingham Caravans was an offshoot of a coachbuilding business founded by H V Burlingham. In the early 1930s he built a number of caravans to special order, some based on Burlingham motor coach designs and including four-wheeled vans, a production example of which was exhibited at the 1934 Olympia Motor Show. By the second half of the decade he was producing a range of elegant models named after the English lakes as well as continuing to build specials including heavy four-wheeled vans for travelling showmen. Originally located at Addison Road, Preston, Lancashire, by 1938 the works were located at Brook Street, Preston, with a display ground and camp site at the nearby Garstang By-Pass.

The 1939 range comprised £380 18ft Langdale, £265 15ft Rydal, £182 14ft Thirlmere, £198 13ft 6in Rydal Junior, £168 12ft Lyndale, £198 Grasmere and £138 12ft Derwent – all 4 berth vans apart from the 2 berth Grasmere. The Rydal Junior, developed from the Rydal, had two doors, front end double dinette, rear end kitchen, near side settee extending to form a single bed opposite an off side single bed which folded up into a sideboard. The window frames were chromium plated brass and the interior wall panelling was veneered in hand polished figured oak, although the make was known for internal panelling of hardboard faced with hand stuck leathercloth, giving a lighter interior than veneered walls. Whilst heavy the vans had a reputation for superb craftsmanship with exceptionally good body hardware. Burlingham built

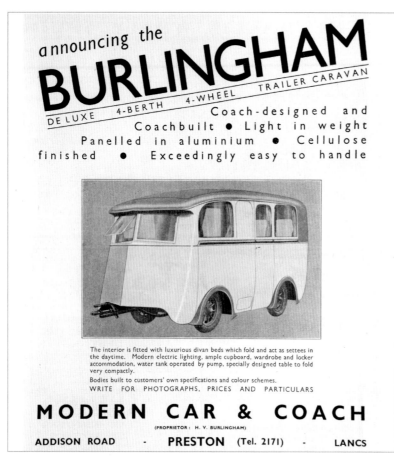

announcing the

BURLINGHAM

DE LUXE · 4-BERTH · 4-WHEEL · TRAILER CARAVAN

Coach-designed and Coachbuilt · Light in weight · Panelled in aluminium · Cellulose finished · Exceedingly easy to handle

The interior is fitted with luxurious divan beds which fold and act as settees in the daytime. Modern electric lighting, ample cupboard, wardrobe and locker accommodation, water tank operated by pump, specially designed table to fold very compactly.
Bodies built to customers' own specifications and colour schemes.
WRITE FOR PHOTOGRAPHS, PRICES AND PARTICULARS

MODERN CAR & COACH

(PROPRIETOR: H. V. BURLINGHAM)

ADDISON ROAD · PRESTON (Tel. 2171) · LANCS

The 1934 Burlingham four-wheeler was based on the maker's motor coach designs.

1947 Burlingham Rydal, one of the firm's first post-war models.

The 1939 Burlingham Rydal Junior. Whilst heavy the vans had a reputation for superb workmanship with exceptionally good body hardware.

their own chassis and were leading exponents of stiffening drawbars and longitudinal members by trussing. Vans fitted with electric brakes could be supplied to order as early as 1938.

The first post-war models were the Rydal and Langdale of 1946, both 4 berths and costing £842 and £988 respectively. Models exhibited at the 1948 Earl's Court Motor Show were the the 19ft 4 berth Lakeland and 13ft 3in 2 berth Sportsman. The Lakeland was a £1,580 living van, the end kitchen of which had a stainless steel sink with twin draining boards; an ironing board folded down in front of the cooker, which was provided with a supply point for a Calor gas iron. The roof of the £599 Sportsman was designed to carry a 10ft dinghy, available as a £96 extra. H V Burlingham retired in 1948 and the business was carried on by his son-in-law and daughter, Mr & Mrs S Parkinson.

New models in 1949 were the £1,175 17ft 6in Langdale and £695 Lindale. The 14ft 4 berth centre kitchen Lindale could be supplied with leaded windows and 'best quality mattresses' for an extra £27, and was also offered with an alternative layout incorporating a folding toilet compartment. By mid-1951 the range comprised the Sportsman still priced at £599, the Lindale now costing £758, the £935 4 berth 16ft Rydal, the Langdale and the £1,295 22ft Windermere. The Langdale was now 18ft 6in long and cost £1,140 with plain roof or £1,340 with lantern roof and oak veneered interior wall panelling.

Later models were the £895 15ft 4 berth Kendal of 1953 and the 14ft 3in 4 berth Grasmere of 1955. The Grasmere cost £595 with centre kitchen layout or £615 with end kitchen. The last year of production appears to have been 1958, with a model line up comprising 12ft Sportsman costing £825, 14ft 3in Grasmere at £725, 15ft 6in Kendal at £895, 18ft 6in Langdale at £1,095 and 22ft Windermere at £1,495. The firm never appears to have had a dealer network, selling direct to the public from their own sales ground and by 1954 were also selling other makes, a business which continued after Burlingham stopped producing caravans themselves. H V Burlingham retained his interest in caravanning after retirement and still had his own van when he died in 1959 at the age of 82.

CAISLEY

Caisley was a Bristol maker who immediately before the Second World War had produced a prototype with side frames made as complete ovals of laminated wood and hardboard panels glued on without pins and mouldings.

CAMPETTE

Introduced in 1936, the £38 Campette Camping Trailer was manufactured by Campette Trailers, Northfield, Birmingham. The closed dimensions were 6ft 6in long x 4ft 6in wide, opening to 8ft 8in wide on site. The bodywork was constructed of ash, pine and plywood, with medium heavy canvas for the tent top. Equipment included two 6ft 6in x 2ft 6in sprung camp beds, wardrobe cupboard, table and either carpet or linoleum floor covering. Maximum headroom of 6ft 6in was provided on site but when closed the trailer was low enough to allow the driver of the towing car an uninterrupted view of following traffic. By 1937 the price had increased to £40. A 1952 classified advertisement for a secondhand 2 berth Campette folding camping trailer may refer to a model dating from before the Second World War.

The 1936 Campette was a 2 berth model. It is not clear where the other members of the party are going to sleep!

CAR COASTER

Nothing is known of Car Coaster models predating the Second World War but the make was certainly in production in 1939. The vans appear to have been popular with the dealers Yorkshire Caravan & Trailer Co, Bawtry, near Doncaster, who sold the vans both before and after the War. Car Coaster were hardly a local make, their works at Poole, Dorset, being a long way from Yorkshire. A 16ft 3 berth model priced at £895 was available in 1948, and 1951 models were the Sunbeam, Maisonette and 22ft Silver Star, priced at £500, £750 and £1,125 respectively. New in 1952 was the Derby, a 16ft end kitchen van costing £475, followed in 1953 by the £215 9ft CC9. Late in 1956 it was reported that the CC9 would be the only model built for general sale in 1957, with the building of commercial specials occupying the rest of the production capacity. By 1958 the firm had moved

1952 Car Coaster Derby, still with the Art Deco sunburst pattern glazing which had been popular in the 1930s.

to Sandford, Wareham, Dorset, and whilst production of the CC9 continued until 1959 it appears to have been the final model.

CAR CRUISER (COOPER)

CAR CRUISERS

3. New system of insulation for sides, roof and floor.
4. Full-width lantern roof, with separate ventilators to wardrobe and galley.
5. Enclosed galley.
6. Air-shield cooking.
7. Special air supply to prevent floor draughts.
8. "Outside inside" food lockers.
9. Combined folding table and chest of drawers, the last word in table design.
10. Light weight and perfect balance.

1925

The 1925 Car Cruiser was years ahead of its time. The Car Cruiser of to-day is the practice of to-morrow. Here are some exclusive features :—

1. Hook ball joint. Safe, rattleproof, adjustable.
2. Brace-operated screw legs with the roll foot. Efficient at all angles, no jamming or fouling.

1935

CAR CRUISER CARAVANS LIMITED
NORTH HYDE ROAD, HAYES, MIDDLESEX

Phone : Hayes 253

The styling of the 1925 Car Cruiser vans was still very like the original 1920 experimental model but had become much more attractive by 1935.

Eating al fresco outside a 1931 Car Cruiser Type 4.

Major Clifford Fleming-Williams, or 'Flaming Bill' as he was known in caravan circles, had been an illustrator before the First World War. He also had a keen interest in flying and was closely associated with pioneer airmen, several of whom he assisted in the design of their aeroplanes and fittings for them. He was an ardent enthusiast for streamlining and became known amongst the flying fraternity as 'Streamline Bill'. On the outbreak of War he joined the Royal Flying Corps and served with them and the Royal Air Force until the Armistice. Early in his period of service he had to move a Blériot monoplane by road and did so by dismounting the wings and attaching the tail skid to the back of a car. The plane towed perfectly and this experience led to the construction of light two-wheeled trailers on which to convey crated aeroplanes.

In 1917 he built a large streamlined motor caravan on a Leyland chassis, followed in 1920 by a trailer caravan built in his front garden. This van was mounted on an axle from a De Havilland aircraft, with large section tyres of the type known as balloons, and had a profile said to be derived from an aircraft wing. The flat front end was raked back slightly from bottom to top and the V roof and rear end were in one continuous curve. The shape severely restricted headroom at the rear but this drawback was overcome by the layout. A transverse double bed settee ran across the back end, with two single beds along the side walls at the front end. The full height cooking galley and the wardrobe, which alone required full headroom, were in the middle of the van, giving structural stiffening and good separation of the bed areas. The body had a marked tumble home which reduced weight, and further weight reduction was achieved by the construction. Body skinning comprised mahogany plywood single panelling up to the waist with doped canvas above. The mahogany plywood floor was mounted on wooden chassis longitudinals with a wooden towpole. The obliquely mounted, height adjustable corner legs were also of wood, and the wood framed windows were glazed with very thin glass. Canvas was used for the shelves. All this contributed to getting the weight of the 15ft van down to 9½cwt. Overall height was kept down by fixing the floor below the chassis longitudinals.

This first trailer caravan was used for several years by the Fleming-Williams family and enquiries from friends as to where similar holiday homes could be obtained led to the building of caravans for sale and hire. The vans, which quickly won a reputation for good towing, were initially made at Frensham, but in 1924 a move was made to Cubitt's yacht basin, Chiswick, West London, a quiet hide-out on the Thames where a number of unconventional people had made their homes in boats or caravans. The Fleming-Williams lived on *Flamingo*, a converted First World War motor launch fitted with a streamlined deck house in the style of a Car Cruiser caravan. Reginald Francis Luck ('Lucky'), a trained woodworker and good all-round handyman then aged about 21, who had done a number of jobs modifying and improving *Flamingo*, was invited to join the Car Cruiser team, eventually becoming works manager. At about this time Fleming-Williams met Wing-Commander O G ('Ossie') Lywood who persuaded him to substantially expand the business and provided the necessary financial backing.

By 1928, when a Car Cruiser, still very like the 1920 experiment, was shown at the Ideal Home Exhi-

bition, the works had been moved to Teddington and in 1929 Car Cruiser Caravans Ltd was formed and purchased the freehold of large premises at North Hyde Road, Hayes, Middlesex. Fleming-Williams was managing director of the new company, W E Hellyer, who had joined the firm in the previous year, was company secretary and Mrs Lywood was also a director. The Hayes works were not conducive to efficient production, consisting of various sheds grouped round a yard, and the movement of a half-finished van from one shed to another meant four or five men stopping work to push it up the slight rise involved.

In 1931, when the range comprised the £95 10ft 6in Type 2, 13ft Type 3 and £147 15ft 6in Type 4, the company and caravanning in general received valuable publicity through a series of articles in the *Daily Express* by its motoring editor Harold Pemberton, who described a tour of England in his Car Cruiser, named 'Hedgerow Villa'. By this time the construction had changed to all solid walls of Sundeala pressed fibre board, and the roof, though still of canvas, was double with an air cavity to combat condensation. As a result

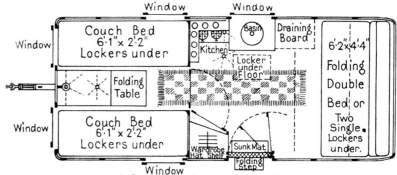

Internal layout of 1931 Car Cruiser Type 4.

In 1933 this Car Cruiser and Hillman Wizard covered 3,000 miles from London to Cairo via Marseilles and Tunis in 21 days.

A sturdy youngster won its first prize at the Rally—the

CAR CRUISER COLT

It is daringly original in conception, and a complete breakaway from conventional design.

It is fitted with two full-sized beds (the table can be converted into a child's cot) and when expanded is roomy and comfortable. When folded there is still head room to sit up in comfort, and it would ride out the worst gale that ever blew. It is so light that it can be towed by the smallest car.

At the price of fully equipped it **£78** should find a ready market.

When in camp the Car Cruiser Colt is neat, smart and roomy. The roof can be lowered from outside or inside. In rough weather you can sit and sleep inside with the roof down.

1935 Car Cruiser Colt, in which it was supposed to be possible to sit up in comfort with the roof lowered in high winds!

the weight of the largest model had increased to 10½cwt, but the basic design continued until the late 1930s, although just prior to the 1931 Motor Show a curve was added to the front end and solid roof panelling was introduced in 1932. Prior to 1933 there had been no windows in the rear end, provoking some critical references to 'the Black Hole of Calcutta', and for 1934 the curved rear end with two tiny windows was replaced on some models with a more vertical back wall with one large window, a change that was

first seen at the Motor Show in 1933.

In the early years anyone might be involved in anything at the works, and R F Luck, though a woodworker, found himself fitting axles, painting – even Mrs. Fleming-Williams took a hand in this – or dealing with customers for the large hire fleet which, in common with other manufacturers of the period, Car Cruisers operated in the early 1930s. Hire charges in 1931 were 3½ guineas per week for the Type 2 and 5 guineas for the Type 4. The first complete caravan designed by Luck was a small lantern roof model of about 1934. Models exhibited at the 1934 Motor Show were the £125 10cwt Featherweight, £175 12cwt 15ft 6in Airflow Four, and £198 14½ cwt Airflow Insulated, which was fully insulated including the floor and was the first model to feature a full width lantern roof. Other Car Cruiser innovations included a fitted spirit level to help in setting the legs as early as 1933, air pressure water feed and an underfloor ice chest in 1934, Alfol reflecting foil insulation in 1935, a cabinet for cutlery incorporated in the draining board, washing up utensils clipped to the underside of the sink cover, and cooling the larder by using the drop in temperature at the gas cylinder caused by the evaporation of the gas from its liquid state.

At the Camping Club meet celebrating King George V's Silver Jubilee in 1935 Car Cruisers won first prize with a prototype called the Rally Four, 18ft long but weighing only 15¾cwt. This van had a full width lantern roof and a central compartment with two pairs of double doors, separating it when necessary from the bedroom areas at the ends but allowing access to the occupants of each. This compartment contained a washbasin, floor bath, second wardrobe

The 1937 Car Cruiser Double Saloon Four. By this date some models had a more vertical back wall with one large window.

with a commode sliding out from beneath, and wet coat hanging over a drip tray and drain. In production form, reduced to 17ft, the Rally Four appeared in the 1936 range at £255. Another 1935 model was the £78 Colt (one source refers to this model as the Cub), a 10ft 6in single panelled van with hinged rising roof and canvas infills to upper front and side walls. It was claimed to be still possible to sit up in comfort with the roof lowered in high winds.

Models exhibited at the 1937 Motor Show were the £345 17ft 6in Astoria, £298 16ft Light Rally Four and £165 12ft 6in 2-3-4. Other models in the range at this time were the £252 15ft 6in Double Saloon Four, £230 12ft 6in All Season Four, a single panelled version of the 2-3-4 at £135 and the Colt, now costing £110. The Astoria was the first end kitchen model. The kitchen was at the front end and other features were a built-in Aladdin oil-fired radiator with airing cupboard, air pressurised water feed to the sink with a pedal pump to top up the pressure, gas-fired water heater, refuse bin, clock and barometer. When the Second World War was imminent O G Lywood rejoined the Royal Air Force in an administrative role and Fleming-Williams took up a post as an art master in Cambridge, selling his interest in the company to the Lywood family, although the company name does not appear to have changed from Car Cruiser Caravans Ltd to O G Lywood Limited until around 1948.

Terence D McCarthy and R F Luck became responsible for the activities of the company both during the War and for a number of years afterwards. Early in 1940 a utility 14ft 6in Vacuation Van with an anthracite stove was produced and in 1942, by which time little could be done to meet civilian needs, a starkly functional 18ft unit called the Billivan was being built. These vans had no permanent chassis, the idea being that one chassis could be used to move a fleet of Billivans one at a time. Numerous special purpose units were built during the War, such as powder vans for the transport of explosives and others which were cloaked in secrecy at the time. There was even a type of mobile strongpoint built for the defence of airfields against airborne assault. This had inner and outer walls of 3/4in marine plywood enclosing a cavity filled with pea gravel. When the British Army and the Royal Air Force were officially equipped with commanders' caravans for the Normandy landings, only Car Cruisers, of the firms experienced in caravan building, received an order.

The first post-war model was a coach shaped van of 1946-47 with anthracite stove and rear end kitchen. This was followed in 1948 by the more conventionally shaped 18ft 9in Adelphi priced at £1,125 and the 15ft 3in Splendide at £550. When the National Caravan

Council formed a Trade Division on 3rd December 1948 Terence McCarthy was the first chairman. Further new models were the £335 14ft 3in Cadet of 1950 and the 17ft 6in Mayfair of 1951 priced at £675 or £750 in de luxe form. Clubman model is a term which came to be applied to any caravan of high

1939 Car Cruiser 2-3-4, streamlined but without the restricted headroom imposed by the curved rear end of earlier models.

1947 Car Cruiser, a sign of post-war austerity!

quality which performed well on the road, was suitable for entertaining in at rallies and satisfied pride of ownership, but which originated as a Car Cruiser model name with the £525 14ft 9in Clubman Major also introduced in 1951. Car Cruisers were very popular with Caravan Club members and together with Cheltenhams were seen at Club rallies in numbers out of proportion to their overall market share. R F Luck built two vans for his own use which he took to National Rallies as well as on tour, the 10ft 8½cwt Red Rover seen at the 1952 Caravan Club National Rally and the later 12ft Grey Squirrel from which the Carousel was developed. Luck fully subscribed to Fleming-Williams' ideals of weight saving but often found his intentions frustrated by the demand of Car Cruiser customers for fine quality oak furniture and de luxe specifications. The only 22ft model built was the Olympian living van of 1952. An advertisement in August of that year offered the only six examples made for sale at a less than cost price of £875, saying that no more would be produced because the company was to play an important part in the cold war rearmament programme.

A very striking van designed by Luck was the 13ft 6in Lynx exhibited at the 1953 Motor Show. Developed from a 12ft prototype made earlier in the year,

the Lynx was offered as a £625 end kitchen 2 berth or £575 centre kitchen 4 berth. Low wrap-round end windows gave excellent view through from the tow car, the body corners were rounded with double radius roof and ends, the whole shell being an outstanding example of coach building in aluminium. A 13ft 9in Clubman model introduced in 1954 had composite floor construction of the same type as the Lynx with two full length channel steel longitudinal members running above the floor, concealed from view by the furniture units and a raised floor at the entrance. Under the ¼in phenol-bonded plywood floor and integral with it were seven timber cross members and eleven closely spaced full length floor bearers. A typical piece of Car Cruiser practicality on this model was the table, attached to the front end cupboard by a positive metal screw device and which could be swung up vertically and secured to the ceiling with a leather strap and turnbutton when not required. A combined meat and bread board, Formica faced on one side, slid under the table when not in use.

The 10ft Carousel in 2 and 4 berth versions, exhibited at the 1957 Motor Show, also had a composite floor and the 18 gauge unpainted bright aluminium exterior wall panelling had an embossed stucco effect finish whilst the 20 gauge roof panelling was painted 'baby pink' although cream was available as an alternative. A contemporary report on the van praised the quality of workmanship and finish. The beds in the 4 berth version give an indication of the thoughtfulness which had gone into the design. To avoid making the daytime backrests too bulky the double bed provided 5in of mattress under shoulders, hips and knees with 3in under pillows and feet, whilst the lower bunk bed had a 5in mattress, the upper having a 3in mattress on Pirelli strapping. New at the Caravan Exhibition in 1960 and, unusually for a small van, creating quite a stir was the stylish 10ft Carissima, probably the last Car Cruiser designed by Luck. Headroom of 6ft 1in was achieved within an overall height of only 7ft 2in and the ex-works weight was around 8cwt.

Post-war Car Cruiser innovations included a trial of Moulton Flexitor suspension units when they became available for caravans in 1950, the one-hand operated 'brolly' roof vent and leathercloth finish to the internal walls both first seen on the Clubman Major of 1951, plastic foam mattresses in 1957 and Rubery Owen torsion bar suspension on the Carissima. As well as caravans the firm continued to produce special purpose units such as Automobile Association offices, propaganda vans for various marketing boards, survey vans for Africa and the Near East, trailers unfolding into elaborate stands for agricultural shows, mobile canteens for the Ministry of Supply and Post Office units.

At some point D W Gumbley, a retired top civil servant, invested capital in the company and was described as joint managing director in 1953. O G Lywood's son Allan, after war service as a Fleet Air Arm pilot, stayed in the forces and even after the death of his father took little active interest in the business. When he left the forces in the late 1950s the firm had been making little or no profit for a number of years and, although taking up a position with a large printing concern in the south-west, he began to take more serious interest. An accountant was appointed to look into the company's affairs, and acting on his recommendations a number of changes were made. Terence McCarthy, who was a director of the company as well as its general manager, left in 1961 and joined the dealers Pilgrim Caravans Ltd of Ringwood, Hants, as sales manager, and R F Luck was appointed buyer, taking no further part in the overall administration of the company. A young ex-apprentice, D Adams, became general manager and a new board of directors comprised Allan Lywood by virtue of his own shareholding, Jim (later Lord) Prior who was married to Allan Lywood's sister Jane and represented the interests of his wife and O G Lywood's widow, and D W Gumbley. Following the demise of

The 1957 Car Cruiser Carousel had unpainted bright aluminium exterior wall panelling with an embossed stucco effect finish and 'baby pink' roof.

Berkeley a former employee of that company, R J Cooper, was appointed sales manager in 1962.

By the beginning of 1963, following a compulsory purchase order on the North Hyde Road premises, the company had moved to Coldhams Road in Cambridge. Very few members of staff moved with the firm and a number of ex-Berkeley employees were recruited together with various tradesmen who had received coachbuilding experience with Marshall's, the Cambridge bodybuilders. D Adams left in that year to pursue his interest in rock climbing and R J Cooper became general manager. Initial production in Cambridge consisted of 10ft and 12ft Carissimas and 12ft, 14ft and 16ft Carousels. There were some problems with quality but these seem to have been overcome and the first new models after the move were the 12ft Carnelian and 15ft Cambridge of 1964. Primrose Caravan Holdings Ltd, who were a subsidiary of Trafalgar House and controlled a group of sites and sales depots mainly in the south of England, took over the company in 1964. A new board of directors comprised D R Freemantle (chairman), R J Cooper (managing director) and Allan Lywood. R F Luck left the company in mid-1965. The new owners invested money in the company and work was actually started on a new 10,000sq ft factory, but late in 1965 it was announced that production was to cease due to continued rising costs and impending reorganisation.

R J Cooper set up his own company, Cooper Coachworks Ltd, Shuttleworth Road, Bedford, building specialist units and caravans to individual requirements and stocking Car Cruiser spares. A 13ft 2 berth prototype with very angular lines won the Design Award competition at the 1967 British Caravan Road Rally but in 1968 it was reported that Coopers were to start manufacturing Car Cruisers again and vans in the traditional styling were produced at least until 1973 at a rate of around 160 per year, but were eventually discontinued because they were unprofitable, production being subsidised by the specialist units.

CAR TRAILERS

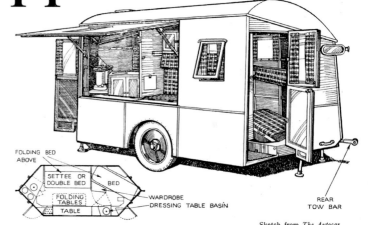

COUNTY — The Caravan of the Year

YOU are out of doors but under cover with this special County sunflap design. There are no man-handling difficulties —a tow bar is fitted at each end. The larger model has five beds —two wash basins—two compartments — two doors — real privacy. For 12 h.p. cars. The price is £175. The smaller model has three beds, two wash basins and the sunflap. For 9 h.p. cars. Price £135. Popular Models also available.

Our List No. 35c fully describes both models and details of the attractive hire terms.

FOR THE CAMPER we have our well-known *County* TENT AND LUGGAGE TRAILERS, List No. 30c.

FOLDING BED ABOVE

SETTEE OR DOUBLE BED — BED

FOLDING TABLES — TABLE

WARDROBE
DRESSING TABLE BASIN

REAR TOW BAR

Sketch from *The Autocar*

CAR TRAILERS LIMITED
HIGH STREET, HARPENDEN, Herts. Phone: HARPENDEN 388

1933 Car Trailers County – no need to reverse, just couple up at the opposite end.

1949 Car Trailers County, with the signature Car Trailers sunflap.

A former artillery officer, Major F A Arnold-Foster, whose company Car Trailers Ltd, of Harpenden, Hertfordshire, had been producing the County tent trailer since 1927, introduced his unorthodox County caravan in 1928. Originally the van was pointed at both ends and the towpole ran full, with coupling and braking gear at each end so that reversing was unnecessary. There was a door in each of the V ends and on the nearside was a large sunflap – a feature of Car Trailers vans for many years. The V rear end was

deleted on a new version introduced in the second half of 1933. In 1939 the range comprised the tent trailer with prices starting at 50 guineas, the 8ft lantern roof Countess at £90, or £105 with double panelling and gas fire, and the County with full width lantern roof and prices ranging from £125 for the 2 berth model to £195 for the 4 berth. The company also operated a hire fleet of their caravans and tent trailers.

Production of caravans ceased during the Second World War but recommenced in 1946 with the 13ft x 6ft 2in Countess and 16ft 6in x 6ft 6n County. Both vans had flat front ends and lantern roofs with very small lantern lights. The Countess had its door at the rear whilst the County had both nearside and rear doors. By 1949 the County had a further door at the rear, giving access to a toilet compartment which had no door to the interior of the van. Late in 1949 a new 14ft Countess was introduced, now with nearside door and rear sunflap.

A 1951 advertisement by Masonite Ltd, who manufactured the hardboard with which the exterior of the vans was panelled, shows a line of Countess models built for service in Jordan, and in a 1952 advertisement Car Trailers claimed to have been exporting their vans since 1930. At the 1952 Motor Show Car Trailers exhibited the County tent trailer in production again for the first time since 1939. Also on

The 1953 Car Trailers Zephyr: the name had to be changed after complaints from the Ford Motor Co.

the stand were a Countess and a Countess Special model built for the Swiss market and including 5 berths, hot and cold water systems, toilet room, foot bath, refrigerator and a cellar for bottles. Although Arnold-Foster was still managing director, Colonel G E Walker of Car Trailers was appointed a manufacturer member of the Trade Division Committee of the National Caravan Council in 1952.

The 1953 Motor Show saw the introduction of the 10ft Zephyr, a streamlined model radically different in appearance from previous Car Trailers. The name was quickly changed to the Countess Minor after the Ford Motor Co pointed to possible confusion with one of their cars. At the end of 1954 Car Trailers were advertising their range for 1955 as the County tent trailer at £175, Countess Minor at £265 and Countess at £395. New in 1955 was the 11ft 3in Carnival, a very plain 4 berth van with a roof curved from end to end. Shortly after the introduction of the Carnival the business was acquired by F H Babcock, production being transferred to Branch Road, Parkstreet Village, St Albans, Hertfordshire, from which address Babcock's company Self Drive Caravans Ltd had been operating a hire fleet of Car Trailers vans since 1952. In August 1956 it was reported that Car Trailers had resigned from the National Caravan Council as they were no longer producing vans.

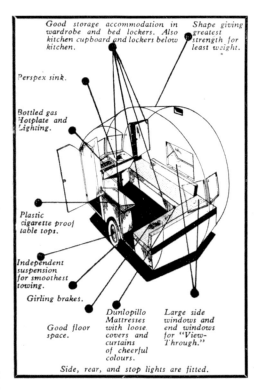

CARATENT

The 1938 Caratent tent trailer was manufactured by Jordans, Chestnut Road, Northampton, and cost 70 guineas. Closed dimensions were 7ft 4in long x 5ft 5in wide x 4ft 6in high, opening on site to provide a floor space of 13ft 6in x 5ft with headroom of 6ft 10in at the centre and 6ft 1in at the ends. Cellu-

1938 Caratent tent trailer. The rear end of the trailer could be detached to form the top of a toilet or kitchen tent in conjunction with the curtains provided.

loid windows were fitted and equipment included two beds, folding table and lockers. The rear end of the trailer could be detached to form the top of a toilet or kitchen tent in conjunction with the curtains provided.

CARLIGHT (CLASSIC)

Carlight Lincoln Imp and Rolls-Royce at The Autocar Rally, Minehead 1932. (LAT Photographic)

WR ('Bob') Earl was an auctioneer and estate agent in Sleaford, Lincolnshire. Having first taken up camping, in 1930 he decided to build himself a caravan which so impressed fellow campers that within a few weeks he had received unsolicited orders for a number of vans. Having no facilities to fulfil these orders himself he engaged a local wheelwright to build the vans for him. The following year Earl opened a small workshop and started production of Carlight caravans on his own account, although the

date when the business started was later said to be 21 July 1932 – presumably when the company Carlight Caravans Ltd (later Carlight Trailers Ltd) was formed. Progress was modest, with turnover rising from £1,500 in the first year to £10,000 by 1936. The early models were square-ended with roofs bowed from side to side, a Lincoln Imp van of this type attending the rally organised by *The Autocar* at Minehead in August 1932. In 1933 the Lincoln Imp range cost between £85 and £117 5s, with Nymph semi-streamlined vans

1935 Carlight Light Four, described as in the 'Super Streamline' style, and with 'compact cooking locker'.

priced from £77 10s to £128 10s, but following a visit to nearby RAF Cranwell Earl built a 'super-stream-lined' 15ft 6in model for the rally held by the RAC at Cheltenham in May of that year. This van had an aerofoil profile, one continuous curve from C-shaped front to floor level at the rear. A study of aircraft construction led to the introduction of much lighter bodies relying for strength on bracing provided by the furniture.

By 1934 there was a range of four 'Super Stream-line' models, a 10ft 6in 2 berth at £109, 13ft 4 berth at £145, 14ft 4 berth at £150 and 15ft 6in 4 berth at £157. The New Light Four of 1934-35 was a £149 13ft four berth weighing only 11½cwt and featuring a new 'compact cooking locker' kitchen design. The Century, which had both roof and walls panelled with single sheets of hardboard, was the fulfilment of Earl's ambition to build a well-finished 4 berth van which could be sold for £100. By 1937 the price had increased to 105 guineas, but like other makers Earl came to realise that making very cheap vans was not an economic business when big turnover was frustrated by the amount of hand work and the small size of the market.

A new lantern roof model exhibited at the 1937 Motor Show was the £350 19ft Colonial. The living space was divisible into two rooms, each having a double bed, wardrobe, washbasin and chest of drawers. The chest in the rear room had a bureau top and the double bed in this room was made up from a conventional dinette, but the bed in the centre room was made up from a three seater dinette, with trans-verse two person settee, armchair and Pullman type table. The well fitted separate front kitchen had a serving hatch and the van was fitted with both gas and battery lighting along with a trickle charger. Reflecting the revulsion still felt by many caravanners, this ultra luxurious van did not have a toilet room. 1939 models comprised the Colonial at £450 (now available with lavatory at £460), Commander £395, 17ft Colonial

Carlight maker W R Earl with wife Ann and Light Four at the Haggerston Rally in 1936.

THE CARLIGHT "CONTINENTAL"

(Model 7)

17' 3"
Luxury
Caravan

"Continette" De Luxe, similar to the Model 7. Lantern-roof, double-panelled in oak, £195.

One of the finest Caravans on the road

£267 10s.

THE MARVELLOUS "CENTURY"
15 ft. 2-room. The first real complete caravan for £100. So great is the demand that we must respectfully ask customers to order well in advance.

The CARLIGHT STREAMLINE Range

The "Century" on view at the Yorkshire Caravan Company, Bawtry, Yorks.

The Light 4, 13 ft., 2-room 4-berth (improved lay-out) - - - £149 10s.
The Model 5, 15 ft. 6 in., 2-room 4-berth (entirely new lay-out) - £175
The Model 5 LR, Lantern Roof, oak-panelled, 4-berth - - - £225
All the above are equipped with Clyde Cookers. Supplied in the "Century" £4 13s. extra.

Fit a Clyde Cooker in your caravan; it's worth it. Come and inspect, weekdays or week-ends; we shall be pleased to see you.

"Century" Light 4 and "Continental" on view at Land Yachts Limited, Ormonde Lodge, Egham, Surrey

CARLIGHT TRAILERS LTD., SLEAFORD, LINCS.

1939 Carlight Colonial Minor – less streamlining provided more internal space.

Motor Show priced at £1,400 and £1,425 respectively, the more expensive model having a foldaway double bed. The Colonial II introduced a classic shape, with curved V front and a lantern roof extending to full width over the rear end kitchen, which was to remain basically unchanged for a number of years.

For 1951, production was concentrated on a Mark V version of the Colonial, 22ft long x 7ft 2in wide, weighing 38cwt and costing £1,650. A 1953 test report on this model gives some idea of the conscientious construction reflected in the price. The double floor had 3in deep joists with 12mm thick plywood above and 4mm thick below, and was so strong that the steel chassis needed no transverse members. The square beam axle was mounted on 42in long 11-leaf underslung half-elliptic springs, the 12in Girling brakes were operated by Clayton Dewandre vacuum servo equipment, and the 25 x 6 Dunlop truck tyres were inflated to 90psi. The exterior wall panelling was 18 gauge aluminium on keruing hardwood framing. Two layers of waterproof kraft paper divided the wall thickness into three cavities, the centre one containing pads of fibreglass or Isoflex insulation (Isoflex where fibreglass might shake down during towing). The exterior panelling on the upper part of the lantern roof was canvas covered Masonite, with aluminium panelling on the shoulders. The ceiling and the interior walls to the kitchen were panelled in hardboard, with oak plywood panelling to the remainder of the interior walls. The ten frameless perspex lantern roof lights had outside louvres to prevent rain bouncing in

Minor £339, Lincoln Challenger £239 and Coronet Major at £155 double panelled or £140 single panelled. How long manufacture continued into the Second World War is not known but models in production early in the War were the 16ft Conqueror, available with plain or lantern roof, 17ft Colonial Minor and 21ft Commander.

1946 models were the 20ft Colonial II and the 16ft Carholme, whilst vans exhibited at the 1948 Motor Show were the 15ft 6in Commonwealth, £1,150 16ft 6in Colonial Minor II and £1,385 20ft 8in Colonial III. The Commonwealth had oil cooking and an export price of £495 (home market price £675!). The Colonial was seen in IVa and IVb versions at the 1949

off the roof shoulders, and the two perspex rooflights were operated by winding gear. The high quality finish to the furniture extended to the inside faces, and wardrobe doors were of warp proof sandwich construction with a core of Dufaylite – a honeycomb of resin impregnated paper. The water system included a 20 gallon main tank, 4½ gallon header tank and 8 gallon hot water tank heated by the Pither's stove. There were nine electric and six gas lights, and toilet room equipment included a washbasin and shower. A thoughtful touch was the inclusion of a kettle to make sure the user had a type which could be filled from the mixing faucet over the sink. At this period however, even at this price level, an Astral refrigerator was an optional extra.

New in 1952 was the export only 16ft 9in Type X, designed for use under rough conditions abroad and available for general sale as the Cosmopolitan by the time of the introduction of the £975 17ft Continental in 1953. The Continental had an ex-works weight of only 22½ cwt, unprecedented for a van of this size and specification. Chassis steel was reduced to the drawbar and a small sub-frame on which were mounted the Bramber Flexitor rubber independent suspension units, though these were later replaced by conventional half-elliptic leaf springs and axle. The plywood floor was carried on six timber joists, with a wooden triangular box assembly providing an anchorage for the drawbar. Exterior wall panelling was 18 gauge aluminium and the oak plywood interior wall panelling was glued to the hardwood frame. The walls were insulated with Isoflex and the fibreglass insulated roof was panelled externally with canvas covered marine plywood. Dixon-Bate quick-action corner legs with integral handles were fitted. Bob Earl's wife slept in the Continental entered in the 1955 British Caravan Road Rally during the 200 mile night section. The next new model was the £950 15ft Caribbean of 1955, followed late in 1957 by a new Cosmopolitan, a 15ft 3in four berth claimed to have been towed at a speed in excess of 85mph on a German *Autobahn*. This van had been designed with an eye on the Continental market, with particular regard to the Swiss size limits of 19ft 8in long including drawbar and 6ft 6in wide. On export models a German made Atlas balanced flue convector heater was fitted.

The canvas covered roof was reported to be so well finished that even on close inspection it looked like an aluminium roof – a finish achieved by filling the texture of the canvas and applying the final coat of paint by hot spraying.

A new Carlight product in 1959 was a stabilizer based on the American style of equalizing hitch. Priced at £15, two quarter-elliptic leaf springs attached to the towing car were connected to the van drawbar by means of chains, adjustment of which allowed the degree of tension in the springs to be varied. The device resisted any sag at the hitch due to the caravan noseweight and pitching, maintaining front wheel adhesion and also resisting any tendency to snaking. At this time Carlight also made towing brackets and roller flyscreens for general sale. The Carabase also of 1959 was a Carlight design manufactured by T Bath & Co Ltd, Norwood Road, London SE24. Priced at £295, this comprised a 25ft x 9ft garage/store with walls clad in western red cedar, and a 10ft wide side canopy to provide shelter for a caravan.

Reports on the vans in the 1950s, as well as praising the superb workmanship and finish, pointed to evidence of research and development pursued with an intensive thoroughness equalled by few other

1948 Carlight Commonwealth. The export price was £495 but on the home market it cost £675!

The 1955 Carlight Caribbean had classic styling.

at the 1960 International Caravan Exhibition at Olympia. This van featured a change to Carlight practice, shared with the other models, in that the canvas roof covering was abandoned in favour of glassfibre fabric bedded on resin. Demand for the other models however was such that the Caspian was not built for the 1961 season but was in production in time for the 1961 Earl's Court Caravan Show. Prices at this time were £875 for the Caspian, £1,085 for the Cosmopolitan, £1,195 for the Caribbean, £1,295 for the Continental and £1,950 for the Mark VII Colonial. A new Carlight accessory in 1964 was an electrically operated reversing stop costing 10 guineas.

Also new that year was the Casetta, a 14ft 3in van weighing 17cwt. Whilst styled like the other models, this van had a completely new body of virtually frameless construction, the side walls and lantern roof consisting of a bonded sandwich with GRP outer skin – flat on the sides and moulded on the roof – a 1in thick core of expanded PVC and an inner skin of melamine laminate. The end walls also had moulded GRP outer and melamine laminate inner skins but on timber framing with fibreglass insulation. The construction of the end walls was integral with the furniture, the front end cocktail cabinet and rear end kitchen contributing to body strength. Timber inserts in the sandwiches provided anchorage points for

makers, even much larger and wealthier ones. Bob Earl's post-war partner was Cyril Gregory, a former RAF pilot, and both men flew the Taylorcraft purchased by the company for business purposes in 1947 in various air races during the 1950s. A 1954 report on a meet of the East Midlands Centre of the Caravan Club at Carlight's Sleaford airfield mentions members being taken up for flights.

A new 14ft 3in model, the Caspian, was exhibited

1955 Carlight Caribbean. Few vans had built-in flued gas fires at the time.

furniture and other fittings, and the sides had a timber edging for securing the ends and roof which overlapped the sides. The outer floor joists were split lengthwise, one half being bonded into the bottom skirt of the side wall and joined to the other half when the wall was attached to the floor. Underfloor strength was provided by the six 2in x 1in floor joists resin bonded to the ½in plywood floor, and a triangular plywood box assembly under the front bay. There was no conventional chassis, just a gun-carriage type frame and drawbar of 3in x 2in x ¼in aluminium channel. Independent suspension was provided by Rubery Owen torsion bars with telescopic shock absorbers. The basic price of £1,225 included a Whale foot pump, 8 gallon underfloor aluminium water tank, Racasan Paragon chemical closet, built-in flued gas fire and three Morco No. 1 gas lights as standard equipment, but various extras were available – a 33 piece china service, Minimain gas water heater, 2.2cu ft Astral refrigerator, two 20 watt 12 volt fluorescent lights, flyscreens, all-round awning channel and folding step. The smallest post-war model was the 12ft Casalette of 1970, a £995 2 berth weighing 13½cwt. 1973 vans were the Casalette at £1240, Casetta £1770, Caribbean £2150 and Continental £2300. Whilst the smaller vans had Rubery Owen suspension the two larger models still had beam axle and semi-elliptic leaf springs.

By 1983 a new shape had been introduced and the four model Commander range comprised the 13ft 2in 132 at £8165, 15ft 154 at £8924, 15ft 152 at £8464 and 18ft 6in 184 at £12995. The vans were still mounted on an own-make chassis, fully galvanised, but with Al-Ko running gear and axle. The GRP ends and lantern roof were laminated to the timber framing, which had halved, screwed and glued joints, and the exterior wall panelling was 20g aluminium. The mattresses were made from three layers of varying density foam and the customer had 22 different choices of carpet and 100 options each for curtains and upholstery. Each van took between 500 and 600 man hours to build. Surprisingly at this price level, flyscreens and spare wheel carrier were extras.

For 1987 the company had decided to sell the vans direct from the factory rather than through a dealer network and also to sell factory refurbished Carlights. By this time Robert Hodgson, step grandson of Bob Earl, was Managing Director – his father John being Chairman. Production ceased early in 2003, the cost of the labour involved in manufacture having pushed the price of the cheapest van in the six model Commander range to £35,985 and literally priced Carlight out of the market. Manager Neil Cook continued to run the business as a service, repair and refurbishment operation. In mid-2003 it was reported that Tommy Green of Vanmaster was working on designs for a new Carlight range to be produced at Vanmaster's Lancashire factory and sold from there and Sleaford, with the first model due in early 2004. Nothing appears to have come of this but in the second half of 2006 it was reported that production had restarted at Sleaford, with Neil Cook making a five model range priced from £30,500 in small numbers. New van building, refurbishment and servicing being undertaken by a staff of nine. In mid-2007 the firm moved to new premises at Heath Farm, North Rauceby, Sleaford and in December 2008 went into administration, but an anonymous investor provided funds to allow the company to continue trading, with Bob Black, former chairman of the Caravan Club and longstanding Carlight owner, named as the new chairman and Neil and Julie Cook remaining responsible for the day-to-day running of the business. Renamed Classic Caravans Ltd, the firm was to specialise in servicing and refurbishing older Carlights, only building new vans to special order – a five model standard range costing between £43,450 and £44,950.

CARLTON

Carlton Caravans, Carlton Fredricks Studios and Works, Weston-super-Mare, were producing four models in 1936-37, the 9ft 6in 2-3 berth Bijou costing from 50 guineas, 12ft 6in 4 berth Clipper in standard and de luxe versions costing 75 and 85 guineas respectively, and the £100 15ft 4 berth lantern roof Privateer. 1950s advertisements have been found for second hand 16ft and 18ft Carltons which may refer to vans dating from before the Second World War.

A 1937 Carlton, justly claimed to be of 'distinctive appearance'!

CAROVER

Manufactured by The Springvale Company, Great West Road, Brentford, Middlesex, the 85 guinea 2/3 berth Carover collapsible caravan had independent suspension and was exhibited at the 1934 Motor Show at Olympia. Closed for towing the Carover was 9ft 4in long x 5ft 6in wide x 3ft 6in high but on site the width increased to 7ft 6in with 5ft 10in headroom, and the canvas sides could be lifted and supported on poles to form sun awnings.

The First De Luxe Collapsible

The Carover de luxe 2/3 berth Collapsible Caravan

SALIENT FEATURES:

1. The independent springing of the Trailer wheels effect—low centre of gravity ● ample road clearance ● the maximum of roadability and safety. The coach-built Airline body allows the minimum of wind resistance ● provides an unrestricted view of following traffic above the closed caravan.

2. Easily and quickly prepared for living by one person. Overall dimensions : closed 9ft. 4ins. long by 5ft. 6ins. wide and 3ft. 6ins. high. When erected the width is increased by 2ft. to 7ft. 6ins., and head-room throughout is 5ft. 10ins.

3. The flexible weather-resistant wall sections are easily detached so that any one side can be opened to form a sun-flap and verandah. The lock-up glazed two-section door at rear, and the window at front end, provide the comfort which can be found with the conventional fixed-wall type of caravan.

PRICE EX-WORKS 85 GNS. NETT

Carover Caravans may be purchased on a special plan of extended payments.

A fully detailed specification is contained in our illustrated prospectus. Send to the builders for your copy. The Springvale Company, Great West Road, Brentford, Middlesex.

See this Caravan demonstrated ● Stand No. 237, Grand Hall Annexe ● Motor Exhibition, Olympia, adjacent to the "Caravan & Trailer" Stand

THE CAROVER
COLLAPSIBLE CARAVANS

1934 Carover. The canvas sides could be lifted to provide sun awnings.

CHALOSS CRUISERS

After building caravans to special order for some years, the motor body and commercial vehicle builders, Challands, Ross & Co Ltd, Canal Street, Nottingham, introduced the Chaloss Cruiser in 1934. This £195 4 berth 15ft van was 6ft 6in wide at floor level, tumblehome reducing this to 6ft at roof level. A side extension of the lantern roof increased headroom above the entrance door.

"Chaloss" Cruisers

Reg. Designs
Nos. 784937 & 786235

DISTINCTIVE FEATURES

Light in weight, easy to handle.
Plenty of head room throughout.
Full length, comfortable beds.
Steel sub frame, twin steel tow pole.
Patent quick-action ball hitch.
Streamlined to resist wind and suction.
Low centre of gravity and overall height.
Rides steadily, no pitching, side rock or tail wag.
Lantern roof with double lining.
Air spaces between lining prevent condensation.
Top ventilation without draught.
Rigidly supported when standing.
Four berth, two separate rooms.
Windows at both ends permit view of following traffic.

£195 At Works

28 Canal Street **Challands. Ross** & Co., Ltd **Nottingham**
Telephone : Nottingham 40095.
Telegrams : Chaloss, Nottingham.

1934 Chaloss Cruiser, manufactured by a motor body and commercial vehicle builder.

CHARNWOOD *See* RITE

CHELTENHAM

In 1920, having just been demobbed from the Army and wanting to take a holiday, Arthur E Gardner decided to build a motor caravan, which he constructed in one of his stables with assistance from the gardener and the village blacksmith. A friend showed great interest in the project and offered to join him on the holiday tour when the vehicle was complete. The friend's daughter Joy was also very interested and offered a number of helpful and practical suggestions. As a result of shortcomings experienced during the tour Gardner started to reconstruct the van, a process which continued at intervals for the next three years before he decided that it would be a lot less trouble to build a trailer caravan. A small works was taken in Cheltenham in 1924 and, trading as Summerfield Caravans, the first trailer caravan was built, though this was hired out rather than being sold. Total production for that year was three vans and the business continued in a small way until 1926

when Gardner married the friend's daughter who had taken such an interest in the original motor caravan, and naturally they went on a caravan honeymoon.

In 1927, by which time the name had been

The 1928 Cheltenham had typical 1920s styling.

Before You Make Your All-Important Decision
BE SURE TO SEE THE
CHELTENHAM RANGE
—particularly the Moose and Stag models

Here is the famous Stag Model. It has full accommodation for 4 persons, is double-panelled, and with gas cooking, costs **£175**

The Eland— Cheltenham's masterpiece with end kitchen, bath, gas lighting and cooking, toilet room and wireless. Price **£265**

★ See the special Cheltenham Display at the LONDON CARAVAN COMPANY'S Big Exhibition — March 21st—27th
—or send a postcard for our full catalogue of all models:

THE CHELTENHAM CARAVAN CO. LTD.
Maida Vale Works, Naunton Lane, Cheltenham

1938 Cheltenham advertisement. The firm had evolved their own distinctive style of streamlining in the early 1930s.

changed to the Cheltenham Caravan Co, a move was made to larger premises, followed by a further move in 1928. The early vans were boxy lightweights about 8ft in length and were traditionally shaped lantern roof models. When Cheltenham introduced streamlining they at first followed the Car Cruiser shape before evolving their own distinctive style in the early 1930s. Large low end windows giving a view through from the towing car were used in conjunction with measures to lower the floor, involving cranked axles, underslung springs, 'bumped' chassis and floors mounted below the main joists. A Cheltenham Silver Chalet with bright aluminium exterior panelling was seen at the world's first trailer caravan rally held at Minehead in August 1932 and a new 15ft model with an elegant streamlined lantern roof made a big impression at a rally held by the RAC in Cheltenham in May 1933. Features of this model included stop light and direction indicators (not then a legal requirement), locker for golf clubs and fishing rods, walnut interior panelling, floor well for storage, bath, hot and cold water system, stainless steel cooking recess, fitted radio

with roof aerial, and a fire extinguisher. Starting in 1933 with a tour of Morocco, the Gardners began a practice of testing new models on arduous overseas trips. Vans exhibited at the Motor Show in 1934 were the Air-o-lite 10ft 2 berth costing £78 and a large luxury model featuring a separate room for maid or chauffeur. Equipment on this van included hot and cold water supply, full size bath under one of the berths and stainless steel fittings.

Cheltenham were instrumental in bringing about the changeover from oil to LPG for cooking and lighting – Major Henry Presland of the dealers P & P Motor Co, later The London Caravan Co, attended the 1936 Caravan Club National Rally with a Cheltenham Special fitted with gas cooking, lighting and central heating with hot water radiators. This model was marketed in the 1937 range priced at £320 and featured a centre toilet room of semi-circular shape to minimise its obtrusiveness, full size bath under one of the single beds, dressing table with triple mirrors, and cocktail cabinet. In 1935 the firm operated a hire fleet of 25 vans but by 1937 demand was such that all vans built were sold and vans were being hired out on behalf of customers.

The six model range in 1939 included the £85 10ft Fawn, £175 13ft 9in Stag, 16ft Gnu and £275 17ft 6in Eland. The Stag was a double panelled 4 berth with insulated floor, gas cooking and lighting as well as electric lighting. A saving of £12 was made if the gas equipment was omitted, oil stoves being provided for cooking. The Eland had a front bay window and the beds, with Dunlopillo mattresses, could be arranged as one double and two singles or four singles, and under the offside front bed was a bath. Furnishings included writing desk, china cupboard and fitted cocktail cabinet, and the comprehensive equipment ranged from hot and cold water systems, two gas heaters – one for each compartment – ventilated food safe, metal rubbish bin and a radio to a complete set of crockery, cooking pots, pans, cutlery, paper rack, flower vases, towel rail, tooth glass, tea strainer, mop and dishcloth. Design features of Cheltenhams in the 1930s included friction damping to control the overrun braking system (from 1933), their own design of ball coupling and early use of synthetic enamel for exterior finish (from around 1934). Apart from wheels and hubs all parts needed were made in the works, stocks being built up during the winter so that the summer months could be devoted to building caravans. The vans were designed by Arthur, with Joy choosing fabrics, generally supervising the interiors and handling sales.

Before caravan production ceased during the Second World War, a 1940 16ft 3 berth model offered

A 1939 Cheltenham Fawn at Cheddar, Whitsun 1940. Note the wartime headlamp shield on the car at the right hand bottom corner.

permanent living accommodation with two doors, two wardrobes, washbasin as well as sink, toilet room, coal stove and blackout panels to the windows. Production soon resumed after the War and by 1948 the models available were the £460 14ft 4 berth Reindeer, £650 16ft 4 berth Gnu and £785 17ft 3in 4 berth Eland. The Gnu was a coach-shaped van and the Eland a V-fronted lantern roof model. Reflecting uncertainty at the time as to whether roof and wall cavities should be sealed or ventilated, the roof on the Gnu provided a one inch air space open all round the edges, the single panelled inner roof lining being integrated with the fibreglass insulated walls. A new model in 1949 was the £285 12ft 3 berth Gazelle, and by 1950 the Reindeer had been replaced by the £345 15ft Antelope. In September 1950, to mark 30 years of caravan building (the advertising actually said the 30th anniversary of Cheltenham Caravan Company Ltd), the Gardners invited all Cheltenham owners to a rally at their home, Southfield Farm, Cheltenham, and a Cheltenham Owners Club was formed. The original Club Officers were Arthur Gardner, President; Ralph Lee, Chairman; Cecil H Gardner (Arthur's son), Honorary Secretary: and Joy Gardner, Honorary Treasurer.

1951 started with a five model range: Gazelle, Antelope, Gnu, Eland and the £675 20ft 5 berth Elk, though by the middle of the year the Gnu had been dropped and later in the year the Deer – a 2 berth version of the Gazelle – was added. The Elk was dropped towards the end of 1952 and a new £485 15ft 4in 4 berth van introduced. This was the end kitchen Bison with toilet room and two double beds, and featuring wall lining and furniture in limed oak. When the 1955 range was announced towards the end of 1954 it comprised the Deer, Antelope, Bison, Eland and a new luxury 14ft 6in 2 berth end kitchen lantern roof model, the Impala, priced at £650 with hardboard exterior panelling or £665 with 18 gauge aluminium panelling, though even on the aluminium panelled vans only the roof shoulders were in aluminium, the raised part of the lantern roof being traditionally constructed of canvas bedded in white lead on insulation board. Equipment included a rotating cocktail cabinet, panel gas fire, refrigerator, roller action top over sink and drainer, wash basin in toilet compartment, electric and gas lights, and folding step. This van also featured seat backs hinged to the walls at the top so that during the day they provided raked backrests whilst folding flat to the wall at night so as not to reduce the available width of the beds.

A completely new range of vans was exhibited at the 1955 Motor Show, the most significant feature of which was the introduction of GRP mouldings for the front ends, roofs and doors, and the adoption of a body style which was to continue with little change until the end of production. The new models were the £355 12ft 2 berth Deer, £435 14ft 4 berth Stag, £565 14ft 2 or 3 berth Klipspringer and the £595 15ft 8in 4 berth Springbok. To minimise the number of moulds required all models utilized the same ones, the roof being in front and rear halves made in the same mould. On the Deer the two halves joined directly together, an opening being cut in the middle for a conventional rooflight. On the 14ft vans the 2ft gap between the halves was bridged by a Morlite GRP

A 1952 Cheltenham Eland hitched up to a Standard Vanguard.

The 1954 Cheltenham Impala. Even with the optional aluminium exterior panelling, the raised part of the lantern roof was still traditionally constructed, with canvas bedded on white lead on insulation board.

rising roof section the full width of the van, and the Springbok had a huge 4ft Morlite. Hardboard was finally abandoned in favour of aluminium for the exterior wall panelling, with bowed side walls on the Klipspringer and Springbok. To improve seating and bed comfort the 4in thick Dunlopillo mattresses were supported on transverse coil springs. A fifth model added to the range at the end of 1955 was the 12ft Sable. After operating from premises at both Naunton Lane and Leckhampton Road, Cheltenham, for many years, the Naunton Lane factory was closed in 1956. Cecil Gardner married Ralph Lee's daughter Patricia in 1957.

For 1958 the range was reduced to three models – the £465 12ft 9in 4 berth Waterbuck, £475 12ft 9in 2 berth Sable and £645 15ft 8in 4 berth Springbok – all now with moulded GRP rear ends, and on the Waterbuck and Sable the moulded ends were curved around the corners to form part of the side walls. Foamed plastic had replaced Dunlopillo for the mattresses, with Dunlopillo strapping replacing the coil springs, and the steel frame previously used to resist the tension of the springs was replaced by a much lighter duralumin frame. The next major innovation was the

fitting of independent suspension to the Springbok for 1959. The 1959 models also featured moulded GRP drawbar shrouds. New for 1960 was the £550 14ft 2in 4 berth Kudu with the full width rising roof of the earlier 14ft models replaced by a large central rooflight. This van and the Sable were fitted with the independent suspension previously introduced on the Springbok. The 1961 Puku was a 14ft 4in 2 berth costing £600 and a 4 berth version exhibited at the 1961 Earl's Court Caravan Exhibition was equipped with refrigerator and shower, though these were optional extras adding £38 and £35 respectively to the basic price of £595. Apart from the Waterbuck, 1962 models were fitted with hydraulically damped overrun braking of Cheltenham's own design.

For 1963 the Waterbuck was fitted with independent suspension and hydraulically damped coupling like the rest of the range, and the £425 10ft 7in 2 berth Fawn was introduced, the Kudu being discontinued. A new after-sales service scheme, then unique, was also introduced whereby after 500 miles of towing or within one month of purchase owners of new vans could return the caravan to the supplying dealer for checking and adjustment including brakes, chassis, cupboard catches, drawer retainers, gas and electric systems, Cheltenham paying the dealer to carry out this service. For 1965 1/2in thick expanded polystyrene insulation replaced aluminium foil, but this was only fitted behind the aluminium panelling, an air cavity still being relied on for insulation behind the GRP mouldings. An extra first introduced at that year's Earl's Court Caravan Exhibition was a solenoid-operated reversing catch controlled from the dashboard of the tow car. Costing around £6, the accessory was designed specifically for the Cheltenham coupling. For 1967 there was a new 15ft model, the £685 4 berth Nyala, the Springbok was fitted with a moulded GRP lantern roof, unusually extending to full width at the offside rear only over the toilet compartment, and all models now had polystyrene insulation in roof and ends as well as the side walls.

The Gardners also had site and dealership interests, being mentioned as the owners of Rushford Warren Camp, between Mudeford and Christchurch, in 1953. In 1962 they acquired the Berkshire dealers, Wallingford Caravans, followed in 1967 by Yeovil Caravan Co and West of England Caravans (Devizes) – the three dealerships becoming The Cross Country Group. Whilst the vans were conscientiously constructed, with comfortable, well thought out layouts, several reports commented that the quality of the interior finish was below what might be expected at the price level. Cheltenham owners however were noted for 'brand loyalty' and like Car Cruisers the vans were seen at Caravan Club rallies in numbers out of proportion to their overall market share. At the International Rally held in Israel in 1964 half the British vans attending were Cheltenhams. Cheaper Explorer models were added to the range in 1972 but production at Cheltenham ended in 1974. The name and moulds for the GRP bodywork were acquired by Stephens and West, manufacturers of Stirling Caravans, who restarted production before selling the name and moulds on to Ferndown Caravans, a Kent dealership, following which Roger Launder, a former Cheltenham employee, started production, building vans in small numbers until the early 1980s. Between 1981 and 2003 John and Tina Bradley of Christchurch operated a caravan restoration business specialising in Cheltenham vans.

The Cheltenham Springbok of 1963. Utilising the same mould for the front and rear halves of the GRP roof on different lengths of van resulted in a huge 'Morlite' rising roof section on this model.

CHILTERN *See* PALADIN

CLASSIC *See* CARLIGHT

CLIFFE

A 1920s maker building vans in a style typical of the period with square ends, bowed sides and lantern roof.

CLIFTON (1)

A design for an extending trailer caravan houseboat, patented by W E Clifton of Birmingham in 1923.

CLIFTON (2) *See* ECONOMY

COLLAPSIVAN

This folding caravan, designed for towing behind a motorcycle combination, was produced by the Collapsivan Company of Westminster around 1929. The make does not appear to have been in production for very long but W S Greening took an example to the Caravan Rally organised by *The Autocar* at Minehead in August 1932. Later in the 1930s Mr Greening went into production with the Fohlo, a design derived from the Collapsivan.

COMPACTO

The 1934 Compacto was still 4ft 10in high when closed for towing.

Costing 75 guineas, the 1934 3 berth Compacto collapsible caravan was manufactured by John Kitcher, Gosbrook Street, Caversham, Reading. Closed for towing the dimensions were 8ft long x 6ft wide x 4ft 10in high, opening on site to 12ft 6in long x 6ft 3in high.

CONDOR

Condor caravans were built by J C Chick at Cambridge Road, Southampton in the period 1935-39. Models in early 1937 were the £98 Condette with 2 or 3 berths, and 13ft 6in, 15ft and 17ft 6in 4 berth vans priced at £125, £145 and £245 respectively. Mr Chick appears to have been a keen rally-goer – his attendance at a Caravan Club rally at Greta Bridge, Co Durham in 1936 reportedly involving a round trip of 640 miles. Mr and Mrs Chick were also reported to have attended a rally at Lulworth in June 1939.

1937 Condor advertisement. Its maker J C Chick appears to have been a keen rally-goer.

COOPER *See* CAR CRUISER

Introducing a New Baby

£98

The "CONDETTE"

A compact 2 or 3 berth van with pleasing lines for the small car

STEEL CHASSIS OF ROBUST DESIGN, DOUBLE PANELLED, RACO BEDS, PRESSURE FED WATER SYSTEM, EIGHT GALLON TANK. ALL FITTINGS STAINLESS, WHEEL DISCS.

OTHER MODELS—ALL DOUBLE PANELLED—
13 ft. 6 in.   4 BERTH **£125**
15 ft. 0 in.   4 BERTH **£145**
17 ft. 6 in.   4 BERTH **£245**

We have an interesting catalogue if you care to apply for it:

CONDOR CARAVANS

CAMBRIDGE ROAD :: SOUTHAMPTON

Telephone : 2518

COTSWOLD

When Cotswold Caravans Ltd, Francis Street, Cheltenham, commenced production in 1938, the vans were advertised as being 'Designed and built under the personal supervision of a practical and experienced caravan manufacturer'. This refers to W A Adams, who started Cotswold shortly after resigning his directorship of Adams Caravans Ltd. There were five models in 1939 – the 14ft 6in 4 berth Emerald, 12ft 6in 4 berth Sapphire, 10ft 6in 3 berth Ruby and 10ft 6in 2 berth Moonstone, priced respectively at £115, £112 10s, £95 and £85 with single panelling or £127, £123 10s, £102 and £92 with double panelling. There was also a 9ft 2 berth van, the Gem. Interestingly, the vans had Brockhouse undergear although Adams Caravans had been wound up on the petition of J Brockhouse & Co Ltd. Due to the limited supply of materials when manufacture re-started at Charlton Kings, Cheltenham in 1946 the only model was the 4 berth Emerald costing £551 3s 4d. By the beginning of 1951 the firm had moved to Kingsditch Lane,

1946 Cotswold Emerald, the first postwar model.

COTSWOLD "SAPPHIRE 49"

FULLY INSULATED. 14' 6" x 6' 4",
4 berth, 2 room, Chromium Plated
Windows, Jockey Wheel, etc., and
Gas Equipped.

Price **£498** Inc. Tax, Ex Works.

THE PERFECT HOME —
— FOR THE OPEN ROAD

Cheltenham and the 14ft 6in 4 berth Sapphire had succeeded the Emerald. This was joined in 1952 by the 9ft 3in 2 berth Cosyvan priced at £225 – a 3 berth version cost £238. The Sapphire cost £460 in 1952 and was framed in hardwood with 20 gauge aluminium exterior roof and wall panelling, painted hardboard interior panelling and Isoflex insulation. Production does not appear to have continued beyond 1952.

1949 Cotswold Sapphire – the maker had previously built Adams caravans.

COUNTRY LIFE

When Country Life Caravans started production at Slough, Buckinghamshire, in the latter part of 1936, one of the principals was reported to be G W Bush, former works manager at the Car Cruiser factory, who had also worked for Carlight and Eccles. 1937 models were the £135 13ft Canterbury, £149 15ft Durham, £154 15ft 6in Salisbury and £210 17ft 6in lantern roof Exeter. The price of the Exeter included gas cooking and lighting but this was an £8 extra on the other vans. By 1938, trading as Country Life Caravans (Mobile Luxury Flats Ltd), the firm had moved to London Road, Ashford, Middlesex, and the range comprised the £145 12ft Durham, £175 14ft Salisbury, £225 16ft Exeter and £300 18ft Windsor Super. All these vans had 4 berths with full width lantern roof and all except the Durham were double panelled.

After the Second World War Country Life models were built by the Rolfe family, who ran a car business at Romsey, Hampshire. Whilst the firm was aid to have

1937 Country Life advertisement. The firm had previously been located at Slough and later moved to Ashford. During this year the Exeter was replaced by the Windsor Super and the price of the other models was increased.

Whether or not you plan to buy a new caravan you will enjoy looking over the new COUNTRY LIFE models. They can be seen either at EGHAM or at

CARA-CARS LTD.
ILKLEY, YORKS.
and
ASSOCIATED BRITISH CARAVANS, LTD.
CHURCH END, FINCHLEY

THE "CANTERBURY". Single-panelled, furnished in mahogany. Four-berth, oil stoves, electric and oil lighting. 13 ft. long by 6 ft. 4 in. wide, weight 12 cwt. Towable by 10 h.p. PRICE **£145.**

THE "DURHAM". Double panelled, furnished in oak or mahogany. Four-berth, Bottogas cooking, electric and gas lighting. 15 ft. long by 6 ft. 6 in. wide, weight 13 cwt. Towable by 12 h.p. PRICE **£175.**

THE "SALISBURY". Double-panelled, furnished in oak or mahogany. Four-berth, Bottogas cooking, electric and gas lighting. 16 ft. 6 in. long by 6 ft. 6 in. wide, weight 15 cwt. Towable by 14 h.p. PRICE **£230.**

THE "WINDSOR SUPER". Treble-panelled, furnished in oak, mahogany or walnut. Four-berth, Bottogas cooking and heating, electric, gas and oil lighting. End kitchen, shower bath and geyser, front and rear doors, awning and latrine with tent. 18 ft. long by 6 ft. 9 in. wide, weight 17½ cwt. Towable by 16 to 18 h.p. PRICE **£350.**

COUNTRY LIFE CARAVANS are built with steel under-carriage, ash frame, Sundeala panelling, Godins windows and Insulwood roof, and are fitted with Rex mattresses.
The larger models are all equipped with full-width lantern roof.

THE COUNTRY LIFE CARAVAN CO.
WHITE LION WORKS, EGHAM, SURREY

Phone: EGHAM 623

THE LANGUARD 48

CENTRE KITCHEN   ELSAN CLOSET
REAR   SELF - CONTAINED   BEDROOM
COAL   HEATING   STOVE   GAS   MATTRESSES
CURTAINS   CARPETS   ETC.

£888

OVERSEAS   INQUIRIES   WELCOMED

THE COUNTRY LIFE CARAVAN CO., ROMSEY

The 1948 Country Life Languard was a pioneering living van design.

1951 Country Life Lancraft. Several makers introduced short-lived two-storey models at the time.

The 1952 Country Life Lanliner, an exceptionally large van at the time and not legally towable.

built horse-drawn caravans from 1918, this may have been under the Rolfe name rather than Country Life and this early caravan building was probably superseded by the motor business at some point. The Rolfes do not appear to have had any connection with GW Bush's company. The first post-war van appears to have been the Cub of 1946, which had exterior panelling consisting of vertical strips of aluminium with folded edges which were riveted together and dispensed with most of the usual body framing. At a period when there was enormous demand for caravans as homes, the Languard of 1947 was a pioneering design, very different from the traditional touring caravan based designs being produced by the old-established makers but suiting the taste of many people who were looking for an alternative to a house. Originally 19ft long, later increased to 22ft, the living room had a solid fuel stove angled across one corner with an open doorway leading to a large well-appointed kitchen from which a passageway between the nearside wall and a round-ended toilet room on the offside led to a separate bedroom. The toilet room was equipped with a chemical closet and hanging for wet coats, and later a washbasin. The interiors were painted in pastel colours. Another 1947 model was the 15ft 6in Daydream. In 1949 the range comprised the 22ft Languard 49 at £798, 22ft Diplomat at £780, 17ft 6in Cruis-alon at £598, 15ft 6in Daydream at £695 and the 12ft 6in Cub, available unfurnished at £298, or furnished (gas, mattresses, curtains, etc) at £338.

Country Life also produced vans fitted for use as canteens, fish fryers and for ice cream vending. By 1951 three models were available, the Languard 51 unchanged in length or price, Lanclipper 51 18ft long in standard or de luxe form at £498 or £535 respectively, and the 13ft Langull in 3 or 4 berth standard or de luxe versions priced between £338 and £375. When Berkeley introduced the Statesman double-decker in 1951 Country Life was one of several makers to hastily produce a two-storey model, the £1,195 22ft Lancraft with two upstairs bedrooms. Sufficient headroom on the ground floor was provided by using the space which would otherwise have been under-bed lockers upstairs, resulting in very limited floor space in the bedrooms. An unusual feature for the period was double glazing, though only to the main side windows. This design did not attract buyers and was soon dropped. The 30ft Lanliner would have been considered an exceptionally large van when it was introduced in 1952 – being in excess of the maximum length of trailer permitted to be towed under the Motor Vehicles (Construction and Use) Regulations. Layout featured a front end double bedroom, central lounge 16½ft long with single bed settee and a double bed which by day slid away, ready-

made, under the bed in the front bedroom. The kitchen and bathroom shared the width at the rear end. The firm also produced a large motor caravan named the So-long, but probably in very small numbers.

Several makers were influenced by an American fashion which owed something to the cherished symbol of the covered wagon and took the form of roof and sides extending as a hood over the front window. This generally featured on living vans but Country Life applied it to both ends of the 13ft 6in Silver Langull and 16ft Golden Lancrest introduced in 1957. This was a curious feature on a touring van and must have had a very adverse effect on aerodynamic efficiency although four vents were provided in the front projection to relieve air pressure – a feature inducing an audible whistle at low speeds. Strangely the shape was not adopted for the only other model available in 1957, the 22ft Languard living van, now with a double bed which rolled away with bedding in-situ under a Welsh dresser. The Lancrest body was also

offered as a demonstration unit or mobile office. It was reported late in 1959 that Country Life were to continue manufacturing these three models unchanged for 1960 but production appears to have been discontinued around this time.

COVENTRY STEEL

Following the failure of his Airlite company in 1938, Clifford R Dawtrey formed Coventry Steel Caravans Ltd, with solicitor A E Spaven as fellow director, and launched the 16ft Phantom Knight priced at £285. The Ovoid steel body was manufactured by Rubery Owen from rolled-out sections welded together to produce a smooth one piece shell with no mouldings. The edges of the rolled sections were turned in to carry wooden fillets for mounting the inner panelling and furniture, and the windows slid down into the bodywork on leather straps in railway carriage style. Introduced at the same time was the 13ft Silent Knight priced at £115. The shape of this model was more conventional but the parana pine

body frame had the sides and ends panelled in 20 gauge steel overlaid with an insulating layer of felt and outer covering of leathercloth, the roof being covered with leathercloth laid over closely spaced light spars. There was also a 15ft Silent Knight model, and a modified version of the Phantom Knight was sold by the dealers Bransby Bros, of Butley, near Macclesfield, as the Bransby Special. Dawtrey was an original thinking, forward looking, technological pioneer, but by temperament he was impetuous and, having formed the company and advertised 'caravans of steel', he soon had to abandon steel in favour of aluminium due to excessive weight – the Phantom Knight panelled in 18 gauge aluminium being about 3cwt

CARAVANS OF STEEL

THE "PHANTOM KNIGHT" CARAVAN

Inside there are three rooms, a lounge, dining room and central kitchen compartment. The room at the rear end provides a double or two single beds, and the room at the front end provides a double bed, which in the day time becomes a lounge seat. The whole interior is divided off in two rooms by the wardrobe door.

In the central kitchen is a large gas cooker and oven with complete equipment of cooking utensils, and there is a large sink with a small bowl inside and water tanks with a gravity feed to the sink, and a complete equipment of crockery supplied.

Standard equipment includes an all-wave wireless set, clock, gas-lights and a gas fire. A large outside locker provides accommodation for a complete chemical toilet cabinet, tents, deck chairs, etc.

The length—16 feet, width 6 feet 6 inches, and head room inside 6 feet 3 inches.   PRICE **£285**

An exceedingly strong chassis is manufactured by this Company which ensures perfect towing at all speeds.

The "Phantom Knight" exterior is entirely steel, welded together in one piece without any joints or mouldings whatsoever, and painted and finished with a high-class varnish.

THE "SILENT KNIGHT" CARAVAN

The body frame is constructed of Parana Pine, covered with steel panels which, in turn, are covered with a layer of felt, and finally with an outer cover of high quality leather-cloth fabric, forming insulated walls. Oil lighting and cooking stoves, and a complete central kitchen equipped with sink, draining boards, water tank, cooking utensils, crockery and cutlery, etc., are supplied.

Both the models are similar in appearance and layout.

The length—13 feet, width 6 feet 2 inches, and head room inside 6 feet 3 inches.

The "Silent Knight" is a very light Caravan built for the light car.   PRICE **£115**

The "PHANTOM KNIGHT" layout is illustrated above.
The "SILENT KNIGHT" layout is similar.

Both models are designed for use Winter and Summer.

A Coventry Steel Phantom Knight in the foreground with Home Guard in attendance.

1938 Coventry Steel Phantom Knight. Steel was soon abandoned in favour of aluminium due to excessive weight.

lighter. The £695 Phantom Lounge Car motor caravan was exhibited at the 1938 Motor Show. This had a body styled on the same lines as the Phantom Knight mounted on a 10ft 6in wheelbase Jensen sports chassis with a V8 engine.

Production was devoted to other work during the Second World War including the building of trailer ambulances, and after the premises at Quinton Road, Coventry, suffered bomb damage the company moved to Leek Wootton, Warwick, later acquiring The Old Corn Exchange, Market Place, Warwick. However, caravan development was not neglected during the War and on a visit in 1943 the editor of *The Caravan* found Dawtrey on the roof of his house, checking on samples of aluminium finishes which he was subjecting to an extended weathering test – at a time when most people in caravanning circles had never even heard of anodising. When the Phantom 46 went into production in 1946 it represented a spectacular breakaway from traditional construction methods. The coach shape body, mounted on a rust-proofed chassis, had walls made up of narrow vertical panels alternating with extruded aluminium ribs of complicated cross section made to Dawtrey's own design, which also accommodated strips of Isoflex or Onazote insulating material, faced on the inside with oak veneers. The roof had a band of translucent perspex all round its outer curves and three large skylights on top. Moulded perspex was also used for frameless top-hinged windows. A double bed turned up on end, with bedding in-situ, into a cabinet across the front end, leaving space for a movable easy chair on each side. In the centre were two single beds, one folding to the nearside wall, two large wardrobes, dressing table, bureau-bookcase and a dining table with four chairs. The table was mounted on a false floor of carpeted aluminium so that when all the chairs were pushed under the table the whole unit could be pulled around with one hand. Heating was by oil-fired convectors designed to give a red glow. A swing door led to the rear end kitchen and toilet room, faced and furnished in coloured perspex. The perspex larder had a cooling jacket which was also the water tank, and a wall mounted crockery rack had drain tubes leading down to the sink. A wash basin fitted under the larder slid out for use, and a cupboard beneath this had a chemical toilet mounted on the inside of the door so that it swung out when the door was opened. The toilet could be lifted off the door and placed in an outside compartment or tent, which were offered as optional extras. A section of the floor lifted to reveal a shower tray. Operation of the shower was simple but ingenious – water of the desired temperature was poured into a metal tank mounted on two vertical metal tubes and the tank was then pushed up the tubes to the ceiling, the water flowing by gravity via a flexible hose and hand held shower rose. The toilet/shower area could be separated from the kitchen by a plastic curtain.

Dawtrey impetuosity was demonstrated once again in the Phantom, which was designed as a 19-footer, went into production as a 20-footer and was soon lengthened to 21ft and then 22ft. The exclusive extruded rib section, which had involved a heavy cost in tooling, was altered to eliminate the separate panel strips. Heavy condensation occurred on the ceiling and the roof construction had to be redesigned with a new centre section and 'double glazing' for the perspex band. Even then, for the worst conditions of cold and heat, a supplementary roof was added, mounted a few inches above the integral one. A single branch electric light fitting incorporating a knight in armour motif was designed and, since tooling costs made the unit price for a small quantity excessive, sufficient for several years' production were ordered. Within months the fitting was redesigned with two branches, involving retooling. Again a large order was placed to keep the unit price down and the single branch fittings were left unused in the stores. In November 1945 the van was announced as 'coming soon' at a price of 'something over £700', yet when first delivered in April 1946 it was priced at £1,290 and eventually reached £2,420.

The Phantom, later renamed the Coventry Knight, was however an immediate prestige and sales success, appealing especially to buyers with a taste for the magnificent, such as fairground folk and gypsies. When a drawbar mounting with aluminium covers for two gas cylinders was provided, one of the covers had a built-in heater, similar to a miner's safety lamp, to ensure that the butane gas continued to vaporise in freezing conditions. Changes for 1949 included an insulated, perspex lined self contained toilet compartment, and a more spacious kitchen was fitted with a 45in fold down bath supplied with hot and cold water and incorporating a shower with re-circulating water supply. There was a built-in mains electric refrigerator and the unique Dawtrey water trolley with two containers, one for fresh and one for waste water.

The shell was offered for other purposes, and fitted out as a mobile bank was purchased by most of the major banks. A serious problem occurred when one of the banks, pleased with its purchase, had the van

The 1948 Coventry Steel Knight was a spectacular breakaway from traditional construction methods.

towed through the narrow City of London streets for the directors to view it. A traffic jam resulted, the police arrived and the van was found to exceed the legally permitted width. Dawtrey had not taken into account the projecting door hinges and window hoods. The vans had to go back to the factory and it was just possible to reduce the width sufficiently by modifying the projecting parts. Other uses included dental, X-ray and desert survey units. Countries to which the vans were exported included Egypt, Iran, Saudi Arabia and Turkey. Early in 1949 the factory was said to be turning out two Knights a week with each van taking about two weeks to build.

The short-lived Falstaff Knight was first advertised in the second half 1949 priced at £2,150. The lead covered almost flat roof eliminated the curved band of perspex, which was replaced by a line of shallow opening perspex windows at the tops of the walls. The layout was ingenious but very complicated. The front end lounge area and rearward dining area were each one step down from the central kitchen area. A double bed over the lounge area was lowered from the ceiling by cables. In its lowered position the bed was reached

1950 Coventry Steel Falstaff Knight – an ingenious layout but very complicated.

by stairs at each side and left headroom for the lounge settee to be used as another double bed. Two single beds separated by a central partition were located over the dining area and rear end bathroom. There was a toilet room next to the nearside entrance door and the van was fitted with 14in Warner electric brakes. The 22ft Warwick Knight, first exhibited at the 1950 Motor Show, and the 15ft Silver Knight were similar in appearance to the Falstaff Knight but with fewer top windows, those at the ends being circular. An extra unit was offered to convert any Warwick Knight model from five to seven berths by the addition of a top deck. Overall height increase was kept within 3ft by recessing the floor of this unit through the roof of the lower unit. An alternative unit, costing £440 in 1952, added a sun deck incorporating a sun lounge and roof garden accessed by a ladder from the van interior.

On one visit to the works the editor of *The Caravan* noticed a van with the wheel on one side in a different position from that on the opposite side. Dawtrey explained that he was exploring a theory that by making a close-coupled four-wheel chassis and then eliminating two of the wheels, diagonally selected, he

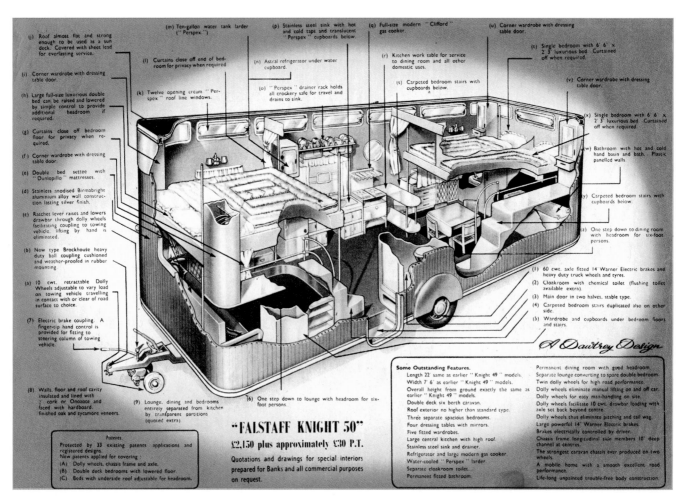

1954 Coventry Steel Kampa Knight, surely the most unorthodox van from a very unorthodox designer.

could obtain the good trailing of a twin-axle chassis without its additional weight and its tyre scrubbing on corners. Nothing further was heard of this van but in 1961 it was reported that a Belgian stabiliser manufacturer was testing several vans with a similar wheel arrangement. The tests are presumed to have been unsatisfactory and nothing more was heard of these vans either.

In 1950 Dawtrey linked up with Tickford Ltd, coach builders, of Newport Pagnell. Production was gradually moved to Newport Pagnell and the Market Place works were put up for sale in 1952. New models introduced in that year were the 22ft Newport Knight and the 12ft 6in Tickford Knight, both with external wall panelling of resin-bonded mahogany plywood finished in clear varnish. Unusual in a small tourer were the free-standing wicker armchairs in the 2 berth version of the Tickford Knight. A new and much cheaper version of the Coventry Knight was introduced in 1953, also with resin-bonded plywood external panelling and featuring a rollaway bed – normal bedding of blankets, sheets and pillows was made up inside a cotton tray and held in place with straps across the top. By day the complete bedding was rolled up from one end and pushed into a recess adjoining the other end, and at night it was simply unrolled ready for immediate use. There was also a new Silver Knight model, 16ft long with aluminium exterior panelling.

1954 saw the introduction of the startlingly unorthodox Kampa Knight, a 12ft 6in V fronted model weighing only 7cwt. The single panelled lower walls and roof were of resin-bonded plywood faced internally with gold coloured aluminium foil for insulation and decoration. Below the waistline the plywood walls were moulded into corrugations and above the waistline the side walls consisted of continuous rubber-tipped wooden louvres which opened and closed to any angle required for ventilation. Dawtrey is reported to have claimed that the use of the foil gave the single wall an insulation value equal to that of a good sealed cavity double panelled wall! In 1955 it was announced that standard caravan production had been suspended due to heavy commitments on commercial trailers, mobile offices and clinics. The Kampa Knight appears to have been the last of Dawtrey's designs for the company and in 1956 he left to set up Silverknight Trailers Ltd. The Coventry Knight body continued to be used – a 1958 photograph shows one fitted as a mobile animal surgery for the Blue Cross, and whilst production was concentrated mainly on special purpose mobile units, the 14ft 3in Liteline tourer was offered in the period 1959-62, although by 1961 it was available only to

order. The angular body reflected its commercial origins and could certainly not be described as aerodynamic – in advertising the company glossed over this by stressing how spacious the van was. The same riveted-up aluminium standard panel assemblies were used for walls, roof and floor. There was no conventional chassis and the interior was lined with leather grained hardboard. Price of the 4 berth van in 1960 was £549 or £385 for an unfurnished shell. Only special units were produced after Liteline production ended. Newport Instruments acquired the company in the 1950s and were themselves taken over by Oxford Instruments Group in the 1970s. Oxford's sold the Coventry Steel business to Caravans International and when that group experienced financial difficulties ownership passed to a banking group who sold it to GRP Massey Group in 1988. The Newport Pagnell factory closed in 1989 and production was transferred to Massey's main plant in Yorkshire. Ownership and location changed again in 1994 when Coventry Steel became a subsidiary of Paneltex Ltd, a commercial body builder in Kingston upon Hull.

The 1959 Coventry Steel Liteline was offered as a touring van!

CRUISER

Classified advertisements in the August 1939 issue of *The Caravan* offer a 1938 4 berth Cruiser for sale and a 4 berth model for hire.

CURZON

Curzon Caravans, Curzon Road, Boscombe, Bournemouth, produced a six van range in 1938. There were three standard models - the 12ft Sunnyside, 13ft 6in Countryside and 15ft Mountainside, priced at £120, £135 and £180 respectively, and three de luxe models – the 12ft Lakeside, 13ft 6in Riverside and 15ft Seaside costing £169, £189 and £250. The standard models featured insulated full width lantern roofs, single panelled walls, oil cooking and electric lighting, whilst the de luxe vans had insulated lantern roofs, double panelling, gas cooking, gas fire and gas as well as electric lighting.

A 1938 Curzon advertisement – in subsequent advertising the price of the de luxe models was increased to include gas equipment as standard.

CURZON CARAVANS

THE CURZON SEASIDE DE-LUXE

15ft. Model Built on Steel Chassis, with Leason ball hitch, panelled in Masonite or Sundeala hardboard with metal windows, beautifully furnished in oak with chromium fittings. Spring interior mattresses are fitted and generous cupboard space is provided. Oil and petrol stoves, gas equipped to order. ... ... Price **£180**

| CURZON RIVERSIDE | ... | ... | ,, | **£135** |
| CURZON LAKESIDE | ... | ... | ,, | **£120** |

Send for illustrated catalogue

CURZON CARAVANS
CURZON ROAD, BOSCOMBE
—BOURNEMOUTH—

DAVAN

A E Davies started building caravans in 1936 – the first one in his front garden – in response to someone telling him he couldn't make one. His company Davan Caravans was located at St George's works, Worle, Weston-Super-Mare, and by 1939 a range of nine models was in production, the Davex 2 berth at 50 guineas, Dainty 2 berth at 55guineas, Davanette 2-3 berth at 65 guineas, Dinkie 2-3 berth at £80, Dandy 3-4 berth at £90, Daydream at 92 guineas, Dauntless 4 berth at £115, Davania 4 berth at £140 and Dane 3 room at £225.

The make was not well known outside the West Country until it was taken up by dealers in other parts of the country in the early 1950s. Details of early post-war models are sparse but the dealers Stafford & Co, Kirkheaton, Huddersfield, were advertising the Davania in 1949, and a 16ft 4 berth and the £285 3 berth Davanette are known to have been in production at that time. The only model around 1951 appears to have been the 15ft 4 berth Dabonair priced at £375 with hardboard exterior panelling, aluminium panelling being a £20 extra. The full width front bay had two windows with imitation diamond pattern leaded panes whilst the window in the entrance door

1939 Davan advertisement. The maker A E Davies built his first caravan in the front garden.

DAY-LIGHT-FULL DAVANS 1939

DAVEX 2 berth	50 gns.
DAINTY 2 berth	55 gns.
DAVANETTE 2-3 berth	65 gns.
DINKIE 2-3 berth	£80
DANDY 3-4 berth	£90
DAY-DREAM	92 gns.
DAUNTLESS 4 berth	£115
DAVANIA 4 berth	£140
DANE (3 room)	£225

For full particulars please write or give us a call
DAVAN CARAVANS
St. George's Works, Worle, Weston-s-Mare

had square pattern leaded panes, all the other windows being in plain glass. By Late 1952 a range of seven models was available, the 10ft 2-3 berth Sporterra at £265, 10ft 3 berth Davanette at £295, 14ft 4 berth Delytu at £350, 15ft 4 berth Dabonair now at £420 or £440 with aluminium exterior, 16ft 4 berth Permhome at £440, 20ft Mansionette at £645 and 22ft Mansionette at £725. This last model had bathroom and kitchen at the front end, two single bedrooms at the rear and a central lounge with anthracite stove, movable chairs and a double bed which by day, with bedding in-situ, slid through the partition into the space beneath the single beds. The firm also provided layouts built to individual customers' requirements and fitted out vans for commercial use.

Whilst touring vans continued to feature in the

range for some time, the smaller models gradually disappeared, and by early 1964 no models below 22ft long were listed, although a 10ft Sporterra did feature for a short time at the end of 1964 and was supposed to be joined by 12ft and 14ft models which never materialised. Longer vans were also introduced and early in 1962 the largest model was the 32ft x 9ft Dellarama priced at £960, soon joined by the 28ft x 16ft twin unit Della-Bungalow with lounge, kitchen, bathroom and two bedrooms, priced at £1,550 fully furnished. Around 1964-5 the firm also produced a 34ft x 9ft 6in unit called the Motella. Intended for sale to site owners and holiday camps, this was divided into three separate compartments with sound insulated partitions and the price was £700 unfurnished. A special built in 1964 was an 8 berth dormitory van to provide seaside holidays for children from Sandhill Park Hospital, Bishop's Lydeard, Somerset. In the later 1960s and into the 1970s the firm concentrated on the Mansionette twin unit in various sizes. 1976 was the last year of production, when the available sizes were 30ft x 20ft at £6385 and 38ft x 20ft at £6885. Davan did however continue in business, dealing in other makes.

1953 Davan Dabonair, with leaded light glazing still in evidence.

DAWN

Dawn Caravans started production at Shepreth near Cambridge in 1936. Details of the early models are not known but the firm was certainly selling a 16ft shell to be fitted out by the purchaser in 1936. Models in 1937 were the De Luxe 4 berth priced at £115 with single panelling or £129 10s double panelled, £95 Standard 4 berth, £85 3 berth and £65 2 berth, with a hire fleet also being operated. In 1939 the range comprised the Challenger Light Four at £97 10s, Challenger Supreme at £159 10s, Ultra Lightweight at £69 10s, Family Four at £117 10s and Challenger Minor at £87 10s. All models had a full width lantern roof and dormer type end windows. There was also a de luxe version of the Minor priced at £125. This 10ft 6in 3 berth was fitted with a gas cooker and two gas lights and came complete with crockery for three. The van was double panelled on an ash frame, with figured ash interior panelling and hand polished oak furniture.

The 1939 Dawn Challenger Light Four, with full width lantern roof and dormer type end windows.

DIXIE

The only reference found is in a list of vans attending a rally at Cheltenham in 1938.

DIXON-BATE

Dixon-Bate Ltd, of Chester, is included because of its close involvement with the industry over many years. From the 1920s the firm built chassis both for caravan manufacturers and for amateur caravan builders. Buyers of the chassis could also obtain drawings for the caravan body and furniture. Prior to the universal adoption of the internal expanding brake the firm made its own version of the external contracting band brake, with servo action and operating only in the forward direction, thus simplifying reversing but presenting difficulties when parking on a reverse slope! About 1930 Dixon-Bate introduced a permanently engaged ball joint having protected bearing faces and a separate two-part coupling clamping up solidly. Technically this was good engineering practice but it could not compete with the lower cost and simplicity of the combined make-and-break and universal joint of the cup and ball coupling. A later coupling had a very small ball clamped between two rubber-lined cups, the ball being mounted on the caravan rather than the car.

After the Second World War the firm continued to make caravan chassis as well as couplings, jockey wheels and a new quick-action corner leg. In this design the leg was dropped at once to the ground and the screw, turned by a permanently attached handle, engaged with a half nut and began to work only when the leg took up the load. Camping, cattle and boat trailers were also built. A 40cwt caravan chassis displayed at the 1951 and 1952 Motor Shows was fitted with electrically operated brakes. In the period 1945-50 Colin Witter, sales director of Dixon-Bate, campaigned on behalf of the trailer committee of the SMMT for better towing brackets, winning co-operation from car manufacturers and encouraging them to make brackets themselves or issue designs and instructions. In 1950 Witter set up his own company to make pre-fabricated brackets and Dixon-Bate also took up manufacture. From 1959 the firm also produced a stabilizer incorporating a pair of specially designed Girling telescopic hydraulic dampers.

As well as all this caravan-related activity Dixon-Bate did actually build two experimental caravans in the early 1930s. When *The Autocar* announced that it

Dixon-Bate produced this construction drawing for amateur caravan builders, available to purchasers of Dixon-Bate chassis. (Courtesy of Bradley Doublelock Ltd)

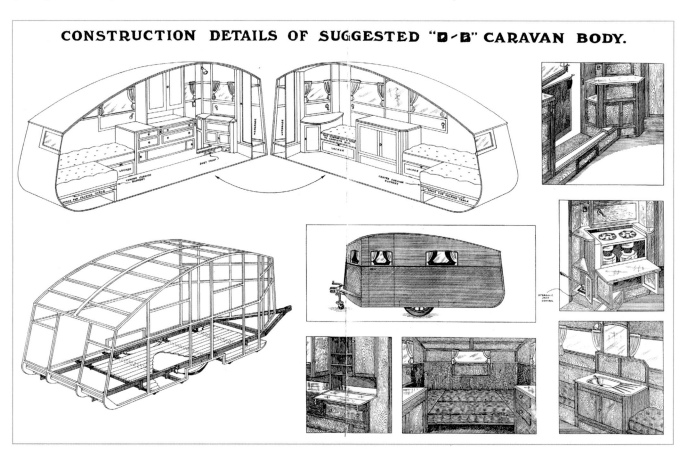

CONSTRUCTION DETAILS OF SUGGESTED "D-B" CARAVAN BODY.

was organising a caravan rally at Minehead in August 1932 (the first trailer caravan rally in the world) the firm decided to design and build a van to take to the rally and won first prize in the 2 berth class. This van had a V front with a curved roof, and leaded light windows in a design representing the setting sun. In May of the following year the RAC organised a rally at Cheltenham and Dixon-Bate took another van, which had railway type sash windows and utilised Jackall hydraulic car jack units for corner legs and axle levelling. Neither of these vans appears to have been put into production although a 2 berth camping trailer was made in the mid-1930s and various luggage and utility trailers were also produced.

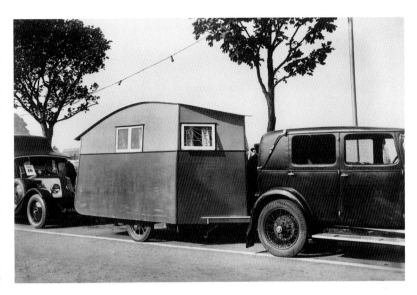

Dixon-Bate experimental van at The Autocar Rally, Minehead, 1932. (Courtesy of Bradley Doublelock Ltd)

DORMY HUT

Designed and marketed by Lt Col Guy Liddell, Hatch Beauchamp, Taunton, Somerset, and built by a Bridgewater firm of woodworkers, the 1935 Dormy Hut was primarily a folding hut weighing 4cwt which could be used as a summerhouse or shed but was also available with a 2cwt trailer enabling it to be used as a 2 berth folding caravan. Unpacking and erection by one man was said to take five minutes, and when set up on its floor, which formed part of the trailer on the road, the hut measured 7ft x 7ft with headroom at the centre of nearly 7ft.

DOVEDALE

Although Dovedale were in production in the late 1930s nothing is known of the vans from this period. Manufacture after the Second World War appears to have started around 1950, the first model being a 15ft 6in x 6ft 10in 4 berth centre kitchen van costing £299. Dovedales were made by R Mitchell of Cowley Road, Marton, Blackpool. Initially the sole concessionaires were Northern Caravan Distributors Ltd, Handforth, Cheshire, who quickly established a dealer network, advertised in *The Caravan* for June 1951 in a six-page Dovedale caravan dealer supplement. There were four models at this time, the above 15ft 6in van now named the Standard at £320, a de luxe version of the same van at £365, 22ft x 7ft 6in 4 berth Bungalow at £495 and 12ft 6in x 6ft 6in 4 berth Traveller at £237 10s. The extra cost of the de luxe model provided polished metal window frames in lieu of wood, fitted carpet, upholstered backrests and a full cooker. Later in 1951 the Traveller was replaced by the 13ft 6in x 6ft 6in Minor, beginning a practice of most model names starting with the letter M.

The range for 1953 was the Standard, now priced at £300, a 16ft end kitchen 4 berth at £320 and 22ft 4 berth Major at £500 with a settee double bed or £515 with a drop down double bed. By the end of 1953 Dovedale were advertising in their own right and the six model range comprised the 12ft Minx, Standard, 17ft Marvel, 18ft Monarch, 20ft Majestic and 22ft Marquis, to which were added in the early part of 1954 the 16ft Merlin, 22ft Bungalow and 22ft Family Bungalow with two separate single bedrooms.

By mid-1955 the range had expanded to 12 models, with two of these also available in a de luxe version, and a further two offered with the choice of settee or foldaway double bed. Reporting on a visit to the factory around this time, the editor of *The Caravan* expressed surprise, in view of the sizeable output achieved by 80 hour a week shift working, that the vans were hand painted in Dulux and the furniture was all hand french polished. The same report mentions another model, an unusual 4 berth touring van with a front end door leading into a porch

TAKE YOUR PICK FROM "Dovedale"

MAMMOTH
FAB. 35 FT. 6 BERTH
£1650
DELIVERED

BUNGALOW
22 FT. 4 BERTH
£557-10s.

MIRAMAR
FAB. 22 FT. 4 BERTH
£650

MYSTIC
19 FT. 4 BERTH
£475

NEW MONARCH
20 FT. 4 BERTH
£530

MAJOR
FAB. 22 FT. 5 BERTH
£615

MASTER
FAB. 22 FT. 4 BERTH
£575

MINOR
14 FT. 4 BERTH
£335

MERLIN
16 FT. 4 BERTH
£389
ALSO MODEST
16 FT. 4 BERTH
£410

MARVEL
17 FT. 4 BERTH
£422

MARQUIS
FAB. 22 FT. 4 BERTH
£590

All above prices ex works, except the "MAMMOTH".

If you have any difficulty, write to the Manufacturers for Illustrated Leaflet and full details.

R. MITCHELL · DOVEDALE CARAVANS · MARTON · BLACKPOOL

Tel. Blackpool S/S. 41297

1958 Dovedale advertisement. In 1966 the firm was sold to Pemberton who soon phased out the Dovedale name.

through which one entered a normal layout with a side kitchen, but with a toilet room also leading off the porch, though nothing further appears to have been heard of this van.

It was Dovedale's custom to display a number of their vans at Cluny Mews near Earl's Court each year during the Motor Show, and in 1957 the display included the 35ft Mammoth, the company's first model to exceed the legally towable length of 22ft. The 12-strong range for 1958 comprised the £335 14ft Minor, £389 16ft Merlin, £410 16ft Modest, £422 17ft Marvel, £475 19ft Mystic, £530 20ft New Monarch, and five 22ft vans: the £557 10s Bungalow, £615 Major, £590 Marquis, £575 Master, £650

Miramar, and £1,650 Mammoth. All these prices were the usual 'ex works' except the Mammoth, which included delivery, and all the vans had 4 berths except the 5 berth Major and 6 berth Mammoth. These were joined by yet another 22ft van in mid-1958, the £575 5 berth Marina, and later in the year by the 32ft end-to-end twin unit Mercury at £800, available as either a 5 berth with bathroom or 6 berth with a single bedroom in place of the bathroom. By the time of the 1958 Cluny Mews display there was also a new 28ft model, the £825 4 berth Miami, a new tourer, the £299 10s 12ft 3 berth Mynx, and a 24ft version of the Marina with 6 berths and costing £610. Early in 1959 there was also a 28ft version of the Marina, a 6 berth van costing £730.

In 1960 the company moved to a new factory at Mitcham Road, also in Marton, Blackpool, and to mark the occasion introduced a further 28ft model named the Mitcham, a £639 10s 6 berth. 1961 advertisements invited enquiries from individuals for any size of van or special layout. In 1965, the last year of independent production, there were 15 models: the £205 8ft 6in Minim, £295 10ft Midge, £325 12ft Minor, £340 14ft Minor, £425 16ft Merlin, £455 18ft Merlin, 20ft Mammon, 7ft 6in or 8ft 6in wide at £475, £505 20ft Monarch, £510 22ft Mammon, £535 23ft Manry, £645 26ft Maribou, £760 30ft Manhatton, £899 32ft Melvin Super and £905 32ft Markalin.

At the beginning of 1966 Dovedale was sold to Pemberton, R Mitchell retiring from the business though still operating a fleet of static hire vans on south coast and Isle of Wight sites. By early 1967 the Dovedale name had been phased out and the production capacity was used to manufacture Pemberton models.

Dovedale produced large numbers of vans including tourers and mobile homes, though static holiday vans probably represented the bulk of the output, and whilst in the low price range they incorporated some conscientious construction details. The hand painting and hand french polishing have already been noted, but in the mid-1950s the roof construction involved not only an insulation board ceiling under the framing but also a further layer of insulation board above the cavity, in contact with the aluminium exterior panelling, to prevent condensation forming on the underside of the aluminium. The walls had a vapour seal of bituminised paper next to the aluminium, an air cavity and insulation board lining, faced where necessary with veneered plywood. The later residential models featured an insulated double floor at a time when this was by no means a standard feature on higher priced makes.

DYSON

R A Dyson & Company Ltd, Grafton Street, Liverpool, were one of a number of manufacturers in the 1920s and early 1930s producing vans typical of the period with square ends, bowed sides and lantern roof. The company also operated a hire fleet of its vans.

The 1931 Dyson was an example of classic 1920s styling carried over into the 1930s.

ECCLES

Eccles Motor Transport Ltd was formed in March 1919 by W A J Riley (d.1932) and his son W J 'Bill' Riley (d.1968) to take over a moribund haulage business run by H A Eccles from ramshackle premises at Gosta Green, Birmingham. The Rileys thought that caravan building would reinforce the haulage business, but the father, who had built a motor caravan in 1913, thought that the way forward lay with this type, whilst the son, who had served in the Royal Flying Corps, was influenced by the wartime use of trailers for ambulances and other purposes and saw better prospects for trailer caravans. They displayed both the 1913 motor caravan and a new trailer caravan at a garage near the Motor Show in 1919, and whilst there was little public interest, they sold the trailer to Sybil, Dowager Viscountess Rhondda, a leading figure in South Wales finance, industry, mining, shipbuilding, etc.

On the strength of this sale they decided to go into production with the trailer. The body was made of steel sheets soldered together, screwed to a metal reinforced wood framework and lined internally with three-ply polished mahogany over a layer of felt, with a white enamelled ceiling. Externally the walls were finished in dark green with a stone coloured roof. Equipment included two 6ft 6in beds, paraffin gas stove in a fireproof compartment, aluminium cooking utensils stored in a locker over the stove, tip-up lavatory basin, mirror, lockers for clothes, food, bedding, etc., and a folding table. The van rode on Sankey steel wheels with pneumatic tyres of the same size as those used on the rear wheels of Ford cars and was fitted with internal expanding brakes operated by means of a

cable from the towing car, though as early as 1920 Eccles were using an overrun mechanism to actuate the brakes. A patented cantilever spring coupling absorbed shocks from the road and three legs kept the van level on site. A ring was fitted at each corner so that guy ropes could be attached for additional stability in strong winds.

At first the Rileys made little progress, for the van was unattractive and the steel bodywork was expensive to make as well as heavy, but a change was soon made to light plywood bodies, which were bought in from William Turner, a wheelwright of Old Hill, Staffordshire, the axles and interior fittings being added at Gosta Green. Following encouraging publicity at the British Industries Fair in Birmingham in 1921, serious production started in 1922 with a planned output of

The original 1919 Eccles and a 12hp Rover. This van was sold to the Dowager Countess Rhondda.

An Eccles of around 1926, showing the classic 1920s styling closely associated with the make.

1925 Eccles Jacobean models featured dark oak internal walls and furniture, with diamond pane imitation leaded windows.

A 1929 Eccles camping trailer with a Norton motorcycle. Tent trailers were also made for and to the 1921 patent of A G Cocks, who ran a hire fleet of them from Aberdovey.

50 vans. H A Eccles was bought out, William Turner joined the firm and the body building was moved to Gosta Green. Eccles exhibited at the 1922 Motor Show at its White City overflow, and during the Show they appointed their first dealers, Herbert Woolley of Woolley Bros (Bristol) Ltd and Henry Presland of the P & P Motor Co (later The London Caravan Co).

The first successful models were very small vans, 7 to 8ft in length, very light and priced from £75 upwards. The profile of the boxy plywood body was softened slightly by rounding the corners in plan, the roof – cambered from side to side – projected at both ends and the door was at the rear. This shape was retained for the smallest vans until 1932, but at the 1923 Motor Show Eccles introduced more ambitious models, de luxe vans reminiscent of horse caravans, at prices from about £185. These had square cornered bodies 9 to 12ft, occasionally 14ft, in length, slightly bowed sides, an imposing lantern roof overhanging both ends and a bay window at the front. They brought greater success and created an image of what a good caravan should look like which lasted for the rest of the 1920s – an image so closely associated with the make that any surviving van of the 1920s with this styling is likely to be labelled an Eccles even though several makers produced similar designs.

Eccles also made tent trailers for and to the 1921 patent of A G Cocks, a well known motorcyclist who ran a hire fleet of them from Aberdovey, as well as their own camping trailers, 6ft long x 4ft 8in wide, equipped with two single beds, hook-on table and

Camping scene illustrating "Eccles" 9 ft. 6 ins. de Luxe and "Eccles" 7 ft. 3 ins. Caravans

IF YOU ARE INTERESTED SEND FOR ILLUSTRATED CATALOGUE AND NAME OF NEAREST AGENT

A 1929 Eccles leaflet. 'Motor caravan' was the firm's name for a motor drawn trailer caravan.

roof locker. Single panelled up to waist level in plywood covered in canvas, which continued to form the upper walls and roof, these trailers cost £65 in 1928-29. Whilst most caravan manufacturers bought in chassis from one of the specialist makers Eccles made their own frames, only buying in axle and suspension sets, although integrated design was so far from caravan practice at the time that for some years a cranked axle was offered as an optional extra. A patented feature of de luxe models in the 1920s, eventually discontinued on cost grounds, was reversible mattresses. Domed cushions formed raked seats and backrests to the settees by day, and at night they were turned over to form beds with a flat surface and weaker springs.

Once securely launched the company dropped transport activities and in 1926 became Eccles Motor Caravans Ltd, 'motor caravan' being its name for a motor-drawn trailer caravan. In 1927 Eccles moved to Stirchley, Birmingham, to the first factory in the world built specifically for caravan manufacture. Within six years this factory was increased from 14,000 to 24,000 square feet.

1927 saw the police at Honiton, Devon, prosecute a number of caravanners in connection with the use of overrun brakes, the legality of which was uncertain.

The 1929 Eccelite, seen here with a Morris Cowley two-seater, was a weak concession to the streamline fashion.

.. Finally you'll choose

"The Joys of ECCLES Caravanning"
is the title of a free booklet we should
like to send you. It illustrates 1934
Eccles Caravans, from £110, and tells
you much about caravanning the Eccles
way. We have a booklet on Luggage
Trailers, too.

*The Eccles Organization covers the country.
Let us put you in touch with your nearest
Eccles distributor who can give you any advice
or help you need.*

The Eccles Model 40 of 1934, forerunner of the 1935 Road Nymph. The vans of the French manufacturer Notin still bore a family resemblance to Eccles of this period into the late 1960s.

Bill Riley drove down to Honiton with one of his vans and gave a demonstration of the braking to the police on Honiton Hill. After this and a lengthy hearing the Bench dismissed the charges, and as a result of widespread newspaper reports other police forces were deterred from bringing similar prosecutions. A series of articles on a tour of England with a large four-wheeled Eccles, written by the American Sinclair Lewis and published in the London *Evening News* in 1928, was very effective in publicising the caravan movement, and in 1932, in collaboration with the Hillman Motor Company, an Eccles was entered in the Monte Carlo Rally. Starting from Glasgow and driven by Dudley Noble, publicity manager of the Humber-Hillman Group, and A Clive Scarff of the Nomad Caravan Co, dealers on the Surrey fringe of London, the outfit finished sixth out of the 35 British entries (only 19 reached Monte Carlo) and 35th overall, covering 1,550 miles at an average speed of 24mph in very bad conditions. An interesting special of 1929 was the 9ft lantern roof model presented to Lord Baden-Powell by the Boy Scout Movement along with a Rolls-Royce towing car. The single berth van was equipped with desk and sink but no stove – presumably cooking was done over the camp fire.

Whilst Eccles had created the two most successful styles of the 1920s, after 1930 their styling was conservative, their layouts and interior equipment tended to

follow that of other manufacturers and the vans were only averagely good on tow, but in a period when many ill-qualified builders were starting caravan production Eccles were unrivalled as manufacturers, building up a great reputation for workmanship, finish and reliability. They were far ahead of other makers in industrial methods and factory organisation, and the Stirchley factory was an impressive manufacturing unit at a time when most other makers, even those producing very good vans, had premises not far removed from backyard sheds. Although the factory was the most advanced of its day, so much hand work was still involved that large batch production was ruled out, while the market was too small for a maker with so much capacity to neglect any sector of it for the sake of rationalisation. As a result nearly 50 per cent of production was devoted to specials – motor caravans, heavy four-wheel vans for travelling showmen, special purpose units for missions, commercial concerns and charities, and luxury vans for the nobility and Indian Maharajahs. Even the extensive 'standard' range of models was offered with various options – several could be ordered with plain or lantern roof and rigid or collapsible bodies, where the upper part lowered over the lower and was raised by chain-driven winding gear. There was also a choice of single or double panelled walls and, in de luxe models, of light oak or Jacobean interior, the latter featuring dark oak walls and furniture with diamond pane imitation leaded windows. Concerned by rising competition, Eccles introduced the lightweight Eccelite in 1929. A weak concession to the streamline fashion, this stark looking van had a plain box body with a fore and aft curved roof and was followed in 1931 with a moderately streamlined design.

Before building a new model Bill Riley would draw the outline full size on a wall and look at it daily for weeks. As a result Eccles designs generally looked assured and competent if only rarely achieving the elegance of Bertram Hutchings's Winchesters. So the new 1931 design had relatively bluff ends and looked less stylish than the contemporary Car Cruisers and Winchesters, but the characteristic profiles which the industry adopted in the 1950s and 1960s were very similar. For 1934 Eccles introduced the Model 40, a streamlined lantern roof van and forerunner of the 1935 Road Nymph. Several British makers were exporting vans to France and the designs, particularly Eccles, were copied by French manufacturers. Notin claimed to be the oldest French maker and when he died in the late 1960s his vans still bore a family resemblance to the Eccles designs of the Road Nymph era.

Another customer for an Eccles special was F L M

'Mit' Harris, editor of *The Caravan & Trailer*, forerunner of *The Caravan*. Having predicted the triumph of streamlining, he continued using old style Eccles vans (a 12ft 6in model purchased second hand for £100 in 1933 and a 14ft 6in model in 1934) before owning a 15ft 6in streamlined Car Cruiser in 1935, and eventually had the semi-streamlined 13ft 6in 'Liberty Hall IV' built to his specification by Eccles in 1936 at a cost of £425. Exterior wall panelling was 2½mm aluminium and the heavy lantern roof ended short of the front end in a glazed V. The upper roof was of 3/8in oak boarding, with the lower part of Lloyd hardboard. Wall and roof cavities were insulated with Alfol reflective aluminium foil and the floor was 5/8in 5 ply birch overlaid with Lloyd hardboard. The inner walls were panelled in 6mm 3 ply teak, and cream painted 5/8in Lloyd insulating board was used for the ceiling. Teak was used for the furniture, door frame and lantern roof frame. There was a bay window at the front and the axle was set back to balance the formidable weight of a Diamond coal range under the rear window. The flue from this range was cranked and carried forward within the lantern roof to emerge at the front end. No doubt the weight and location of the range contributed to the appalling road performance of this van, which W M Whiteman described as 'a superbly made monstrosity'.

By 1936 four assembly lines were in operation at the Stirchley works, though without strict continuity of models, and Eccles were in the forefront of the development of pre-fabricated furniture, which cut down the delays and frustrations caused by men getting in each other's way when furniture was built in situ. The company stood alone in the industry in having a large building with open floor area, capable of being laid out for rational progress from unloading bay and mill to paint shop, finishing and despatch, with furniture making, upholstery and other departments feeding their output into the production lines from the sides. Bill Riley monitored progress with the aid of a chart showing every caravan going through, its timetable for all major operations, and whether the timetable was being kept.

The 1936 Imperial was a £530 18ft lantern roof model planned as a living van. The kitchen occupied over 7ft of the length at the rear end and could be separated from the rest of the van by three-fold wardrobe doors. The comprehensive equipment included a domestic type kitchen cabinet, cooking recess with roller shutter front, sink and drainer, oil-fired water heater and refrigerator, 12 gallon water tank and pump, floor bath, lady's dressing companion, battery, electric lights and built-in radio. A toilet room opened off the kitchen and also had an external door.

Facing settees in the centre of the van formed a double bed at night and a dinette by day with a freestanding table – a feature used by several makers over the years despite the obvious disadvantages of having a bed and dinette straddling the middle of the van. Further multi-fold wardrobe doors separated the front end, which featured a double bed settee and external door. Up to 1937 the fashionable streamlined styling featured roofs whose lines flowed smoothly through into the end walls, but Eccles were in the forefront by replacing this continuous outline with boldly projecting ends to the roof. The 1938 range comprised the £170 12ft No 55, £195 15ft No 65, £298 16ft Independent, £330 16ft 6in President, £357 16ft Aristocrat and £440 17ft 9in Senator. All except the No 55 and No 65 were double panelled.

The standard of workmanship was of the very highest order but Bill Riley came to realize that having the largest and best planned factory in the industry was best suited not to largely hand made de luxe models but to popular models produced in quantities for the growing numbers of middle class motorists. In 1939 Eccles were suffering from a boycott as a result of a dispute with the big distributors and agents and could not sell the de luxe models in sufficient numbers. The company responded with their new National model, built in unprecedented batches of 50, a 14ft 6in 4 berth with double panelled walls and roof costing only £130 oil equipped. A family size Eccles at this price carried such weight with the public that the big dealers could not ignore it and the organiser of the boycott was the first to place an order. The National was a success despite problems with the first batch, which had to be recalled and re-panelled. After building and testing two successive prototypes a switch was made to a cheaper panelling material before production started, but this was found to disintegrate easily. A larger version, the 16ft New Imperial followed. In 1939, to reflect its diversification into light steel fabrications, school furniture and Government contracts, the company name was changed to Eccles (Birmingham) Ltd. The company was fully engaged on Government contracts during the Second World War, ending the war with an expanded and well equipped factory.

In the early post-war period supplies of many of the materials used in caravan construction were government controlled, but Eccles received allocations which allowed them to resume production on a modest industrial scale. The first post-war model was the Enterprise, introduced in January 1946. Whilst the use of jig-built body sections was not new, the technique was taken much further than hitherto, jigs being used for all the body sections and for all body

The 1946 Eccles Enterprise, although only 14ft 9in long, was supplied in quantity for housing at the US base at Burtonwood, Lancs.

and furniture components that could be built separately, including wooden window and skylight frames, furniture sides and doors, and seat locker lids. A 1946 press article reports that 147 vans had been built up to the end of June and it was expected that the Ministry of Supply allocation of 260 would be completed by the end of September, with a further allocation taking the total to 350. Eccles had found that 72 per cent of vans so far supplied were for use as living vans – although only 14ft 9in long the Enterprise was supplied in quantity for housing at the US base at Burtonwood, Lancs.

In 1948 the cost of the Enterprise was £534 13s with oil cooking. A gas installation with two lights, hotplate and two gas cylinders cost approximately £30 extra. In the same year the range was extended to include the £355 13ft Active and £715 17ft Progress. The 1949 Active was a £348 8s 14ft 6in van with two double beds, and the similar Alert cost £338 8s and had a double and two single beds. 1950-51 models were a 14ft Mark II version of the Alert and the Advance, an 18ft living van. For 1951-52 there was a Mark III version of the Alert and the £850 18ft Adventure. A report in *The Caravan* for February 1952, whilst acknowledging that the Adventure was suitable for all the year round use, suggested that it also made a comfortable touring van – the manufacturers claimed an ex-works weight of 31cwt! A substantial chassis with steel members 3/16in and 1/4in thick overlaid with 7/8in tongued and grooved boarding, a 2in square axle and 44in x 2in x 3/8in eight-leaf springs no doubt constituted a significant proportion of this weight. The walls were panelled externally with aluminium, internally with oak faced ply, and the roof of aluminium painted canvas on hardboard had a cream painted hardboard ceiling. A Vanesse solid fuel stove with a three gallon polished

copper water tank around the flue provided heating and hot water, and a five gallon under floor tank supplied cold water via a hand pump mounted alongside the sink.

For 1952-53 the Adventure was replaced by the much cheaper £460 New Imperial, the Alert went into a Mark IV version and a new lightweight van, the 12ft Coronation was introduced. Up to this point all the post-war vans had had a roof curved both lengthways and widthways but the Coronation and New Imperial had a new roof profile, curved lengthways but with a V shape across the width. These two vans continued in Mark II versions for 1953-54 together with a Mark V Alert and two new models, the £225 10ft 3 berth Coronet and 16ft 6in New Democrat. The Coronet and New Democrat appear to be the first models with aluminium panelled roofs. For 1954-55 the range extended to six models – Coronet Mark II, 12ft Bounty, Alert Mark VI, Democrat Mark II, 18ft 6in Eversure and 22ft Fortune. 1955-56 models were the £265 Coronet Mark III, £310 Bounty Mark II, £450 15ft 6in Aristocrat and £540 Eversure Mark II, joined early in 1956 by the £382 14ft Dominant. When the 1957 models were announced towards the end of 1956 there were two new models, the 10ft 3-4 berth E10 and 16ft 4 berth E16 together with Mark II versions of the Dominant and Aristocrat, and Mark III versions of the Bounty and Eversure. For 1957-58 the E10 and E16 continued with Mark III Dominant and Aristocrat, and Mark IV Bounty and Eversure, with a new 4 berth 22ft van, the E22.

Although Eccles had been manufacturer members of the National Caravan Council their membership had lapsed, but in 1958 when it was proposed that NCC members should adopt Mutual Trading (NCC manufacturers and dealers not trading with non-NCC members) Eccles, then with an output of 2,000 vans per year, were reported as having agreed to re-enter the Council if Mutual Trading were adopted. When the 1959 range was advertised towards the end of 1958 only the Eversure was retained, in a Mark V 20ft version available in Traveller or Standard models. All the other models were new: £215 8ft 6in Nipper, £265 10ft 6in Nymphette, £315 12ft 6in Avenger, £365 15ft Landfarer, £675 16ft 6in Enchantress and £430 17ft 6in Leader. The £648 22ft Endeavour replaced the Eversure early in 1959. New models at the 1959 Caravan Exhibition were a de luxe 2 berth version of the Avenger and the 16ft Elegance which replaced the Enchantress. The Nipper was dropped from the range for 1960, and the inevitable Mark II versions of the Nymphette, Avenger, Landfarer, Leader and Endeavour appeared.

Bill Riley's son John had been a director of Eccles

1964 Eccles Moonstone, one of three new models introduced in 1961 after the firm was acquired by Sprite and said to have 'the best furniture and décor in the modern idiom yet seen in a production tourer'.

1964 Eccles Emerald, with the same interior styling as the Moonstone.

but after his death his father sold the company to Sprite in 1960, and early in 1961 the caravan side of the business was moved to a new factory at The Pines, Newmarket, Suffolk, two miles away from the Sprite factory at The Oaks. The Birmingham works had 62,000 square feet of production space, employed 60 caravan production workers and had a potential output of 3,000 vans per year, although the actual rate, more realistically coupled to the market for Eccles, was around 1,000 vans. It was expected that the new factory, with less than half the space and 40 production workers, could produce 1,000 vans per year. The 1961 models were the £312 10ft Echo, £422 12ft 6in Avenger, £473 15ft Landfarer, £629 16ft Elegance and £698 22ft Endeavour, though during the year the latter was replaced by the £1,275 20ft Traveller. The range introduced at the 1961 Caravan Exhibition comprised three new vans, the £290 10ft GT305, £400 13ft Moonstone and £470 16ft Sapphire. Internally colour, texture and simplicity of line were combined to present what was described as 'the best furniture and décor in the modern idiom yet seen in a production tourer'. The new vans were designed by Reg Dean, originally a freelance furniture designer and illustrator. Dean had joined Sprite in 1957 as interior designer although he had no previous experience of caravans. He was an influential designer who was involved with various makes over a period of about 30 years. A new model introduced towards the end of 1962 was the 22ft Emerald, with the same interior styling as the other new vans.

In 1963 Sprite and Bluebird merged to form Caravans International Ltd.

ECCLES **emerald**

SPECIFICATION

A Toilet compartment
B Bay window
C Table
D Roof locker
F Dinette seats
G Wardrobe
H Kitchen unit
K Tip-up bed
M Sideboard
O Dividing curtain
P Double bed settee
S Day seat
U Solid fuel stove, airing cupboard
Gas lights

DIMENSIONS
Body length: 22' overall.
Body width: 7' 4½".
Good headroom throughout.

SHIPPING SIZES
Length: 24' 7".
Width: 7' 4½".
Height, from ground to roof: 8' 3".
Weight: 24 cwt. 1 qr.

UNDER GEAR
All steel chassis with adjustable corner steadies. Semi-elliptic springs. Solid straight axle. Delta Mk. 10 coupling. 6.50 x 16 tyres.

BODY CONSTRUCTION
Double panelled throughout. All aluminium exterior. Body framing half-lapped. Screwed and glued. Insulated with fibreglass. One glazed stable door. One full door.

WINDOWS AND VENTILATION
Six Eccles adjustable ventilators. Eight opening windows including front easy view picture window.

EXTERIOR LIGHTS
Front lights. Stop/Tail/Reflector combination. Direction indicators. Number plate illuminator.

EQUIPMENT
Foam bedding. 50mm. towing ball. Leg brace. Full oven cooker. Foot water pump. Four gas lights. Screw type jockey wheel. Carpet in lounge. Vynelay in kitchen. Gas bottle compartment. Division curtain. Wheel embellishers.

INTERIOR FINISH
Afrormosia furniture. Plastic working surfaces. Interior panelling – plastic faced hardboard.

EXTERIOR FINISH
Two-tone Eccles colour scheme.

INTERIOR LAY-OUT
'U'-shaped settee making double bed. Sideboard. Solid fue stove. Airing cupboard. Wardrobe. Day seat. End kitchen. Toilet. Breakfast bar, making single bed. Folding table. Mirror. Full width front and rear lockers. Tip-up bed.

Specification subject to alteration from time to time.

ECLIPSE

*1956 11ft 6in Eclipse Norvic.
This Norfolk manufacturer
started production c.1931.*

Eclipse caravans were built from around 1931 by Smith & Moor Ltd, London Road, Wymondham, Norfolk, though nothing is known of vans dating from before the Second World War. The firm appear to have sold direct to the public rather than through dealers, and in addition to a standard range of models built vans to the requirements of individual customers. A hire fleet was also operated. A 15ft model is known to have been in production in 1947 and towards the end of 1948 the Hethersett living van was introduced. This 22ft van was equipped with a settee convertible to either a double bed or easy chairs, radio and Barralet water heater, as well as a Pither's stove with hot water tank. There was also a bathroom fitted with washbasin, 4ft 6in bath, shower and running hot and cold water. The basic range in 1951 comprised the Norvic, in lengths from 10ft to 12ft 6in and priced from £400, the Wymondham, in lengths from 13ft to 15ft 6in and priced from £500, the £760 16ft Kimberley and the £900 17ft 6in Broads Special. The 1954 15ft 6in model weighed 23cwt and cost £850. Thoughtful features included wet clothes hanging space just inside the entrance door with metal drip tray and drain underneath, boxing under the sink to prevent heat from the hot water affecting the food in the metal larder below, shutter over the larder floor vent to keep out dust on the road, ventilated bedding lockers with both top and front access, and Celotex insulation to the toilet room. There was also a bath let into the floor. Production continued until around 1958 when the available models were the 10ft 6in Norvic at £250, 12ft 9in Wymondham at £385, 16ft 6in Kimberley at £550, 18ft Kimberley 18 at £650 and 20ft Twenty at £760.

ECONOMY (CLIFTON 2)

*1934 Clifton was produced by
the makers of Economy trailers.*

In 1933 W A Greenslade, St Thomas Street, Bristol, in addition to a range of Economy trailers, was producing a 12ft caravan with a side extension. Berths for four were provided in the van itself, with room for two camp beds in the annexe. The price of around £160 included complete equipment and utensils for six. The streamlined £152 10s 15ft 4 berth Clifton was introduced in 1934.

ENSOR

Alfred Ensor, after living in America for some years, returned to Shropshire and commenced building caravans at Ketley, near Wellington, in 1928. He made models with outer skins of stretched canvas which could be dismantled and packed flat for winter storage, folding bungalows, knockdown models for export and camping trailers. There were also models with the rear end opening out as a kitchen, canvas forming the fourth wall.

His most successful design was the Wrekin of 1935 onwards, which had a kitchen annexe folding flat against the offside wall for towing, the cooking stove, sink and cupboards being recessed into the caravan area inside a false sideboard. Later models also had a folding toilet room though this was only accessible from outside the van and had no floor; a chemical toilet stood on the ground, the space from the bottom of the walls to the ground being closed with canvas brailing.

His other ideas were wide ranging. He experimented early with independent suspension and produced a three-wheeled caravan with the front wheel mounted in motorcycle forks as well as one with a movable axle so that with the axle forward the caravan had a low nose weight for coupling up, and with the axle set back the nose weight could be regulated to suit the towing car's suspension and ensure the best towing. He claimed to have made the first fold-away bed, the first balanced bed settee for finger-light conversion from one state to the other, and he also designed a large skylight mounted on four springs which rose automatically when released, but his partner, A Clayfield, had great difficulty in getting him to see that new inventions were loss-making unless they led to sufficient production. Subscribing to the argument that a two-wheeled trailer supported at three points would ride steadily on any surface, the tyres being sufficient to absorb shocks and avoid bounce, the 1933 catalogue ignored the legal obligation to fit 'suitable and sufficient springs' and boasted that Ensor's £94 4 berth had no springs. This was claimed to eliminate all roll, with vibration being taken up by large low-pressure tyres. Ensor even wrote a promotional song 'The Ensor Way' for which he obtained permission to use the tune of 'The Gay Caballero'.

THE "ENSOR" TWO-ROOMED TRAILER BUNGALOW

SMALL IN TOW : 9 ft. × 6 ft.

PRICE £150 COMPLETE

LARGE WHEN ERECTED : 12 ft. × 9 ft.

Apply for Full Details to—

C. A. ENSOR WELLINGTON SALOP

With the coming of the Second World War orders were received for nearly 100 ambulance trailers, some two dozen motor ambulances and a number of canteens. Building these necessitated twelve-hour shifts, seven days a week, leaving little time to spend at Ensor's Wellington home, so he built an elaborate folding bungalow in which he and his wife lived on the firm's display site from the early part of 1940.

A 1931 Ensor advertisement. Alfred Ensor was much attached to folding and extending arrangements.

Tireless inventor Alfred Ensor in front of his 1936 three-wheeled caravan, with kitchen extension erected. The front wheel was mounted on motorcycle forks

WINTER STORAGE HINTS

NOVEMBER 1946 6ᴰ

The CARAVAN

INCORPORATING
"THE CARAVAN & TRAILER" and "THE CARAVAN WORLD"
The Premier Caravan and Light Trailer Journal of the World

THE WREKIN

THE CARAVAN WITH
THE FOLDING KITCHEN
AND
LAVATORY COMPARTMENT

IT IS SO SIMPLE
TO HAVE SO MUCH
EXTRA SPACE

ENSOR CARAVANS LIMITED
369 HIGH STREET, WEST BROMWICH, STAFFS.
TELEPHONE: WEST BROMWICH 0300

The 1946 Ensor Wrekin was basically unchanged from the pre-war model.

Interior view of the Wrekin's kitchen extension.

From a closed size of 18ft x 7ft 6in, annexes opening on either side gave a total floor area of 297 square feet. Accommodation comprised a large lounge, two bedrooms, kitchen and toilet room. By 1942 a development of this model – the Wellington Chalet – had been designed ready for immediate post-war production. A single van with exterior panelling in laminated plastic, the first to utilise this type of panelling, was also built during the war.

Having built several caravans to special order for individual customers, as well as a van for personal use, J E 'Joe' Bissell of the coachbuilders Benson Motor Body Co Ltd, High Street, West Bromwich, had intended to start regular caravan production in 1939. This was prevented by the outbreak of war, but in 1944 he met Alfred Ensor, who was looking for someone to take over manufacture of his designs. The first post-war model to emerge from the West Bromwich factory in 1946 was the Wrekin, basically unchanged from the pre-war model and costing £650. A Wrekin was exhibited at the first Motor Show to be held at Earl's Court after the war in November 1948 and the van remained in production until 1953.

Prohibitive costs ruled out production of the Wellington Chalet and a proposed camping trailer. The first new design appears to have been the Light Four of mid-1949, a 13ft 6in x 6ft 5in 4 berth weighing 13cwt. Mounted on an aluminium chassis, finished externally with aluminium paint, with double panelled walls and insulated roof and floor, the cost was £380 with cream painted interior panelling and polished plywood furniture, or £390 with interior panelling also in polished plywood. A further new van introduced later in 1949 was the 16ft 4 berth centre kitchen Beacon priced at £475. Alfred Ensor died suddenly on the eve of the 1950 Motor Show. New models in 1951 were the 16ft 6in Summit, unusual in having a layout which divided into three compartments allowing the double and two single beds to be accommodated in separate rooms, and the £750 22ft Home, a 4 berth living van with rear end kitchen, bath and folding easy chairs.

By late 1954 the range comprised the £425 12ft Elf, £360 14ft Light Four, £550 16ft 4in Elite and £750 22ft Home, the Light Four being replaced by the £430 14ft Elect towards the end of 1955. Joe Bissell was one of only a few post-war manufacturers who, producing small numbers of vans and on terms of personal friendship with his customers, personified the Ensor brand in the pre-war fashion. He tested 2 berth prototypes personally, and his son R J 'Bob' Bissell and family tested the larger vans. Bob Bissell also competed in the Caravan Club's British Caravan Road Rallies from their inception in 1954, his outfit in that year being a Light Four towed by an Austin A40 Countryman with an ash frame body built by Benson Motor Body Co Ltd; his co-driver was the works foreman. GRP mouldings made an appearance in 1956, used for various body parts such as window louvres, rooflights and part of the bay window on the Elect. GRP was also used for sink-drainer units and a tip-up washbasin in the Elf. A new van in 1958 was the £418 10ft 3in 3 berth Kiwi weighing 10½cwt and followed in 1959 by the Eden, a 2 berth model of the same length. Also introduced in 1959 was a de luxe version of the Elite with GRP roof and ends.

A feature of Ensor vans over a number of years was the fitting of exclusive patented design windows. Fitted just to the sides in later years, these wooden framed windows pivoted at the bottom to open inwards and could be slid up to give ventilation top and bottom or lifted out completely. A feature contributing to good roadholding was the fitting of a long drawbar, and from the second half of the 1950s the channels forming the drawbar continued right to the rear corners of the body, replacing conventional chassis longitudinal members. In 1962 the Kiwi and Eden were the first Ensors to be fitted with Rubery Owen torsion bar independent suspension instead of the traditional beam axle and leaf springs. This suspension was also used on a new model in 1962, the

14ft 4 berth Compact, first winner of the Hennessy Design Award at that year's British Caravan Road Rally. This Award was presented for the best prototype or special competing in the Rally. The Compact was fitted with an updated version of the patent widow design to all windows except the front bay. Spring clips held frameless safety glass into a 90-degree outward opening frame with sliding stays of Ensor's own make, but by releasing the clips the glass could tilt inwards to direct fresh air upwards without a draught. Another new van was introduced towards the end of 1964, the 16ft Merit, a 5 berth costing £745. The other models in the range at this time were the Kiwi 3/4 berth and Eden 2 berth, both 10ft 9in long and costing £485, Elf 12ft 6in 2 berth at £570, and Compact 14ft in 2 and 4 berth versions both at £585. All were now fitted with torsion bar suspension.

Ensors were straightforward craftsman built gimmick-free vans noted for their solid construction and proven towing qualities, reflected in higher than average second hand values. Joe Bissell was 70 in 1971 and to enable him to retire it was decided to sell both Benson Motor Body Co Ltd and Ensor Caravans. Buyers were found for both firms but the prospective purchaser of Ensor withdrew at the last minute and production ceased at the end of 1972. Joe Bissell died in 1985.

ESSEX

E Maritaux, the founder of Essex Caravans Ltd, London Road, Copford, near Colchester, Essex, started production around 1932-33. 1933 models were a £70 non-streamlined 7¼cwt 8ft 2 berth, £80 10ft and £100 12ft semi-lantern roof vans, and £140 13ft and £165 15ft 6in streamlined vans.

A 16ft streamlined lantern roof model, later known as the Monarch, was awarded the Coachmaker's Cup by the Institute of British Carriage & Automobile Manufacturers at the 1933 Motor Show. This was an elaborately equipped double panelled centre kitchen 4 berth van featuring a duck tail, copied from a contemporary American caravan style, which incorporated a locker with external door. There was a settee double bed at the front and two single beds at the rear which folded up to form lounge seats, with an extending legless table between them. Interior width was 6ft 3in with 6ft 7in headroom, there were two wardrobes with sliding doors which divided the van into two bedrooms at night, and the toilet room was acoustically insulated and had a sealed door. Other furniture

ESSEX CARAVANS
for
COMFORT, DURABILITY
and VALUE

STREAMLINE SUPER DE LUXE CARAVANS, FULLY FURNISHED AND EQUIPPED

15ft. 6in. Model, 4 Berths, 2 Rooms, £165
13ft. Model, 4 Berths, 2 Rooms . . £140
Other Models from £70

ALL MODELS FULLY GUARANTEED

ESSEX CARAVANS

Excessive streamlining on some 1933 Essex models affected headroom and furniture design at the ends.

1934 ESSEX CARAVANS

The best equipped and the best value. The latest design in caravans

DE LUXE MODELS

16 ft. 2 rooms, 4 berths	**£220**
13 ft. 2 rooms, 4 berths	**£175**
10 ft. 1 room, 2 berths	**£145**

SUPER DE LUXE MODELS

Incorporating wireless set, chemical closet, electric fan, etc.

16 ft. Model	**£250**
13 ft. Model	**£205**
10 ft. Model	**£175**

Send for Catalogue :

ESSEX CARAVANS
COPFORD, ESSEX

The duck tail on 1934 Essex vans was copied from a contemorary American fashion.

included stores cupboard, chest of drawers, ventilated food cupboard, airing cupboard and well fitted crockery and hardware cupboards. The kitchen was fitted with a sink and drainer, and a two-burner oil stove was enclosed in a recess lined with stainless steel. Fittings included a 12 gallon water tank with pump, Dunlopillo mattresses, eight day clock, a battery charged from the towing car serving four flambeau-style fixed lights, table lamp, fan and fitted radio. The full equipment inventory included toothbrush rack and ashtray. Internally the walls were lined with cream leathercloth and the furniture was hand polished. The entrance door slid on ball-bearing runners and the window frames were chromium plated brass. The body was finished with five coats of lead paint followed by a synthetic enamel. The standard finish was light grey with light blue mouldings, but provided notification was received two weeks before the date of delivery the van could be painted in the customer's chosen colour at no extra cost. The corner legs were self adjusting with an automatic ratchet. Once sited the legs were allowed to drop to the ground and adjusted themselves as the occupants moved about inside the van, though this may have worked better in theory than in practice.

1938 vans, looking very like the 1934 models, were the £120 2 or 3 berth My Lady, £150 4 berth Duchess, £162 10s 4 berth Princess and £310 4 berth Monarch. However when the 1939 range was announced in October 1938 the style was less streamlined, with a full width lantern roof, the models being the 10ft 3 berth My Lady at £115 single panelled or £125 double panelled, 12ft Duchess at £125 or £137 10s, 14ft Princess at £135 or £150 and 17ft double panelled Monarch at £300.

EVERYMAN *See* THOMSON

EVERYMAN'S

The Bramber Engineering Company Ltd, Waterloo Road, Cricklewood, London NW2, well known for the manufacture of trailer chassis and undergear, also produced small basic caravans in 1938-39. Not to be confused with the Everyman caravan manufactured for the camping equipment suppliers Black's of Greenock by Thomson, Bramber's vans comprised the Everyman's caravan, measuring 8ft x 4ft 6in, and costing £39 15s for the standard version in 1939, or £45 10s for a de luxe version with mattresses, extension cover, lighting, box seats, table and Primus stove. In addition there was the Every-other-man's model, an unfitted shell 11ft long and costing £55 at the beginning of 1939 but increased to a 12ft van costing £62 10s later in the year.

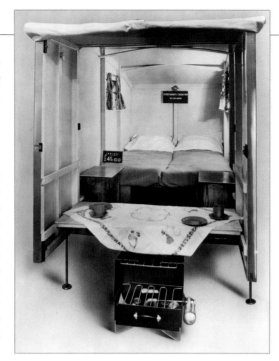

1939 Everyman's de luxe, not to be confused with the Everyman caravan made by Thomson for the camping equipment suppliers Blacks of Greenock.

EXTENSICAR

John and Mary Purdey of Wolverhampton were granted a patent for the Extensicar in 1930. The van had a rectangular box body, and when a handle at the rear end was turned a rack and pinion mechanism caused almost the whole length of both sides to slide out. This resulted in a large floor area but layout was restricted because only moveable furniture could be placed in the centre section. A licence was granted to Holbrook & Taylor Ltd, also of Wolverhampton, who built a small number of Extensicars, possibly only three or four. A licence was also granted to D H Morgan in connection with his Fairway extending vans.

FAIRWAY

DH Morgan started building Fairway caravans in 1935 at Deganwy, near Llandudno, North Wales, and from 1936 specialised in vans with extending bays sliding out from the sides. The first such model was the £135 15ft 6in Caernarvon Castle, which had a slide-out toilet room with doors to the outside and into the van. This was followed in 1937 by the similar £175 16ft 6in Harlech Castle, and in that year, taking out a licence under the Extensicar patent, Mr Morgan started to build vans with larger extensions. 1939 models included the Harlech Castle with large extensions on both sides. The vans had lantern roofs and a unique design of window which opened on either top or side hinges. An 18ft 6in van built for the actor Claude Dampier had four extensions, two each side, to front and rear of the wheel arch, while a special with five separate compartments, built in 1939, had an extending toilet room and two rooms in the middle, each containing a 4ft 6in double bed, as well as a rear end kitchen and a room at the front with a single bed, bureau and other furniture. Production did not start again after the Second World War.

This 1939 Fairway advertisement shows the extending side bays that were a feature of this make.

FAIRWAY'S CARAVANS

are far superior, more thoughtfully planned, better equipped, cost less and are fitted with a **Patent Toilet Room** which does not take any floor space in the van, and when the van is pitched it is extended outwards just where the toilet ought to be (for health's sake) outside the van, more especially away from the kitchen. This Toilet has interior and exterior entrances. It can also be used when withdrawn into the van for travelling, so before you decide on your type of winter model see our literature of models ranging from **£140** to **£350**, they are brimming with ideas for practical use. Our **CONWAY CASTLE** model with extended Bays is having a wonderful reception with old and new caravanners, they marvel at the wonderful floor space and the airy atmosphere. The ordinary type of caravan is as a corridor compared to this model. We do modify this model as a six-berth.

ABOVE:
The **HARLECH CASTLE** shown with extending Bays withdrawn and ready for the road.

LEFT:
HARLECH CASTLE Illustration showing centre of van and toilet extended when pitched.

RIGHT:
Interior of the **HARLECH CASTLE**. The end compartment, with Bureau, etc., which is the usual width of a caravan. Note the difference in width when Bays are extended. These are partly shown in Photograph.

Birmingham Agent:
Mr. SHUCK, 83, Warren Road, Erdington.

Please write for catalogue — you will be interested.

D. H. MORGAN, "Fairway," Deganwy, North Wales
Works : LLANDUDNO JUNCTION, Telephone 81195   Telephone 237

FEU

Feu Engineering Works Co, Davidson Road, Croydon, manufactured trailers and caravan chassis. In 1936 they also produced a sleeping trailer costing £17.

The 1936 Feu sleeping trailer offered basic shelter for £17.

FLATAVAN

Melville Hart, AMINA, was a naval architect-cum-caravan designer. Working in the period 1923-34 from an office at St Stephen's House, Victoria Embankment, London SW1, he designed his Flatavans to meet the customer's needs, from a simple two-wheel trailer to a double-decker motor caravan, from a caravan-houseboat to a train of three four-wheelers drawn by a motor tractor, and then found a builder. Caravans which he made for Indian Maharajahs and other wealthy clients were taken to Buckingham Palace and the Houses of Parliament to be viewed by the King and the Speaker. Typical of his work for the ordinary caravanner was 'Colomen Wen' (Welsh for 'White Dove') built at Godalming, Surrey, in 1926 for Sir Harry (then Mr) Brittain, later a vice-president of the Caravan Club for many years. The heavy plain box body, very tall on 15in wheels, was nearly 16ft long. A short passage led from the rear

1926 Flatavan, designed by a naval-architect-cum-caravan-designer. Enjoying tea here are well-dressed caravanners Sir Harry and Lady Brittain.

door into the saloon. To right and left of the passage were the kitchen with oil stove and a toilet room with flush lavatory and wash basin. Both rooms were served with running water from overhead tanks filled by means of a semi-rotary pump. The saloon had a Columbian coal stove in one corner and a double bed settee across the front end. A then novel feature was a nearside settee converting into two-tier bunks and screened by a curtain at night. The van must have been very comfortable for its time but the design looked back to the horse-drawn caravan rather than forward into the motoring age. In a message sent to the 1969 Annual Members Meeting of the Caravan Club Sir Harry, then aged 95, said that the van was still valiantly holding its own in the garden of his country cottage where it was used as a summer house.

FLEETWING

Fleetwings were manufactured by W Langton of High Street, Uttoxeter, Staffordshire from 1938. The £130 Nippy was an 11ft 8in long x 5ft 8in wide 3 or 4 berth doubled panelled van with lantern roof which could be finished to match the colour of a purchaser's car at no extra cost. Other models priced between £85 and £185 were also available.

FOHLO

WS Greening of Clapham Road, Stockwell, London SW6, had owned a Collapsivan folding caravan in the early 1930s. Later in the decade he went into production with the Fohlo, a design derived from the Collapsivan. The mostly single-skinned body was panelled in Masonite on an ash frame. Folded for towing the van was 7ft 6in long x 4ft wide x 3ft 7in high but when erected was 7ft 6in wide with 6ft 2in headroom. A three-drawer unit, table and worktops stowed on the floor when the van was folded and there were external lockers along the sides with a front end locker accessible from inside. Weight was around 7cwt and the price in 1938 was £125. The time taken to fold the van was advertised as five minutes. Production continued until the outbreak of the Second World War.

The purchaser of a 1939 Fleetwing Nippy could have it painted to match the colour of his car at no extra cost, and then, according to the bold advertising claims, confidently take to 'some of the worst roads in Scotland'.

1938-39 Fohlo. The design was derived from the earlier Collapsivan folding caravan.

FOLDAVAN

The Foldavan Company of Stobcross Street, Glasgow C3, started production in mid-1939 with the 4 berth Mushroom folding caravan. Closed for towing the van measured 7ft long x 5ft wide x 4ft 6in high. When extended the width increased to 10ft with 6ft 4in headroom. The roof was raised on six uprights by means of DWS hydraulic jacks, lifting with it the two large hinged panels which formed the sides of the van when closed. These panels swung outwards to form extended sleeping bays on each side. The bottom of each bay, on which the mattresses rested, was hinged to the side panel and pulled up into position with it. Lockers, racks and a shelf were built in. The Mushroom weighed approximately 10cwt and the price of £125 included a two-burner petrol stove, electric lighting and a table. A Calor Gas stove was available at extra cost. The eve of the Second World War was not the most opportune time to introduce a new van and nothing more was heard of the Mushroom.

1939 Foldavan Mushroom and a Wolseley. Unfortunately, this was not the best time to be introducing a new make.

FREEMAN

1949 Freeman Wel-Four, built for the dealers Welfords Caravans of Warninglid.

Both before and after the Second World War, John O Freeman of Stoke Golding, Nuneaton, built vans under the Wel-Four name (Welfour in some sources) exclusively for the dealers Welfords Caravans of Warninglid, Sussex. In 1939 the D P (double panelled) Wel-Four was a 14ft x 6ft 2in 4 berth costing £115. Mounted on Brockhouse undergear with body framing of seasoned ash, the walls were panelled externally with Sundeala hardboard with oak internal lining to walls and ceiling. Lantern roof vans

were also built before the War but no details are known.

Production restarted in 1946 with the Wel-Four, and in 1948 the 12ft x 6ft 3 berth Wel-Free cost £495, the 17ft x 6ft 6in 4 berth Wel-Four costing £785. In the 1949 edition of *The Caravan Manual* Welfords were still advertising themselves as 'sole distributors of Wel-Four and Wel-Free caravans' but by mid-1949 Freeman were advertising in their own right though still using the Wel-Free and Wel-Four names, and by the beginning of 1951 the vans were being sold through other dealers as well as by Welfords. The range at this time comprised the 26cwt 17ft Wel-Four de luxe at £825, 24½cwt Wel-Four Standard at £750, and the 16½cwt 12ft 3 or 4 berth Wel-Free at £495. The price of the de luxe model reflected its solid construction, luxurious appointments and comprehensive equipment. Mounted on a chassis made by Freeman with Bramber or Boden-Davis axle and leaf springs, the hardwood framed body had almond green painted aluminium exterior wall panelling with 1/2in insulation board roof panelling covered with cream painted stretched duck material. Interior wall panelling was oak faced plywood, with Masonite hardboard ceiling treated with Spraytex – a sprayed on coat of tinted adhesive followed by spraying with tiny particles of rayon of the same colour – to resist condensation. Insulation was by Tropal (kapok) blanket, and tongued and grooved boarding was used for the floor. The windows were a special Freeman design of frameless moulded perspex. A bulge at the bottom of the windows, in conjunction with anodised aluminium linings to the openings, lipped on the inner edge, ensured that any condensation was collected and prevented from dripping into the van. Division for sleeping was by a concertina-type partition, and a two-fold door shut off the rear end kitchen, in which all the fittings were made of perspex or anodised aluminium. Equipment included 7in Rex spring interior mattresses, solid fuel stove with hot water tank, Crossland gas fire, Eltex splash proof chemical toilet, box step, built-in radio, 10 gallon cold water tank, Royston gas cooker and rubbish chute. The kitchen and toilet compartment had cork composition floor covering, the rest of the van having a fitted carpet laid on underfelt and secured by press studs. Four gas lights and one battery electric light were provided.

By 1952 the Wel-Free was no longer in production and new models were the 14ft 2 berth Huntsman priced at £850 and the 19ft 4 berth Talisman weighing 30cwt and costing £1,050. John Freeman attended the Caravan Club's National Rally with a Talisman in 1952 and the Club's vice-chairman, W P Stote, brought a 14ft 9in 3 berth Freeman special to the same rally.

A major change came in 1955 when GRP bodywork was adopted for two new lantern roof vans, the 2 berth Atholl and 4 berth Glencairn, both 16ft 6in long with an ex-works weight of 24cwt and costing £1,095. Mounted on a conventional chassis and with hardwood body framing, the shell was moulded in left and right hand halves which were cemented together. The ceiling was lined with another moulding finished with Spraytex, and creosoted tongued and grooved boarding formed the floor. Insulation was provided by a sealed cavity in walls and roof, and the high quality furniture was in limed oak with matt cellulose spray finish. The kitchen had Formica covered walls and perspex furniture. Equipment included a 22-piece Freeman crockery service fitted in a roof locker with a leaded glass front, built-in radio, aluminium bread bin, fold-down bread/chopping board, detachable refuse bin, Eltex chemical toilet and pull-out perspex washbasin in the toilet room, 12 gallon water tank, three electric lights and four gas lights. A fitted gas fire

1956 Freeman Atholl. The company's GRP expertise was later used for boat building.

was mounted on a small tiled plinth, ventilated to draw fresh air from below the floor, with a built-in flue – then an unusual feature – leading through the airing cupboard and terminating in a 'mushroom' vent on the roof. Surprisingly for such a luxury van, only a hotplate was fitted, with no oven. Attention to detail was shown in the design of the toilet room in the rear off-side corner, the rear wall of which incorporated an obscured glass window and was positioned a few inches clear of the van's rear wall, maintaining the symmetry of the exterior by allowing one of the larger twin clear glass rear windows to extend behind the toilet room. As well as the high quality of the interior fittings, the high weight was attributable to the 1/8in thickness of the body moulding – John Freeman would not sacrifice constructional strength in order to make the van lighter.

A further GRP van was added to the range in 1956, the 13ft 6in 2 berth Leveret with similar styling to the Atholl and Glencairn but without the lantern roof. Unfortunately buyers of high quality vans such as the Freeman tended to have conservative tastes and they were also critical of the minute imperfections of the finish of GRP, which could not quite reach the standard of the best aluminium coachwork, so whilst the Leveret continued in production into 1958 the other GRP models had been discontinued by 1957, and in November 1958 it was reported that only the 19ft 6in Talisman and 15ft 6in Clansman – both with conventional body construction of aluminium external panelling on hardwood framing – would be produced in 1959.

The company's GRP expertise was diverted into boat building, a 22ft Freeman cabin cruiser being exhibited in the boat section of the 1957 Motor Show. Around 1960 caravan production was phased out completely and production concentrated on boat building, though the 1964 and 1968 rallies of Les Amis d'Outre Manche, a fraternity of caravanners who toured on the continent, were held at Leicester Grange, Nuneaton, the home of John Freeman and his wife. At the 1968 rally participants were able to look around the Freeman marine factory.

GIBBS

1936 Gibbs dental clinic. Although caravans were produced, output appears to have been mainly devoted to mobile dental clinics, offices and other functional units.

MG Gibbs Super Caravans, Tarring Road, Worthing, manufactured mobile dental clinics, offices and other functional units. In 1933 they introduced the £295 14ft 4 berth Worthing Special. This was an expensive van for the period and the standard of finish was reported to be excellent, with tongued and grooved oak floor boards and lavish use of chromium plating inside the van. The exterior panelling was aluminium, unusual at the time, but whilst the roof was double panelled the walls were single panelled with a lining of leathercloth fixed with adhesive directly to the aluminium. Later in the 1930s Gibbs also produced panel-beaten steel caravan bodies on box-section steel framing.

GLENDALE

Glendale Caravans, Barrow House, Wooler, Northumberland, were producing three models in 1934.

1934 Glendale advertisement. Presumably the 'exceptionally attractive prices' meant that a photograph for the advertisement was considered a luxury.

GLENDALE STREAMLINE CARAVANS
Comfortable double-panelled models at exceptionally attractive prices

Chemical Toilet Room on all Models

10ft. 2 berth £75
12ft. 3 berth, 2 rooms £95
15ft. 4 berth, 2 rooms £125

Beautifully Equipped

GLENDALE CARAVANS
Barrow House, Wooler, Northumberland

GLIDER

The 1939 Glider Series II was available in single panelled, double panelled and de luxe versions.

RG Stevens, trading as Northampton Caravans Ltd of St Andrew's Street, Northampton, began production of Glider caravans in 1938. Aimed at the growing market for a family van at a popular price, the initial model was a 14ft 6in x 6ft 1in single panelled 4 berth costing £119. Later in the year a 6ft 7in wide double panelled Series II de luxe model, also 14ft 6in long, was introduced. By 1939 the firm had moved to Bridge Street, Northampton, and the Series II was available at £125 single panelled, £140 double panelled or £185 in de luxe form. The vans were mounted on a Brockhouse chassis with English ash framing and Sundeala hardboard wall panelling, and Calor gas equipment was fitted on the de luxe model. All upholstery and beds had 'special de luxe patent mesh springing' and the vans were 'finished throughout in Thomas Parsons & Sons Ltd first class synthetic enamels'.

Post-war models were reported to be in the prototype stage in 1946. The Series III was a 17ft x 7ft 4 berth, fully insulated including the floor, with chromium plated metal frames to the drop type windows, and cost £950 in 1947. By 1948 the company had moved to Kettering Road North, Northampton, and the £889 Glider Supreme Series IV was exhibited at that year's Motor Show. This 17ft

THE GLIDER

SERIES 2

4 Berth Standard £125
or Double-panelled complete - - £140
4 Berth De-Luxe £185

For a delightful holiday — As a weekend cottage or **an emergency house**

4 BERTH STANDARD 14' 6" LONG

Only the finest materials are used in all models—All Upholstery and Beds are special De-Luxe Patent Mesh Springing.

GOODYEAR TYRES as Standard.
SUNDEALA HARDBOARD WALLS—INSULWOOD ROOF.
ENGLISH ASH FRAMEWORK throughout with Limba Panelling.
RAY GAS COOKER on De-Luxe Models.

CALOR GAS exclusively on De-Luxe Models.
EASY-CLEAN WHEELS (Standard).
ALL-STEEL specially designed BROCKHOUSE CHASSIS FINISHED THROUGHOUT in Thomas Parsons & Sons, Ltd., First-Class Synthetic Enamels.

NORTHAMPTON CARAVANS LTD. 73/85 BRIDGE STREET, NORTHAMPTON. TEL: 1471

Write to your Local Agent for details :—
W. WRIGHT & SONS, 147 LOUGHBORO ROAD, LEICESTER

6in end kitchen 4 berth was insulated with Isoflex and equipped with a Pither's solid fuel stove and a small bath. A much cheaper model exhibited at the 1949 Motor Show was the 15ft 3in x 6ft 6in centre kitchen 4 berth Flyte costing £299 15s. By the beginning of 1951 this van was known as the Flyte Series VA 4 berth and cost £307 10s. There was also a Flyte Series VA 2 berth but this £189 10s model was only 9ft 8in long x 5ft 9in wide. There was also a de luxe version of the 4 berth costing £399 10s. The de luxe fittings amounted to a Tayco solid fuel stove with hot water tank, and a Calor gas B500 oven cooker rather than the hotplate fitted to the standard model. The walls were panelled externally with brown painted hardboard and internally with insulation board. The roof panelling was hardboard covered with aluminium painted canvas and the floor was linoleum covered tongued and grooved boarding. A test report of 1951 does not mention any cavity insulation and, whilst generally commenting favourably on the van, noted flimsy support for the shelves above the dinette, the rather dark interior due to the chocolate brown colour of the woodwork, and the substantial noseweight of 2cwt resulting from the positioning of the Tayco stove.

New models exhibited at the 1952 Motor Show were the 10ft 6in x 6ft 6in 4 berth Glider Series VI at £285 and 14ft 6in x 6ft 6in 5 berth Glider Series VI at £370. The vans exhibited at the 1953 Show had aluminium exterior panelling and comprised the 10ft x 6ft 4in Glider Fleetwing Series VII in 2 and 4 berth versions costing £225 and £240 respectively, and the 14ft 6in x 6ft 6in Glider Flyte Series VI 5 berth at £370. A completely new model at the 1954 Show was the Gliderex, a 21ft x 7ft 6in van costing £699 10s which extended on site to 27ft by means of a slide-out rear body section. The company ran into problems with this model, quickly changing the design to slide out at the front end and publishing a notice in the caravan press to the effect that they were not proceeding with the rear extension due to the similarity with Campmaster's Amberley Six. The layout of the Gliderex comprised a separate bedroom with two single beds in the extension, central lounge with fold-away double bed and put-u-up double bed settee, rear end kitchen and toilet room.

A new 16ft 4 berth end kitchen van, the £440 Fantom, was introduced early in 1955. The range for 1956 comprised the 15ft 4 berth Fleetwing Major at £329, Fantom, 20ft 4 berth Fantom Major at £545 and the Gliderex, now costing £799 10s. For 1958 there were only two models, the £435 16ft 6in Glid-away and the £675 22ft Alaskan. A novelty exhibited at the 1961 Caravan Exhibition was the Glider

THE SHAPE OF THINGS TO COME

The style of the 1946 Glider Series III reflects the general move away from streamlining after WWII.

Carafloat caravan/houseboat, a 16ft caravan body mounted on a 25ft x 11ft raft supported by GRP floats. When plans for the 1965 range were reported in November 1964 there was a new tourer, the 12ft Slipstream, a £398 10s 10¼cwt 4 berth with toilet room and mounted on Rubery Owen torsion bar independent suspension, joined towards the end of 1965 by 10ft and 14ft versions. Customers were now offered a choice of Rubery Owen or B & B suspension with transverse swinging arms and coil springs. By 1967, the final year of production, the only model was a Mark II version of the Slipstream 14 priced at £495. At this time the vans were only being sold direct to the public from a showground at the Kettering Road North premises. Customers were offered payment of 6d per mile travelling expenses if an order was placed at the time of their visit!

Originally the extending section of the 1955 Glider Gliderex was at the rear end, but it had to be moved to the front due to the similarity with Campmaster's Amberley Six.

GLOUCESTER

KC Wood started production of Gloucester caravans in 1939 at Copt Elm Road, Charlton Kings, Cheltenham, in premises previously occupied by Adams Caravans Ltd. Former Adams employees were hired and initial models were the Junior 2 berth at prices from £85, Junior 3 berth from £92 10s and Comet 4 berth from £125, all apparently available with steel exterior panelling, the Comet in this case costing £200. Further models were the 16ft lantern roof Courier, from £215, and the Utility, clearly designed with an eye on the likelihood of war. 8ft long x 4ft 6in wide with an overall height of 6ft 3in, the

5cwt Utility cost £52 10s. Body panelling was Sundeala hardboard and the price included mattresses, curtains and equipment for two. Double doors were fitted at the rear and the furniture was removable, allowing use as a delivery van or as an ambulance.

1939 Gloucester Utility: all the furniture was quickly removable, allowing use as a delivery van or an ambulance.

GOOD COMPANION *See* THOMSON

GOODWOOD

Introduced late in 1938, the Goodwood was built by Winchester for the dealers Kingston Caravan Co, but no details are known.

GROSVENOR

G Hay-Moulder, founder of Grosvenor Caravans, Old Church Street, Chelsea, London SW3, was one of the pioneer builders of trailer caravans. Caravan building was carried out in conjunction with a car business and, whilst nothing is known of the early vans, there were two 4 berth models in 1937, 12ft 6in and 14ft 6in, costing £160 and £195 respectively. In 1939 there were three models, the 10ft 6in Sunbird at £95 in 2/3 berth form or £105 as a 4 berth, 13ft 3in

Merlin 3 berth at £125 or 4 berth at £130, and the 15ft 5in 4 or 5 berth Curlew priced from £150. All models were double panelled with Masonite exterior panelling and the vans could also be hired along with suitable towcars.

Production recommenced after the Second World War in 1946 with the Sunbird and Merlin. By 1948 the range comprised the £400 11ft 3 berth Sunbird, £550 14ft 4 berth Merlin and £650 15ft 6in 4 berth

1937 12ft 6in Grosvenor. The founder of this firm, G Hay-Moulder was one of the pioneer builders of trailer caravans.

Curlew. From 1950, whilst still at the same address and producing Grosvenor caravans, the company name had changed to Westminster Carriage Co Ltd (though trading for a time as Westminster Caravans) and, strangely for a business believed to have been producing caravans since 1919, was claiming to have been established for 22 years! By late 1952 the same three models were still in production but the lengths were now 11ft 6in, 14ft 6in and 16ft 6in, increased at the beginning of 1953 to 12ft, 15ft and 17ft, and these were joined later in the year by the 22ft Eagle. The company changed hands about this time but no details are known of the new owners.

A report on the Sunbird in 1954 commented on the sturdy chassis of the company's own manufacture and constructed mostly from 2in x 2in x 1/4in steel angle bolted together with high tensile steel bolts. A hire fleet was still operated and since it was not unknown for a hire van to do a 6,000 to 7,000 mile continental tour on a single let the vans were built to a robust standard. The walls were insulated with fibreglass but the roof was single panelled in Masonite on ash framing. The outer covering of the roof was Egyptian cotton bedded on varnish and finished with four coats of aluminium paint. Pluvex roofing felt was laid between the linoleum and the tongued and grooved floor boarding. The high standard of finish

was said to be what was expected of a company carrying out a lot of car bodywork repairs, and the spring interior mattresses were also made by the firm. From 1956 the Merlin was the only model and production ceased completely after 1958.

1949 Grosvenor advertisement. The model names were bird-themed.

GUILDFORD

RE Gash of The Guildford Motor Body Works, Worplesdon Road, Guildford, Surrey, started building caravans following service in the Royal Naval Air Service during the First World War. Up to about 1930 the vans had the square ends, bowed sides and lantern roof typical of the period, but then a new model was introduced which, whilst retaining a semi-

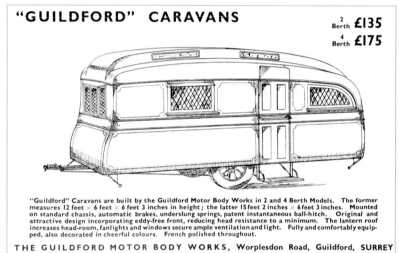

"GUILDFORD" CARAVANS

2 Berth **£135**
4 Berth **£175**

"Guildford" Caravans are built by the Guildford Motor Body Works in 2 and 4 Berth Models. The former measures 12 feet × 6 feet × 6 feet 3 inches in height; the latter 15 feet 2 inches × 6 feet 3 inches. Mounted on standard chassis, automatic brakes, underslung springs, patent instantaneous ball-hitch. Original and attractive design incorporating eddy-free front, reducing head resistance to a minimum. The lantern roof increases head-room, fanlights and windows secure ample ventilation and light. Fully and comfortably equipped, also decorated in cheerful colours. French polished throughout.

THE GUILDFORD MOTOR BODY WORKS, Worplesdon Road, Guildford, SURREY

traditional style, had a streamlined lantern roof. This was followed by 12ft 2 berth and 15ft 4 berth fully streamlined models for 1933 priced at £135 and £175 respectively. Gash continued production until the Second World War, enjoying a sound local reputation, but caravans represented only a small part of the output of the firm.

HAPPEE DAZE

A 1938 advertisement by J Brockhouse & Co Ltd lists a number of caravan makers using Brockhouse chassis including Happee Daze, but no other reference to this manufacturer has been found.

HARCO

WD Harrington started business as a garage proprietor in Bootle in 1924. He began to take an interest in caravans about 1930, manufacturing a van called the Harco. This had the square ends, bowed sides and lantern roof typical of several makes of the 1920s and early 1930s. The van only remained in production for a short period, manufacturing being abandoned in favour of selling other makes. The first distribution depot, at Ormskirk, was started in 1932 or 1933.

The Harco was introduced c.1930 by which time this styling was going out of fashion.

HARLEW

Caravans for Hire Ltd, Alum Rock Road, Saltley, Birmingham, advertised themselves as sole distributors for Harlew streamlined caravans in 1936. The models available comprised a £95 2 berth, £115 3 berth, £135 4 berth and a £160 15ft de luxe 4 berth. By 1937 Harlew Caravans were advertising under their own name from the same address, the name being derived from that of the maker, Harry Lewis, who had started to build caravans in 1933. References have been found to Harlew producing caravans in 1946 and 1952 but nothing is known of the vans from this period.

HARRISON

1934 Harrison Bungalow-Caravan. The firm appears to have originally produced traditional horse drawn caravans.

A E Harrison & Sons, based at Abbott Street, Heanor, Derbyshire, appear to have originally produced traditional horse drawn vans but by the 1920s had turned to making trailer caravans. The firm also made large Bungalow-Caravans more suitable for static use, and built vans to individual customer's requirements for around £160. A famous owner was Harry Wheatcroft, the Nottingham rose grower, who had a van named 'The Rambling Rose' for many years which was used to attend flower shows around the country.

HARVINGTON

J D Lyon-Smith's company, Harvington Trailers Ltd, Harvington, Evesham, Worcestershire, were in production before the Second World War but nothing is known of the vans in this period. Production appears to have restarted around 1949 but again no details of the early post-war models have come to light, although the firm seems to have initially concentrated on living vans. At the beginning of 1951 there was an unnamed £695 4 berth 22ft x 7ft 6in model with open coal fire, end kitchen and toilet room with bath. Early in 1952 there were two living vans, the Lion and Lioness, priced at £775 and £665 respectively, replaced for 1953-54 by the 22ft Tiger. By mid-1954 there was also a 14ft 6in touring van, the 4 berth Romany priced at £395. At this period a solid partition to divide the van at night was still considered essential, so the forward ends of the mattresses on the two 5ft 10in rear end single beds were tapered and extended under the bulkheads dividing off the other part of the van, and were boxed in to form large shelves. The partition was completed by a two-leaf door which stored next to the wardrobe when not in use. There was also a gate-leg table which could be stored in the wardrobe, though where the caravanner was supposed to put his clothes when this happened is not clear!

Models in 1955 were the Romany and the £495 20ft 3in Harmony, and in 1956 the £245 10ft 3 berth Colleen, Romany, £465 18ft Rhapsody and £585 22ft Melody. 1957 models were the £285 Colleen Mk II, £345 12ft 6in Senorita, £499 Rhapsody Mk II and £645 22ft Aladdin. The 16ft Ballerina, introduced late in 1958, had two 6ft x 2ft 3in single beds at the front end, one of which shortened to 4ft for daytime use, allowing a two-leaf partition to fold back against the side wall. It also had a double bed the mattress of which, in three sections stitched together, folded up with space left for bedding into a cabinet about 4ft high. At night the top of the cabinet hinged up, the front let down and slid forward slightly to rest on a dayseat over the offside wheelarch and a hinged support. The foot of the bed extended under a worktop in the kitchen and the side of the bed cabinet hinged open to facilitate bedmaking – usually still involving sheets and blankets at this time. A further dayseat between the single beds provided a U-shaped seating arrangement at the front end. A toilet compartment in the rear nearside corner closed to a triangular space when not in use by means of overlapping doors. The van was panelled externally in aluminium, internally with painted hardboard and was insulated with Alfol aluminium foil. The lounge

1954 Harvington Romany. A solid partition to divide the van at night was still considered essential, resulting in a very complicated arrangement in this 14ft 6in model.

furniture was wax finished oak veneer with solid oak framing. The kitchen furniture had a painted finish and the combined sink and drainer was a GRP moulding. Man-handling must have been quite an effort because the van had no grab handles, and despite a substantial noseweight was only fitted with a slide and clamp jockey wheel rather than a telescopic type. The price was £485, with fitted carpet a £13 extra.

By the end of 1959 the range comprised the Colleen Mk IV, 14ft 4 berth Honey, Ballerina and Aladdin Mk III. New body shapes had been designed for the Colleen and Aladdin, the Honey being a new model which unusually for a van of this size had nine windows. In the days of single glazed glass windows this cannot have made it a comfortable van in cold weather The final range in 1962 comprised the £519 12ft 6in Brigitte, £539 Honey Mk II, £647 Ballerina Mk II, £938 18ft 9in Venus and £1,350 22ft Hall. Towards the end of 1962 it was reported that caravan production was to cease and that the premises were to be converted into a covered showroom, the firm becoming dealers in other makes. The vans were noted for fine craftsmanship but were never manufactured in large numbers.

HEDON

Hedon Aircraft, Hedon, near Hull, East Yorkshire, produced a £105 14ft de luxe 4 berth 'delightfully designed model of aircraft quality' in 1937. 3-4 berth vans costing from £85 were also available.

HIGSONIAN

VE Higson Ltd were toy manufacturers who started building caravans in 1937. The first Higsonian model was a 13ft 6in 4 berth costing £125. Three further models were introduced in mid-1938 – the £97 12ft Minor, £150 14ft 6in Major with full width lantern roof, and 16ft Super with lantern roof and available with alternative layouts costing £185 or £195. 1939 models were the £125 13ft 6in Osborne, £170 14ft 6in Mayfair with full width lantern roof, and £210 16ft lantern roof Dorchester. The Mayfair and Dorchester were both end kitchen vans with two doors. The head office was at Duke Street, Liverpool, with the works at Factory Lane, Rochdale Road, Harpurhey, Manchester. There were no agents, the vans being sold direct to the customer.

1939 Higsonian Dorchester. Toy manufacturers VE Higson Ltd started building caravans in 1937.

HILL

Fred Hill of Swinefleet on the Yorkshire-Lincolnshire border was a well known builder of horse drawn gypsy caravans who also built vans for travelling showmen. Although the last horse drawn van was not built until 1946, demand declined from the 1920s and the firm started to build living van bodies on Ford chassis.

Whether showmen's trailer caravans were also built in any numbers is not known but a two-wheeled model, 10ft long and dating from 1925, is recorded.

HOLGATE

William E Holgate of Arthur Holgate & Son Ltd, Bridge Street, Church, Near Accrington, Lancashire (a family business established in 1890), built his first caravan in 1939. Nothing is known of this van but post-war production started in 1947. The classic body style did not change much over the ensuing years and indeed the photograph which appears in a 1962 advertisement looks little different from that in a 1949 advertisement.

The only model in 1949 was a fully insulated end kitchen van with hot and cold water systems, Dunlopillo mattresses and eight day clock. By 1951 this had been succeeded by the 14ft 4 berth centre kitchen Silver Wings – starting a tradition of 'Silver' model

"HOLGATE"

Caravans of Distinction

- Bay Window
- Separate End Kitchen
- Hot and Cold Water
- Calor Gas
- Dunlopillo Beds
- 8 Day Coach Clock
- Toilet Room
- Full Insulation
- Suitable for Winter Use

A. Holgate & Son, Ltd.

Bridge Street, Church,
Nr. ACCRINGTON, LANCS.

Tels.: *Accrington 39539 and 3309*

1949 Holgate and 1962 Silver Cloud. The classic body styling did not change much in the 13 years between these models.

1962 HOLGATE 1962
BRITAIN'S FINEST TOURING CARAVAN

INTRODUCING THE NEW **SILVER CLOUD**. AN ENTIRELY NEW 16' 0" 4-BERTH CARAVAN WITH INDEPENDENT SUSPENSION AND CONTINENTAL BRAKING WITH A DELIVERED WEIGHT OF **16 CWTS**. MODERN INTERIOR DECOR WITH ALL THE LUXURY FITTINGS OF ITS PREDECESSORS **£650**

A. HOLGATE & SON LTD.
RUSHTON ST. WKS.   GT. HARWOOD
PHONE : GT. HARWOOD 2315

names which continued until the end of production in 1964. When the 1953 range was advertised towards the end of 1952 this van had been joined by the 10ft 2 berth Silver Wren, 16ft 4 berth Silver Arrow and 18ft 4 berth Silver Star, as well as an end kitchen version of the Silver Wings. A 1953 report on the £325 Silver Wren commented on the robustness of the Holgate designed and manufactured chassis, remarkably high gloss finish of the hardboard interior panelling, quality of finish on the furniture and practical workability of the layout. By 1955 the range comprised the £565 14ft Silver Snipe, £610 Silver Arrow and £712 12s 2d

Silver Star, all 4 berths with end kitchen and toilet. When the range for 1957 was reported on towards the end of 1956, in addition to these vans it included a 12ft 6in 2 berth costing £500, or £530 with oak veneered interior walls in lieu of painted hardboard, and a second 16ft model, which whilst maintaining the usual Holgate standard of finish, was a simpler and cheaper van than the Silver Arrow. By 1958 the 12ft 6in Silver Swift cost £550, Silver Snipe £675, Silver Arrow £750 and Silver Star £825, the only other model at this time being a new 22ft x 7ft 6in 4 berth living van with separate end bedroom.

Towards the end of 1958 the company moved to larger premises, a former cinema at Rushton Street, Great Harwood, near Blackburn, Lancashire, and for 1959 the models were restricted to the £579 12ft 6in 2 berth Silver Wren and £775 Silver Arrow. For 1960 the smaller van was discontinued and the Silver Arrow was joined by a new Silver Star model, but by 1961 the range had been expanded again to include the

£590 12ft Silver Wren, £670 14ft 2in Silver Snipe, £770 16ft Silver Speed, £775 16ft Silver Arrow and £875 18ft Silver Star. All were 7ft 2in wide end kitchen vans and apart from the 2 berth Silver Wren were all 4 berth models. From 1962 the vans were fitted with independent suspension for the first time. The final models were the 12ft Silverlight, Silver Wren Mk II, 14ft Silver Snipe, 16ft Silver Cloud and Silver Arrow.

There was an associated company, Holgates Caravan Park Ltd, which operated a site for tourers and static caravans at Silverdale on the Southern fringe of the Lake District, and this continued in business after caravan manufacture ceased, eventually being run by William Holgate's son Frank. The firm's vans were of practical design, soundly built, well finished, roadworthy, and whilst highly regarded by northern buyers of clubman vans were not so well known in the south and consequently never achieved the same overall popularity as other clubman makes.

HOMAWAY

A 1938 classified advertisement refers to a second hand 3 berth Homaway living van.

IDEAL

A 1934 advertisement by the Ideal Caravan Co, Nelson Street, Shotton, Chester, refers to a 15ft 6in 4 berth caravan of 'New Sports Design'. The only other references found to Ideal are a 1936 advertisement by the dealers Cara-Cars Ltd, Ilkley, Yorkshire, which includes Ideal in a list of the makes in stock,

1934 Ideal advertisement. There were also some Balmforth models with this name.

and a 1939 advertisement by the dealers Martins Caravan Co, Exeter, offering a 1938 Ideal Caravan Bungalow, but these may relate to Balmforth models.

ISONIAN

1935 Isonian interior and 1937 Isonian Little Gem. Although standard models were produced, this maker specialised in building owner-designed vans.

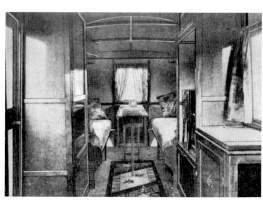

Isonian caravans were produced by C J Ison at Histon, near Cambridge. Although specialising in the building of owner-designed vans there were standard models – a £175 14ft 6in 4 berth in 1935, 2, 3 and 4 berth vans in 1937 and a 3 berth priced from £95 in 1938. The only known model name is the Little Gem of 1937. In July 1938, although the firm was happy to accept orders for 1939, the works were said to be fully occupied with special orders for the rest of 1938. A hire fleet was also operated.

JAFFE

In 1933 M Jaffe, Vauxhall Road, Liverpool, was producing folding 'bungalows' costing from £8 10s which could be carried on a car luggage grid, and trailer bungalows priced from 38 guineas. The largest model was the £150 6 berth Mansion Caravan which when extended formed a three-roomed structure with a small sun verandah.

JENNINGS

Any surviving caravan of the 1920s with square ends, bowed sides and lantern roof is likely to be labelled an Eccles, but several makers of the period were building in the same style. These included J H Jennings & Son Ltd of Sandbach, Cheshire, coachbuilders established in 1764 who had also built horse drawn caravans. The streamlined shape introduced by Bertram Hutchings for his 1930 Winchester was very influential and even such traditionalists as Jennings followed the fashion and introduced streamlined models in 1933, although some vans retained leaded windows. A car-type sliding sunshine roof was a Jennings innovation and a model said to have caused quite a stir at the Motor Show in 1934 was a small 2 berth lantern roof van with rear door, weighing just 5¼ cwt and costing £75. The low weight was achieved by a covering of stretched and painted canvas instead of solid panelling. Exhibited at the same time were 2/3 berth and 4/5 berth models. Later in the 1930s a small van of sheet aluminium lined with leathercloth was introduced. Production of caravans ended in 1939 but Jennings re-entered the caravan field in 1965 with de luxe coach built motor caravans.

1936 Jennings 2 berth, said to have caused quite a stir at the 1934 Motor Show.

Jennings Latest Caravans
FITTED WITH A SUNSHINE ROOF

The lavish equipment includes Float-on-Air Beds, a Monarch Air Extractor, Folding Tables, Wash-bowl and Draining-board, Cooking Stove, Meat Safe, ventilated from outside, numerous Lockers, etc.

Prices from £95

J. H. JENNINGS and Son, Ltd.

Motor Works

SANDBACH

CHESHIRE

The model illustrated is the 4-5 berth de luxe, £154

1933 Jennings advertisement. The car-type sliding sunshine roof was a Jennings innovation.

The ORIGINAL Light 2-Berth
designed and improved by Jennings at the remarkably low

Imitated but never equalled
Can be towed by 8 h.p. car

price of

£95

This caravan is coachbuilt throughout and fitted with chromium framed windows, finished in delicate green and ivory or to choice of colour.

Inside finished in two-tone scheme. Curtains to match.

The only cheap part about it is the price

only **£95**

J. H. JENNINGS & SON LTD.

Sandbach - - - - - Cheshire

JUBILEE

JW Smart was a Birmingham shoe manufacturer who first tried a caravan holiday in the summer of 1930. Having enjoyed the experience, he maintained a casual interest in caravanning and in 1936 decided to start building vans in a spare shed at one of his factories. Soon after taking this decision he met James C Beckett, a sunblind salesman who had previously sold tombstones on hire purchase. A man who could sell him sunblinds at Christmas made quite an impression on Smart, and when progress on the first van needed speeding up he called in Beckett and told him to have the van ready to make its public debut at the Easter Rally of the Caravan Club, only a week away. Assisted by a small staff and working day and night, the van was ready in time despite being hindered by rainy weather – the shed was so low that the van had to be pushed outside to allow work on the roof. Taking the van to the Rally, Smart and Beckett thought it the last word in caravans until they looked at some of the other vans present. A disheartened Smart was ready to give up caravan building but Beckett was keen to continue and the issue was decided on the toss of a coin. Apparently Beckett did not leave the decision entirely to chance – he had a double-headed penny!

Back at the shed in West Bromwich he worked to such effect that in three months a production rate of three vans a week was needed to keep pace with orders. This meant a move to larger premises – a disused garage where a staff of 15 started serious manufacture. By 1937 Jubilee were an important make, having moved to yet larger premises at Bridge Works, Holloway Bank, Wednesbury. They employed a staff of 75 to produce vans at the rate of one a day, with old buildings at the rear of the new works being reconstructed so that production staff could be increased to 120.

Late in 1937 the range comprised the 13ft 6in Firefly, 14ft Butterfly, 15ft 6in Gadfly, 16ft 6in Mayfly, 18ft Dragonfly and the newly introduced 16ft 6in Wasp. All but the Butterfly had lantern roofs, Butterfly, Firefly and Gadfly were available with either single or double panelling and prices ranged from £125 for the single panelled Butterfly to £450 for the Dragonfly Special. The vans, which had drop windows, were robustly constructed and well finished, with practical layouts. The Dragonfly Special was comprehensively equipped, including a hot and cold water system with Maxol geyser and electric pump, and the toilet room was fitted with an American Sanitare chemical closet.

Beckett left in 1938 to join Eccles as sales manager and later set up the dealers Beckett's of Bromsgrove

1937 Jubilee Firefly. Although only starting to build caravans in 1936, Jubilee was an important make by 1937.

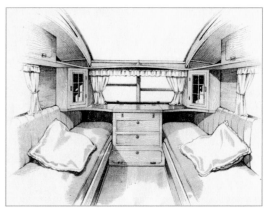

Ltd. He had also worked for the Taplow, Bucks, dealer A S Jenkinson, and in the late 1940s and early 1950s both men's advertising involved a good deal of sniping at the other. Typical examples are Beckett's advertisement in *The Caravan* for May 1949, where he announced great regret at hearing that Jenkinson (whose advertising regularly mentioned that he had lived in a caravan for 12 years) had purchased a house, and in *The Caravan* for September 1953 Jenkinson suggested that 'Not one of Beckett's teeth is real! Just

look at that false smile!' It is difficult to know if this was just good natured rivalry between the two men or whether any real animosity was involved. Beckett's advertising also often featured a drawing showing him wearing a halo, and he attended the 1952 Caravan Club National Rally with a van sporting a neon halo on the roof.

It was reported in August 1938 that E Sumner of Dudley, Worcestershire, who had been the Midland Distributor for Jubilee and Eccles, had purchased the

Jubilee 'Wasp'

FOUR BERTH
CENTRE KITCHEN

The 1939 " Wasp " has been derived from the model so enthusiastically received in 1938, and includes many improvements. It is a four berth caravan which combines daintiness with solidity and considerable care has been taken to ensure that spaciousness be the dominating factor. At the same time it will be observed that the furniture and accommodation is all that could be desired in a caravan of this size. Built for all the year round use the " Wasp " is becoming the home of many whose previous caravanning was limited to " fair weather."

SPECIFICATION

Length	16 ft. 6 in.	Height	8 ft. 2 in.
Breadth	6 ft. 8 in.	Headroom	6 ft. 4½ in.

Lantern roof with ten lights, centre six opening and adjusted with centre fixed chromium quadrant. Roof lockers scribed to lantern roof shoulders with locker bases continued as shelves to ends of caravan. Two single beds with padded sprung back rests. One double extending settee bed. Storage space beneath all beds, easy access by tip-up bed boards and hinged locker bed fronts. Chest of drawers, top compartment containing cutlery beneath lift-up lid. Flush wings to chest of drawers surmounted by bay corner lockers with leaded glass doors. Bowed shelf over lockers extending across double front window. Double front window, rear window, and four side windows full drop. One large wardrobe with division doors and large mirror. One small wardrobe. One large ventilated pantry surmounted by crockery cupboard with leaded glass door. Sideboard furniture and equipment consisting of sink with draining board lid over cupboard containing aluminium cooking utensils, full gas oven in completely metal lined compartment, cupboard containing two copper water containers (total capacity four gallons, approx.) cupboard containing trays, mahogany lined with oak fronts. Two gas lights. Asbestos backed and metal lined gas fire beneath sink. Two gas cylinders and all gas components. Lino and semi-fitted carpet on floor. Two electric lights. Split door. Chromium pulling bar across rear of caravan. Painted, cloth covered, or oak panelled roof interior. Double sided oak clip-on table stored beneath double bed. Neatly mounted clock.

PRICE, Double Panelled **£285**

Nett Ex Works

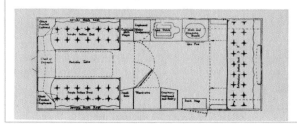

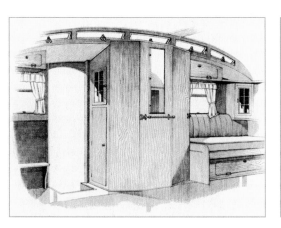

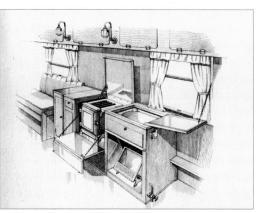

The three drawings on the left nicely illustrate the1939 Jubilee Wasp's interior .

1949 Jubilee Dragonfly showed no sign of the pre-war streamlining and lantern roof.

1954 Jubilee brochure with the slogan 'built for the time of your life' which was used both before and after WWII.

business from the receiver for the debenture holders. He was said at the time to have had long and varied experience in caravan making and distributing but no details of his association with any other make is known. A brochure for 1939 indicates a range comprising the Butterfly, 14ft Queen Bee, Gadfly, Wasp and Dragonfly. Wasp and Dragonfly were available in centre and end kitchen versions and prices ranged from £140 for the single panelled Butterfly to £395 for the de luxe centre kitchen Dragonfly. A further 1939 model was the 14ft double panelled Moth, costing £137 10s with oil equipment or £150 with gas lighting and cooking. The advertising slogan 'Built for the time of your life' was used both before and after the Second World War.

The first post-war model was the Dragonfly, appearing in 1945. This 17ft model had a body bolted up from jig-built sections utilising synthetic resin

The 1949 "Dragonfly"
Now £798 ex works

There is no other caravan of quality to compare in value for money. Be warned in time and see the Jubilee "Dragonfly" at your nearest distributor before deciding on your new caravan—you'll *never* regret buying a Jubilee.

"Built for the time of your life"

JUBILEE CARAVANS LTD
WEDNESBURY :: :: STAFFS
79

glued laminated bends and thermally insulated with 3/4in thick felt, the same material being used for acoustic insulation in the toilet room walls. In production at the beginning of 1949 was the 18ft 3in Dragonfly priced at £798, succeeded later in the year by the 20ft 3in £750 Dragonfly Magna, followed in its turn in 1952 by the 20ft 9in £895 Dragonfly Queen. Three new models were shown at the 1953 Motor Show, the £349 14ft 6in Ladybird, £395 15ft 6in Gadfly and £445 17ft 6in Wasp, joined in 1954 by the £659 10s 21ft 9in Hornet.

The death of E Sumner was reported in 1954 and D G Lloyd Jones is mentioned as a director in 1955. Also in 1955 it was announced that the makers of Jubilee were extending their activities into retail sales, including vans of other makes, by forming a new company, Hillandale Caravans. The 1956 range, introduced late in 1955, comprised the £390 15ft Butterfly, £475 18ft Firefly, £498 18ft Queen Bee and £665 22ft Hornet. Post-war models had V roofs but were rather less streamlined than the Pre-war vans. A front bay appeared on the lantern roofed Dragonfly Queen of 1952 and the 1954 Hornet had front and rear bays, with the other models gaining front bays for

Built for the time of your life

Jubilee Caravans

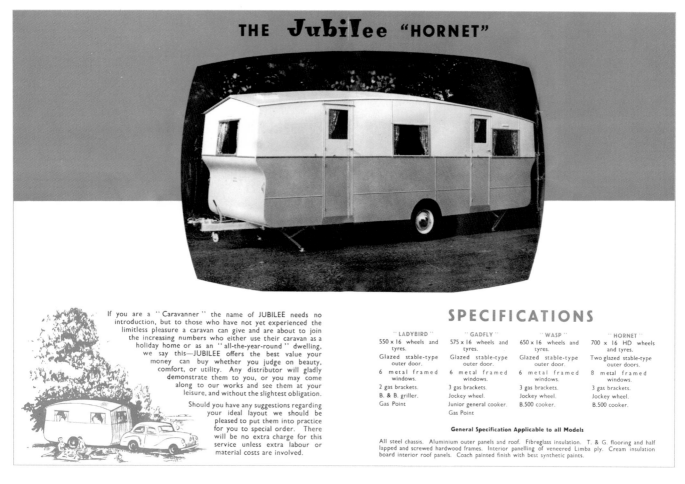

THE Jubilee "HORNET"

SPECIFICATIONS

"LADYBIRD"	"GADFLY"	"WASP"	"HORNET"
550 x 16 wheels and tyres.	575 x 16 wheels and tyres.	650 x 16 wheels and tyres.	700 x 16 HD wheels and tyres.
Glazed stable-type outer door.	Glazed stable-type outer door.	Glazed stable-type outer door.	Two glazed stable-type outer doors.
6 metal framed windows.	6 metal framed windows.	6 metal framed windows.	8 metal framed windows.
2 gas brackets.	3 gas brackets.	3 gas brackets.	3 gas brackets.
B. & B. griller.	Jockey wheel.	Jockey wheel.	Jockey wheel.
Gas Point	Junior general cooker.	B.500 cooker.	B.500 cooker.
	Gas Point		

General Specification Applicable to all Models

All steel chassis. Aluminium outer panels and roof. Fibreglass insulation. T. & G. flooring and half lapped and screwed hardwood frames. Interior panelling of veneered Limba ply. Cream insulation board interior roof panels. Coach painted finish with best synthetic paints.

1956. More pronounced bays front and rear were introduced for 1957. The 1959 range comprised the 18ft Queen Bee, Hornet and Mayfly, both 22ft, and the 26ft Hornet Major.

An interesting feature of the Mayfly was the box containing the foldaway bed which rested against the offside wall by day but pivoted out to form a partition from the forward single beds at night. This was quite a sound idea practically and was also tried by other manufacturers, but the van was only in production for a short period, foundering on the buying public's dislike of contraptions. The 1961 range included a 15ft Firefly model, joined later in the year by the 32ft x 8ft Silver Dragonfly. When the 1963 range was introduced late in 1962 it included two new tourers, the 14ft Firefly and 16ft Mayfly, and a Silver Dragonfly, now 30ft x 9ft 6in. Jubilee also built a considerable number of specials, particularly luxury models for travelling showmen – six artistes of Bertram Mills Circus were reported to be living in Jubilee vans in 1957. After 1964 the smallest model produced was the 19ft Queen Bee and production was concentrated increasingly on specials, with production of all standard vans ending around 1970.

1954 Jubilee Hornet with front and rear bays.

KELSTON

Kelston Caravan Co Ltd, Hambrook, Bristol, whose directors were T H Simmonds and T Partridge, claimed in their advertising to have been established in 1936, although nothing is known of any models produced before the Second World War. Postwar production appears to have started around 1948 with a £500 centre kitchen lantern roof van, joined in mid-1949 by the £375 14ft 4 berth Vacation and later in the year by the £394 17ft Commando. By mid-1950 the Commando, available in end or centre kitchen versions, cost £427, the lantern roof model, now named the Commodore, cost £537 and the Vaca-

1960 Kelston Commodore. From 1960 the firm built Siddall models for the Staffordshire dealers, Gailey Caravan Co Ltd.

tion, now 14ft 6in long, cost £290. At the beginning of 1951 the £675 22ft x 7ft 6in Commandant living van was introduced. This van had kitchen and bathroom sharing the width at the front end, centre lounge with foldaway double bed and rear end bedroom with two-tier bunk beds. New models early in 1952 were the £450 17ft 6in Cossack and £375 14ft Corvette, joined in the middle of the year by the £625 22ft Cossack Major.

The Cossack was intended as a living van and had a front end bedroom fitted with a settee which converted to either two single beds or a double bed. There was a double bed settee flanked by wardrobes at the rear of the van, and a Vanesse solid fuel stove was installed in the bulkhead dividing the bedroom from the living room. The short passageway between the two rooms had doors at either end and formed the toilet compartment. On tow this was occupied by a

chemical toilet set on a hinged and ventilated base, but on site it moved into a wedge-shaped extension which swung out from the side of the van to provide additional floor space, the bedroom door being used to close off the extension and conceal the toilet when not in use. Exterior wall panelling was in tempered Masonite with hardboard interior panelling enclosing fibreglass insulation. The flooring was tongued and grooved boarding and the roof construction comprised aluminium painted canvas on insulation board with a 1/2in cavity above the hardboard ceiling.

Surprisingly, since the Cossack Major had only been introduced in mid-1952, by the early part of 1953 Kelston were advertising a £575 Mk III version, together with an 18ft Mk II version of the Commando priced at £399 10s. There was a new £485 20ft 6in Mk II version of the Commandant in the latter part of 1954, and by early 1956 the range comprised the £425 15ft 6in Vacation, Commandant Mk II, £535 22ft Commandant 22 and £595 22ft Cossack Mk III. By 1957 the models were a £525 de luxe version of the Vacation, £515 20ft Commandant and £549 10s 22ft Commodore Mk II, but the only model listed in 1958 was a £585 Mk VI Commodore.

The Commodore continued in 1959-61 together with the £599 10s 22ft Commandant. Kelston do not appear to have produced vans under their own name after 1961 but from 1960 built Siddalls for the Staffordshire dealers, Gailey Caravan Co Ltd, after Gailey bought the designs, name and right to manufacture from the original maker.

KENTISH

The Electric Welding Co of Maidstone produced the Kentish tent trailer in 1935.

The 1935 Kentish tent trailer was very similar to the Feu sleeping trailer.

KENTISH TENT TRAILERS

Price : **17 Gns.**

Built on our scientifically designed and all welded Triangulated Super Chassis, which gives perfect towing. Fawn "Birkmyre" Cloth Tenting, guaranteed for two years. Excellent for Camping, Bathing or Touring.

Erected in three minutes. Catalogue free.

ELECTRIC WELDING CO. : MAIDSTONE

KILBURN

Gilbert Kilburn, founder of Cara-Cars Ltd, Ilkley, Yorkshire, was one of the earliest caravan dealers, claiming in a 1939 advertisement to have been hiring and selling caravans for two decades. Starting with horse-drawn models before progressing to trailer cara-

vans, he had also built vans for his hire fleet at Dewsbury, Yorkshire.

On arranging to hire a van at a cost of £4 per week in 1927, the nineteen year old H W Marcroft was told that a towing bracket for his father's car would be forwarded to him. This turned out to be a length of angle steel to be cut and drilled as required to bolt to the chassis extension of the luggage grid on the 1926 Morris Oxford tourer. The van was mounted on an axle with Ford wheels and had a wood frame covered with treated canvas. The tubular steel drawbar was flattened at the end and drilled to take a drop bolt. Overrun brakes were fitted and hinged wooden stays acted as corner steadies though apparently they were only usable on level ground and Mr. Marcroft resorted to piles of stones to level the van. Inside, the van was lined with blue tapestry material tacked to the framing ribs. A double bed settee was set across the front of the van with a single settee bed along the offside wall. A cupboard and two-burner Valor oil stove occupied the nearside. A fourth mattress was intended to lie on top

The so-called 'towing bracket' supplied for this 1927 hire van was actually a length of angle steel which the hirer had to cut and drill as required to bolt to the chassis of the towing car.

of the cupboard at night but the occupant of this berth tended to end up on the floor. There was no wardrobe, the door was at the rear and the tail light was an oil lamp.

LAD

LAD Caravans, Rustic Walk, Burnt Hill Road, Lower Bourne, Farnham, Surrey, advertised caravans 'in all states of construction' in 1937. Prices quoted were £39 in skeleton form 'with everything to finish', £55 covered and £65 complete. Vans of any size or design were offered, as well as the streamlining of old vans.

1937 LAD advertisement. It would be interesting to know what the streamlining of old vans involved.

LAMBERT

W& G Lambert Ltd, Thetford, Norfolk, produced Lambert caravans around 1927 but no further details are known.

LANDCRUISER

Although Landcruisers, Mill Lane, Warrington, claimed to have been established in 1923, nothing is known of the make apart from a 1936 advertisement for a £125 18ft streamlined, double panelled four-wheeled caravan with Ackerman steering – said to be the 'only one left'. The same advertisement refers to 15ft and 18ft double panelled shells costing from £85 and the fitting of interiors to clients' plans.

1936 advertisement – only one left!

LANDOVER

1952 Landover Sunlite. Before WWII the firm appears to have traded as the Alconbury Caravan Co.

In 1950 the Landover Caravan Co Ltd, Oundle Road, Peterborough, was claiming 15 years experience in furniture making and body-building, but prior to the Second World War the firm appears to have traded as Alconbury Caravan Co, Great North Road, Upton, near Huntingdon, and the earliest references found are 1938 advertisements. The £108 4 berth Landover Breeze of that year was a double panelled van with full width lantern roof, and a classified advertisement by Alconbury refers to 3-4 berth and 14ft 4 berth Landovers which may be second hand vans taken in part exchange. 1950 model names were the Alconbury, Lanavan, Lancara, Showman and Woodston. The Woodston was a 14ft 4 berth end kitchen model, and the problems manufacturers faced at the time due to increasing material costs are indicated by the pricing of this van – £325 in 1950, £355 in standard or £385 in de luxe version at the beginning of 1951, and £395 or £435 by late 1951. The Lancara was a 19ft 6in 4/5 berth living van priced at £655 or £685 at the beginning of 1951 and the Showman was a 22ft living van costing £895 late in 1951.

In mid-1952 the £330 15ft 9in x 7ft Sunlite was introduced. This was an 18cwt 4 berth end kitchen van, panelled externally in hardboard with a 1/2in plywood floor mounted on a Marshall chassis. The roof was insulated with fibreglass but there was no insulation in the walls. The layout featured a double dinette at the front end with a single bed on either side in the centre of the van. The single beds were mounted on legs to allow suitcases to be stored underneath. An alternative version had a double bed settee in place of the offside single bed facing a sideboard on the nearside. In late 1953 the range comprised the £250 12ft Ballerina, Sunlite, £376 16ft Conquerer, 18ft Lanavan at £450 in standard or £467 in de luxe version, £550 20ft Huntsman living van and the Showman. The company, which was owned by R Boys, also built caravans to customer's requirements and in 1954 produced the 16ft 4 berth Citizen for the Surrey dealers, Hindhead Caravan Company, but this appears to have been the last year of production.

LAYCOCK

The 1930s Car Pup, built by the Laycock Engineering Company, Millhouses, Sheffield 8, was a luggage trailer mounted on a single castor wheel. A development of this was the sleeping trunk camping trailer. Trailers of this type were at a disadvantage because under the Motor Vehicles (Construction and Use) Regulations then in force they were subject to a 20 mph speed limit whilst the limit for two-wheeled trailers was 30 mph.

1935 Laycock Sleeping Trunk. The single wheel meant a 20mph speed limit.

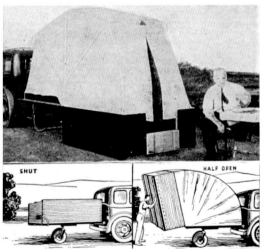

LEADER

The only known model was a 1932 9ft 6in 2 berth which was panelled in hardboard on wooden framing with a double skinned roof and the windows had leaded lights.

LEASON

Joseph Lea & Sons Ltd, Dyche Street, Rochdale Road, Manchester 4, are included because, whilst not caravan manufacturers as such, they had a close involvement with the industry over many years. Established in 1869, the firm originally made parts for horse-drawn caravans before turning to the touring caravan market. The Leason chassis was made for caravan manufacturers and amateur builders, who could also obtain drawings for the caravan body and furniture, with drawings for a 12ft 6in 3 berth, 14ft 6in 4 berth and 16ft 9in 4 berth available in 1939. Lea's are also known to have built three caravans as demonstration models to show prospective purchasers of chassis and plans what the finished product looked like. One of these vans was a mobile showroom, date unknown, and the others were touring models, the Type 18 built in 1938 and the Ellesmere of 1951. The Type 18 was a 15ft 6in 4 berth lantern roofed model with canvas covered roof and 18 gauge aluminium exterior wall panelling – unusual in 1938 when most vans had hardboard panelling. A large Rippingille paraffin cooker was fitted. Lea's had their own design of ball coupling and the 1¼in diameter fitting on the Type 18 was presumably an example of this design. The Ellesmere was a 16ft 4 berth with two doors and a projecting bay at the front. The booklet of plans could be bought separately or obtained free if a chassis was purchased. The Ellesmere was apparently shown at exhibitions until around 1970, by which time the company was trading as Harry Lea & Son. Lea's ceased trading in 1973.

1938 Leason Type 18, made to demonstrate what amateur builders could achieve by following Lea's drawings.

The
Ellesmere
CARAVAN

Built from our plans as advertised.

Designed specially for the Amateur Builder following the successful "Mancunian" design.

The Chassis used is Model 18P, but size can be adapted by the purchaser to suit his own requirements.

The Body is 16 ft. overall × 6 ft. 6 ins. wide. Outer panelling is aluminium, inner panelling in ply or hardboard with cavity 1 in. filled " Isoflex " Insulation.

Layout is two door, end kitchen with toilet room and comprises forward dinette and full centre double bed.

The Booklet is so arranged with drawings to scale of framework, artist's sketches, photos, etc. to enable the builder to read the instructions and follow the design easily, step by step.

The Complete Booklet is given free with order for Chassis, or charged **25/-** (post paid) which may be deducted from the cost of a Chassis if ordered within six months. The design is 1951 and entirely new.

Post-WWII an example of the Leason Ellesmere was also built for demonstration purposes (no connection with the author!).

LEMAC

A 1938 advertisement by Spensers (London) Ltd notes Lemac among makes fitted with Spensers Bottogas LPG equipment.

LION

1938 Lion, whose maker also dealt in tea, ironmongery, drapery, skins, rugs, furs, watches and jewellery.

Albert Harrison, Careless Lane, Ince Bar, Wigan, built vans in the 1934-39 period. Caravans appear to have been something of a sideline since his notepaper was headed 'Wholesale tea merchant, ironmongery and drapery factor, skins, rugs, furs a speciality, watches, jewellery etc'. A 1937 classified advertisement refers to a 4 berth streamline caravan and a 22ft Bungalow-Caravan said to be a 'sacrifice for

quick sale' although no prices are mentioned. There were two Lion models in 1938 – 13ft 6in and 16ft long priced at £125 and £150 respectively.

LOGAN

The Logan Manufacturing Co, Ashford, Middlesex, manufactured a 13ft van in 1931. This featured two slide-out sections, one housing the cooking galley, the other a scullery.

LOLODE

The 1937 Lolode was designed to carry passengers, and the chemical closet was gimbal mounted for use on the move without splashing!

The Low Loading Trailer Co, of Bedford, were builders of horseboxes and applied their experience of close-coupled four-wheel chassis to the highly unorthodox Lolode of 1937-38. Only small numbers of the 19ft long x 7ft wide vans were made. Designed for carrying passengers, features included steel body framing, independent suspension, Lockheed hydraulic brakes actuated by a solenoid fed by electric current from the towing car, a 2in wall cavity, safety glass windows, house type wash basin in addition to the sink, running hot and cold water, gimbal mounted chemical closet for use on the move without splashing, a system of ventilating slots running along both sides, built-in winch to help coupling-up and an externally mounted generator to charge the large battery. Sales were no doubt limited by the weight of nearly two tons and the price of £650 in fully equipped form, as well as by the speed limit of 20mph imposed on four-wheel trailers.

LUXONIC

Manufactured by the Dagenham Caravan Co, New Road, Rainham, Essex, a company established in 1937. The 4 berth Heather of 1938 was a double panelled lantern roof van with leaded light windows costing £115, the same price as the 4 berth Bracken of 1939, at which time 2 and 4 berth vans were also being offered for hire.

No details of the wartime activities of the company are known but by 1949 the 15ft 4 berth centre kitchen Luxonic was being advertised at £400 including full insulation, Calor gas equipment and Dunlopillo mattresses. An 18ft model appears to have been in production in 1951 but nothing is known of the firm after this date.

LYTECRAFT

The original Lytecraft camping trailer of 1938, manufactured by Lytecraft Caravan, Trailer & Accessories Co, South Road, Hailsham, Sussex, was said to be made up from standard components already on the market so that purchasers could buy additional equipment or replacement parts from any of the camping equipment stores. The standard design ridge tent covered an area of 7ft 6in x 6ft 6in when erected. This was superseded later in the year by the Aero Tentrailer which had the tent top supported on pneumatic ribs and cost £38 10s or £44 10s with two Hounsfield camp beds, stove and china. Also introduced later in 1938 was the £68 10s 5½ cwt Sussex Sleepvan, an 8ft x 4ft rigid bodied streamlined sleeping trailer fitted with a Slumberland spring mattress. A door on each side opened into a tent annexe which increased the width on site to 10ft. Lockers built into the sides of the van opened into the annexes and equipment included a two-burner

1939 Lytecraft Sussex Sleepvan. Equipment was accessed from side tent annexes.

Coleman petrol gas stove, china, washbowl and water can. The tents packed away into a large rear locker, accessible from both inside and outside the van. By mid-1939 Lytecraft had also introduced an ambulance trailer with accommodation for four casualties.

MARQUETTE

A late 1920s make of which no details are known.

MARTINETTE

Produced in 1933-34 by R Martin, Lyndhurst Square, London SE15, this double panelled van cost £160. There was a lantern roof and two doors, one at the rear end of the nearside wall and one set in the nearside of the V front end.

The 1933 Martinette's styling was looking out of date by this time.

MERRIE ENGLAND

Merrie England Caravans, Okehampton Street, Exeter, produced a 'Tudor Home on four wheels' (illustrated overleaf) in 1935. Presumably intended as a static weekend cottage rather than as a tourer, this 17ft x 7ft model was fitted out in Tudor style and the double panelled walls with a one inch air space between inner and outer skins were claimed to keep the vans entirely free from condensation. Equipment included wireless, chemical toilet, bath, electric light, Tilley lamps and radiator.

1935 Merrie England, 'A Tudor Home on four wheels'.

MIDLAND *See* BLUEBIRD

MILLER

The only reference found is a 1935 advertisement by the dealers Welford's Caravans for a 1934 Miller 2 berth.

MONKSGATE

Monksgate Garage, Brighton Road, Horsham, Sussex, were advertising caravans for sale or hire in 1939. The vans were available on Brockhouse or Dixon-Bate chassis and had Masonite exterior panelling. Prices were £82 10s for a 2 berth and £182 10s for a 4 berth van.

MONTROSE *See* RAVEN

MOORLAND

The 1935 Moorland Cottage was advertised as towable by a 16hp car!

S Mitchelmore of Moorland Caravan Works, Totnes Road, Newton Abbot, South Devon, produced the four-wheeled £225 17ft Moorland Cottage Caravan in 1935. The van was advertised as towable by a 16hp car, but the intended use can only have been as a static weekend cottage – with pitched roof, gables and exposed timbering the van would certainly have presented an unusual spectacle on the road. Equipment included a two-burner Coleman stove for summer use and a coal stove for the winter. A 15ft two-wheeled model was available at £175 and any special design could be built to order.

The MOORLAND COTTAGE CARAVAN

THE IDEAL CARAVAN FOR SUMMER OR WINTER MONTHS

CAN BE TOWED BY 16-H.P. CAR

There are three compartments: two bedrooms and a kitchenette. The partitions fold back during the day, making one large room. The walls are double-panelled and there is a Coleman two-burner stove for summer use and a coal stove for the winter. There are Moseley draw-out settee beds and the equipment everywhere is of the best quality. The caravan is, of course, wired for electric light. The price for the four-wheel 17-foot model, including the leaded lights, is £225. A 15-foot two-wheel model is available at £175. Any special design built to order.

Send to-day for full particulars to S. MITCHELMORE

MOORLAND CARAVAN WORKS

TOTNES ROAD, NEWTON ABBOT, SOUTH DEVON

MOSELEY

Oliver U Tallett was already an established caravan distributor in 1939 when he and A V Thompson formed Moseley Caravans Ltd, Moseley Road, Birmingham 12, to manufacture caravans. The first model was the £198 15ft 4 berth Golden Star, the lantern roof of which was ash framed, lined internally with ash plywood and externally with plywood overlaid with insulating felt and heavy gauge sheet zinc finished with bronze paint. The walls were panelled externally with Sundeala and internally with ash plywood, enclosing a 1½in cavity. The pine floor was underdrawn with waterproof felt and overlaid with linoleum and carpet. The partition to divide the van into two sleeping compartments at night automatically slid into position when the central settee was pulled out to form a double bed. Equipment included a wash basin in addition to the sink, gas fire, radio, clock, thermometer and two spirit levels. This van was

1939 Moseley Golden Star. The unusual roof covering was heavy gauge sheet zinc finished with bronze paint.

soon followed by the similar Golden Eagle, also costing £198 but with a storage unit in place of the rear offside toilet room. Small numbers of vans also appear to have been produced for a short period after the Second World War but by 1948 Oliver U Tallett Ltd were operating from the Moseley Road address as dealers for other makes.

NAVARAC

As a boy Richard St Barbe Baker made friends with the gypsies of the New Forest and was attracted by their life of mobility. He had already started a degree in forestry at Caius College, Cambridge, when the First World War began. He served as a Captain in the Royal Flying Corps, was invalided out of the Army in April 1918 after being wounded for a second time, and returned to Cambridge to finish his course. Noticing an advertisement of the Government Disposals Board in *The Times* calling for offers for aircraft equipment, he caught the train to London and went to the disposals office at the Waddon dump in Croydon. On the train he had worked out a rough idea of the materials he would need to build a single caravan but discovered on arrival at Waddon that the smallest lots were far in excess of his requirements. Having been handed a tender form he wrote down the prices he would have been prepared to pay for the various materials he needed to build one or two caravans. He signed the form, handed over a cheque, and returned to Cambridge not expecting to hear any more about the matter. Ten days later no fewer than ten railway truck loads of aircraft materials arrived in Cambridge. By the afternoon all had been delivered to a friendly tradesman who was a motor body builder, and that evening Baker set to work and designed his

A Navarac and a modified Model T Ford. In 1919 this was the first ever trailer caravan built for sale, using aircraft materials purchased from the Government Disposals Board. (LAT Photographic)

four-wheeled motor-drawn caravan trailer.

Built on an aeroplane undercarriage, it had a low wide window at the back giving a view through for the driver of the towing car, and a lantern roof with three opening lights on each side. The back and side windows let down into the walls of the caravan in railway carriage fashion and the front end stable type door had a glazed upper part and solid lower part complete with spring-slot letterbox. The timber chassis carried tongued and grooved floorboards with trap-doors giving access to ice-chest, firewood and grocery lockers. A large locker under the chassis took awnings, tents and camp beds, allowing six extra guests to be accommodated in lean-tos on the sides. The van had a gypsy range with double flue going up through a cupboard designed for warming plates. Either side of the range were two hanging cupboards from roof to floor with boot boxes below. On the opposite side a sink, in the centre of a sideboard, was fed with water from a tank in the roof. Hot water was obtained from a kettle made with a copper bottom which fitted into the top of the range. Other fittings included a Russian divan which could be strapped up to the back of the van during the day and a Tudor style bureau. The interior was painted ivory white with mahogany beadings and the exterior finish was Rolls-Royce light grey with black coach-striping.

Baker found that the van could be produced for £300 and registered the Navarac Caravan Company (Navarac being caravan spelt backwards), quickly going into production with what is regarded as the first ever trailer caravan built for sale. When the prototype was taken out for the first time in May 1919 it was followed by a newsreel man and the next evening his film was being shown in cinemas throughout the country. Baker wanted the Navarac to be the Rolls-Royce of caravans, and from the sales manager of Rolls-Royce in Conduit Street, London, he obtained the address of their printer along with permission to adopt the printing style used for publicising Rolls-Royce's latest model.

Underneath his personal van he carried a pair of shafts and a pole so that the caravan could also be pulled by either a single horse or a pair of horses. When the Government held an exhibition of aircraft materials at Olympia the Navarac was put on show and other people took up the idea, soon producing caravans with two wheels and mostly lighter than the 18cwt Navarac. Baker enjoyed building caravans and gave some employment to aircraftsmen who were finding it difficult to get work, but his abiding interest was in forestry. On leaving Cambridge he applied to be Assistant Conservator of Forests in Kenya but was turned down on health grounds and decided to go on a caravan tour to study the trees and forests of Europe. He was about to embark from Southampton when he was summoned back for a further medical examination, and having been pronounced fit he sailed for Africa in 1920. He became well known as founder of *Men of the Trees* and an international expert on afforestation and soil renewal. Interestingly one of his ancestors was Sir Samuel White Baker, a celebrated traveller and explorer, who used a second hand 'gypsy travelling van' as his living quarters when he made a tour of Cyprus in 1879.

NORFOLK

Norfolk Caravans were produced by Martin's at Spooner Row Station, Wymondham, Norfolk, in 1939. 2, 3 and 4 berth models were available, priced at £75 10s, £89 10s and £99 10s respectively.

NORTON

VJ Bevan of Norton Caravans, Norton, Doncaster, Yorkshire, produced the Gnome and Pixie in 1935. The £175 14ft 6in 4 berth Gnome was double panelled with hand french polished walnut interior. A Bosch wireless was a £15 extra. The £150 Pixie differed only in being single panelled above the waistline.

1935 Norton Gnome There was also a Pixie model which only differed in being single panelled above the waistline.

NORWOOD KNIGHT

Norwood Knight Caravans, Norwood Road, West Norwood, London SE27, introduced the £360 15ft 9in 4 berth London in 1937. The van was described as being flush panelled in selected Swedish pine with triple panelled cavity walls and cellulose glazing. Equipment included mains and battery electric lighting, radio, large capacity water tank and a chromium plated radiator. An advertisement refers to a brochure being 'in preparation' but nothing more is known of the make, which presumably did not attract sufficient interest from the caravan buying public.

Norwood Knight London. A brochure was said to be 'in preparation' in 1937 but nothing more is known of this make.

PACKAWAY

Introduced in mid-1939, the 4 berth Packaway was designed by C N Cooper and manufactured by his company, Cooper's Garage (Surbiton) Ltd, Elwell Road, Tolworth, Surrey. The 14ft long x 6ft 2in wide van with 6ft maximum headroom could be dismantled and stored in a garage, projecting only about 18 inches from the wall. The furniture was taken out, roof, sides and ends lifted off, the floor detached from the chassis frame and the wheels taken off – an operation claimed to take a mere 15 minutes! Sides and ends were double panelled, with Sundeala board externally and oak ply internally. The door was normally on the offside, with the nearside wall dividing horizontally and opening to form a verandah with canopy over, but the arrangement could be reversed since the sides were interchangeable. The insulation board roof was secured by six quick-lift catches and in sunny weather could be slid open to any desired extent. Suspension was unusual in having two short coil springs at each side, lateral movement being prevented by flat bearing faces on frame and axle sliding against each other. Extra low pressure Michelin tyres inflated to less than 10psi were fitted, and in its cheapest form at £85 the van was furnished only with a wardrobe or locker on one side and a locker with table attached on the opposite side. A better equipped version weighing 9¼cwt was available, fitted with Carey spring mattresses on the two transverse double beds, wardrobe with mirror and ventilated larder with cutlery drawer above on the offside, a unit comprising

The makers claimed that the 1939 Packaway could be dismantled for storage in around 15 minutes.

enamel sink and metal lined cooking recess with cupboards below on the nearside, and a table hooking onto the side wall next to the front bed settee. This bed could be arranged in dinette fashion with the table between to seat four. Presumably production ceased with the outbreak of the Second World War.

PALADIN

George D Holder built his first caravan at the age of fourteen and produced small numbers of caravans in Lambeth under the Crescent name until 1939

THE 1949-SERIES 5

PALADIN TRAILAVAN

SUPERLATIVE COMFORT
LUXURY FINISH
SUPERB MOBILITY

INCORPORATING THE LATEST DEVELOPMENTS IN
MODERN CARAVANNING

❦

Attractive, strongly constructed shell fully insulated against internal condensation.

Complete isolated end kitchen with pumped hot and cold water. Elsan compartment.

Two luxuriously furnished living compartments, fitted high-grade furniture and interior sprung upholstery. Four comfortable berths.

Pither stove and airing cupboard. 2 wardrobes. 2 chests of drawers. 2 large blanket lockers. 2 china cupboards. 8 spacious drawers under seats.

Gas and electricity cooking, heating and lighting.

Price £1236 *ex works*

PALADIN TRAILAVAN CO.
CRESCENT WORKS, NUNNERY LANE
LUTON, BEDS.   Phone 3258

when the premises were requisitioned. After spending the war years working in an aircraft factory he resumed production at Nunnery Lane, Luton in 1947. Trading as Paladin Trailavan Co, his first model was the 19ft x 7ft Trailavan. The Isoflex insulated coach-shaped body with two nearside doors had walls constructed from narrow vertical aluminium panels with the edges turned in and bolted to T-section aluminium extrusions. The cost in 1948 was £1,236 and in that year the length was increased to 21ft although the price remained unchanged. Gas and mains or battery electric lighting was installed, heating was by a hopper-feed stainless steel Pithers stove which also heated the water, a semi-rotary pump delivered hot or cold water to the kitchen sink, and a drawbar mounted cold water tank, a fire extinguisher and a portable radio were standard equipment. The 1949 version, still 21ft long and costing £1,236, had the front wall curved from side to side, replacing the flat front wall of the earlier models. Confusingly the Taplow, Buckinghamshire, dealer A S Jenkinson advertised the Trailavan as the 'Wonder Paladin' and the 'Perfect Paladin' in 1947-49.

The Trailavan was joined by the semi-streamlined £395 13ft 9in Wisdom in 1949, with similar side wall panels riveted together without the T-sections and dispensing with most of the body framing. This construction was dropped when aluminium became scarce due to Cold-War rearmament, and the panelling was changed first to hardboard, then to pre-finished stove enamelled hardboard, before reverting to aluminium. The Wisdom featured in the Paladin model line-up for several years and in addition to the panelling changes underwent major changes of price, body shape and finish.

Around 1950 the company started production at a second factory at Dunstable Road, Luton. New in 1951 were the conventionally shaped Denizen, a 20ft x 7ft 6in living van originally costing £595, and the 15ft 6in Nomad, priced at £525 and advertised as equally suitable for living or touring! The beginning of 1952 saw the Pixy, definitely not a living van, an 8ft 6in x 6ft 2in four berth costing £199 10s and mounted on very small wheels. The body was single panelled with stove enamelled hardboard. A new £299 10s 14ft x 6ft 9in Wisdom introduced in mid-1952 adopted the same styling as the other models. The construction at this time consisted of tongued and grooved boarding overlaid with hardboard and lino for the floor, walls insulated with Sunfoil reflecting foil

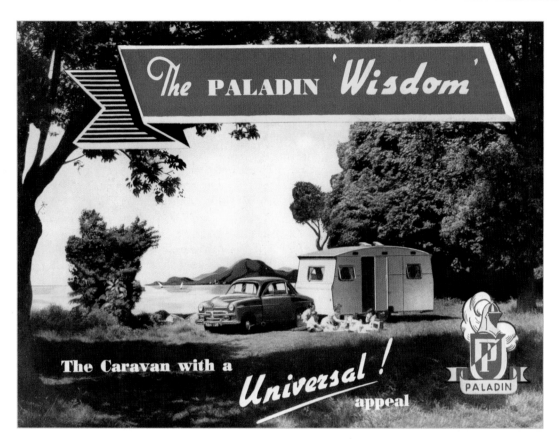

The PALADIN 'Wisdom'

The Caravan with a Universal! appeal

PALADIN

The Paladin Wisdom, this one from 1952, featured in the maker's model line-up for several years whilst undergoing major changes to panelling material, price, body shape and finish.

and double panelled with hardboard, the outer panelling being stove enamelled. The roof comprised hardboard lining, air cavity and insulation board overlaid with aluminium painted leathercloth. The two single berths were each a generous 2ft 3in wide as opposed to the rather narrow 3ft 9in wide double bed. A novel exhibit at the 1952 Motor Show was the Duplex, comprising two modified Wisdoms linked by a covered verandah. One unit had the single beds of a standard Wisdom replaced by a dinette double, providing space for a Tayco solid fuel stove and chest of drawers in the centre of the van. The other unit provided a double and two single beds, centre toilet room, large wardrobe, two chests of drawers and a full size bath under one of the single beds. The theory was that one unit could be taken away on tour leaving the bedroom unit and verandah on site, but very few buyers came forward and the idea was soon dropped.

Mid-1953 saw a new version of the Nomad, 16ft long and costing £309 with stove-enamelled hardboard exterior wall panelling and wood-framed windows. Extras available were aluminium exterior panelling at £20, metal-framed windows at £11 and a Tayco solid fuel stove at £21. Further new models later in the year were the Mercury and the 18ft Forsyth. The Mercury, originally costing £180 with hardboard exterior wall panelling and wood framed windows,

managed to fit a double dinette, two full single berths (not two-tier bunks) and an end kitchen into its 12ft length. All the vans now had aluminium clad roofs with joints double lapped and locked.

Following a fire at the Dunstable Road factory in October 1953 Paladin moved production of the Mercury to new premises at Amersham, Bucks and from 1st January 1954 the company name was changed from Paladin Trailavan Co Ltd to Paladin Coachwork Ltd. New models exhibited at the 1954 Motor Show were two living vans, the 22ft Pacemaker at £565 and the 18ft Mentor at £454 10s, with the Nomad, Wisdom and Mercury continuing in production. Early in 1955 it was reported that the Amersham works were being extended by 10,000sq ft. At that time 10 to 12 Pacemakers per week were being produced at Amersham, with production also continuing at the Nunnery Lane and Dunstable Road factories in Luton. About this time the firm was also building a model known as the Duplex, designed for American forces based in the UK, but few details are known.

Paladin entered an experimental model in the 1955 British Caravan Road Rally. Named the Corsaire, this 11ft van had the complete top half of the body moulded in GRP, but when a £320 12ft production Corsaire was exhibited at the Motor Show that year it had aluminium exterior panelling. Weighing 11cwt ex-works this was a very lightweight van for its size, as was another new model exhibited, the £297 10s 12¾cwt 14ft Buccaneer. Getting two double beds and a toilet compartment as well as two small wardrobes in a van the size of the Corsaire inevitably involved some compromises – the beds were only 3ft 6in and 3ft 9in wide – and lack of insulating material contributed to the light weight. Air cavities were relied on for wall insulation, but the hardboard ceiling was laid over the roof framing and, whilst there was supposedly a 1/8in air cavity, the hardboard was apparently in contact with the aluminium exterior panelling. The only other models at this time were the new £356 16ft Toreador and the £577 Pacemaker, the 18ft Rapier being added at the end of the year.

When the 1957 range was announced towards the end of 1956 it comprised the £350 Corsaire, a new version of the Buccaneer priced at £315, a new 14ft van named the Dolphin costing £415, the Toreador at £366, Rapier at £438 15s, £610 Pacemaker and a new 22ft model, the £580 Commodore, which incorporated a number of unusual features. These included lounge walls veneered up to waist level with wallpaper above, and a double bed which by day slid away, fully made up, under a wardrobe and over a bath in the kitchen, leaving the foot of the bed – which had stronger mattress springs than the rest – to serve in conjunction with a fixed padded backrest as a settee in the lounge. A kitchen worktop covered the head of the bed in its retracted position, and when the bed slid out to reveal the bath this worktop folded down to form a splashback. By March of 1957 the Pacemaker had been replaced by the short-lived £506 Caralina,

also 22ft long. The 1958 range was initially reduced to three models, £325 Buccaneer, £380 Toreador and £589 22ft Liberator. Later in 1958 a Mk II version of the Rapier was added together with a new Pacemaker model having 6 berths including two bunk beds in an end bedroom. There was also a 4 berth version without the separate bedroom. L Rabone, the works manager, became a director of the company in 1959 and later that year Paladin introduced the Pacemaker Kingsize, a 26ft 5/6 berth van costing £697 10s.

New vans for 1961 were the 28ft Super-Solitaire and the Chalet, a 31ft 6in x 9ft 5in living van with 7ft 9in headroom. Caravans exceeding 22ft x 7ft 6in were not lawfully towable and had to be transported on low loaders but, probably in the hope of an increase in the permitted limits, vans such as the Pacemaker Kingsize and Super-Solitaire continued to be built with full size road wheels, springs, brakes and hitch even though towing them was illegal (except to the docks for export). To overcome this difficulty the Chalet was supplied with a 22ft x 7ft 6in chassis designed as a completely separate transporter to which the body was secured by quick action clamps. The law allowed a load to overhang the chassis by 1ft on each side and defined the length as excluding the drawbar. The transporter therefore had a very long drawbar allowing it to accommodate the Chalet's length. The idea seems to have been based on a misconception since a trailer 'constructed and normally used for the conveyance of indivisible loads of exceptional length' was exempt from the 22ft limit. The cost of the Chalet was £866 5s plus £118 15s for the transporter. Small wheels allowed a floor unobstructed by wheel arches and accommodation comprised a 12ft x 9ft lounge with side french windows, 9ft x 7ft 6in kitchen, double bedroom, bunk bedroom and bathroom. Lounge furnishing included a double bed settee and two armchairs, there was a table and four chairs in the kitchen, and a house-type bath and washbasin. Heating was by a solid fuel stove in the lounge which also provided hot water to the kitchen and bathroom. Gas lighting was standard but electric wiring and a flush toilet were optional extras and space for a refrigerator was provided in the kitchen.

By the end of 1961 all the touring vans had been discontinued and the Kingsize and Solitaire replaced by the £727 26ft x 9ft 6in Denizen and £780 28ft x 9ft 6in Super Denizen respectively. There was also a completely new residential model, the Sun Cottage, a 22ft x 19ft twin unit of bungalow appearance with side to side pitched roof, chimney, house-type windows and plumbing, costing £1,310 including transporters. Inside, the accommodation comprised twin bedroom, double bedroom, lounge, kitchen and

ALL THE FEATURES OF A LUXURY MAISONETTE!

1961 Paladin chalet. The separate chassis with extra long drawbar was thought to allow an oversize van to be legally towed!

bathroom fitted with low-level flush toilet.

Following the demise of Berkeley at the beginning of 1961, George Holder formed a new company with former Berkeley managing director Charles Panter. This company operated from premises at Hitchin Street, Biggleswade, and presumably part of this factory was the 16,000 sq ft of production space at Biggleswade which Paladin were reported to be utilising at the end of 1961 to meet delivery dates and ease pressure on the main works at Amersham, orders worth £250,000 having been taken at that year's Caravan Exhibition. Sun Cottages were purchased by the London County Council in 1962 to use as homes on cleared sites owned by the Council which were available pending development for schools or as open spaces two to five years ahead. In mid-1962 came another Paladin touring van, the 425 (4.25 metres) which was designed so that the body complete with all furniture could be mounted either way round on the chassis in order to place the door on the correct side for home or export markets. The layout comprised two single beds, foldaway double bed, centre kitchen, and toilet compartment extending across the entrance door when in use. The cost was £389 15s, and unusually for a van aimed at the export market it had a straight uncranked axle with underslung leaf springs rather than independent suspension.

The range announced for 1963 comprised ten models including three tourers which continued the metric theme as well as reviving familiar names – Pixy 300 at £326 15s, Corsaire 375 at £361 10s and Bucca-

neer 425 at £389 15s. The other models were the Pacemaker at £617, 26ft x 9ft 6in Liberator at £802 10s, Super Denizen at £825, 28ft x 9ft 6in Commodore at £849 10s, Chalet at £910 plus £130 for the transporter, Sun Cottage at £1,222 plus £130 for a pair of transporters, and the Estate House. This last was a 40ft x 19ft twin unit although the two halves could be purchased separately, the basic unit providing lounge, kitchen, bathroom and bedroom, whilst the extension added a further bedroom, lounge extension and roofed verandah. Basic unit prices were £1,348 with gas lighting or £1,388 wired for mains electricity, plus £150 for the transporter, and £2,181 or £2,231 plus £300 for the complete home. The new tourers were only in production for a matter of months and the Estate House was discontinued before the end of 1963.

The Chateau was a new 37ft x 9ft 6in residential model introduced towards the end of 1963 and included a double and two single bedrooms for the

1961 Sun Cottage. A number were purchased by the London County Council and the National Coal Board.

price of £999. Besides the Chateau the 1964 range comprised the Pacemaker, the £587 6 berth 23ft x 9ft 6in Holidaymaker static holiday van, £759 30ft x 9ft 6in Cottage Home and new versions of the Chalet and Sun Cottage. Lengths had increased to 34ft and 26ft respectively and prices were £899 15s and £1,258 15s, but the Sun Cottage no longer had a pitched roof. An order for 150 Sun Cottages was received from the National Coal Board early in 1964. These were to be sited at Radstock, near Bath, to house miners and their families moved down from the Durham coalfield following the closure of several uneconomic collieries, pending the building of new houses. Once on site the Sun Cottages could be ready for occupation in one hour – 56 were sited in one eight day period. At this time the Amersham works were reported to be capable of producing Sun Cottages at the rate of five a day and later in the year it was reported that Paladin were planning an increase of 50% in the production rate at the factory. The Pacemaker was discontinued part way through 1964 and new models for the 1965 season were the £587 23ft Flatlet, £795 32ft 6in Spanish

Villa, £899 15s 36ft Chalet, £999 40ft Chateau and a Mk III version of the Sun Cottage with end to end pitched roof and costing £1,450 with aluminium exterior wall panelling, cedar board cladding being a £50 optional extra.

Early in 1965 it was reported that Paladin were to supply the Army with 160 factory-built homes though these were 36ft x 9ft skid-mounted specials rather than models from the standard range. In 1967 Paladin made their last foray into the touring caravan market with the 10ft Stowaway, a van designed to collapse to a flat pack for storage. There was also a smaller version of the Sun Cottage, the 20ft x 19ft Chiltern Lodge priced at £1,360 complete or £1,195 if supplied without loose furniture, carpets and curtains. Production ceased in mid-1967 but George Holder set up a new company, G D Holder Ltd, and, operating from Hitchin Street, Biggleswade, manufactured mobile classrooms and similar units. Trading as Chiltern Sun Homes, he also entered the mobile home market again in 1980 for a period with a range of 10ft wide single units and 20ft wide twins.

PELHAM

1933 Pelham Princess. Non-streamlined vans were also produced.

Pelhams Caravan Works, Oxford Road, Uxbridge, were producing both streamlined and non-streamlined models in 1933. The non-streamlined vans were the £65 10s 8ft 2 berth Duchess, £99 10s 10ft 3 berth lantern roof Popular, £95 10ft Queen and £113 12ft 6 berth Emperor. This last model had two-tier bunks at each end with a central double bed settee. The streamlined models were 13ft and 15ft vans priced at £117 10s and £129 10s respectively.

PETO

The only reference found to this make is a 1937 classified advertisement by the dealers Welfords Caravans of Warninglid, Sussex, for a new 2 berth model costing £55.

PETONE

A report on the Spring Festival of the Camping Club held at Polesden Lacy, near Dorking, in April 1939 refers to the attendance of a Petone.

PIGGOTT

Piggott Bros of Bishopsgate, London, were already an old-established company noted for camping equipment, marquees and the like in 1920 when they became the first maker to put trailer caravans in the Motor Show. At the White City, an overflow from Olympia, they exhibited two-wheeled models 9, 12 and 17ft long. As well as plywood-walled vans resembling the lighter sort of horse caravan they built ultra-lightweight models inspired by contemporary aircraft construction and covered by a patent. These were based on an oak and ash framework built around two box girders forming the seats and bed boxes and held together with bolts and wing nuts. The walls were of stretched and doped canvas laced up over the framework, and the caravan could be taken to pieces, the canvas rolled up and the lantern roof separated into three sections for winter storage. Some models had the roofs panelled in sheet steel. By 1921 Piggott's were making vans from 9ft x 5ft to 22ft x 6ft 9in with roller bearing hubs, automatic brakes and tyres measuring from 28in x 3½in up to 32in x 4¾in depending on the load. Equipment included curtains, linoleum, mattresses, Valor Perfection oil stoves, cooking utensils, crockery, cutlery and many other items.

Major J Y M Broderip of West London, a pioneer trailer caravanner, bought a 17ft Piggott in 1921 and made his first tour from Egham in Surrey to Seaton, Devon. The van was a rigid panelled model with casement side windows and a stable door at each end. Equipment included four berths, gateleg table, Primus stove, 12 volt electric lighting, and a toilet compartment with a seat and a hole in the floor to line up with a hole in the ground below. Ex-aircraft wire wheels

were fitted instead of the advertised Sankey steel type and two sets of them collapsed in quick succession. Piggott innovations included patented side wall bay windows which folded flat for road travel, legs operated by a spanner to wind up into the body corners, and a canvas extension supported on a framework of rods mounted on a platform with folding legs which slid out from under the floor at the rear end. At the 1925 Motor Show they exhibited a 'Wagon-lit de luxe' 17ft 5 berth claimed to be built very low for towing by a fast touring car and with observation platforms at the ends capable of being converted into additional sleeping accommodation by means of waterproof curtains. Although continuing in their original business Piggott's ceased caravan manufacture after about five years.

1922 Piggott and Armstrong Siddeley. The patented side bay windows folded flat for road travel.

Piggott stand at the 1924 Motor Show. The rear end platform slid out from under the floor.

PILOT

1947 Pilot Panther. Most post-war models had coach shaped bodies.

Trading originally as Pilot Caravans, Roy Pascall started production at Oakengates, Shropshire, in 1937, the first model being a 13ft 6in 4 berth double panelled lantern roof van priced at £125. A claim of 20 years of specialised caravan construction in 1949 presumably refers in part to Pascall's previous employment with Charles Ensor, with whom he attended the

Rally organised by *The Autocar* at Minehead in 1932. 1938 models were a £95 9ft 6in 2 berth, £105 11ft 6in 3 berth, £115 13ft 6in 4 berth and £130 15ft 4 berth. The 16ft Croydon of 1939 had both electric and gas lighting and the 3/4in tongued and grooved floor boarding was overlaid with Celotex, lino and fitted carpet. The cost with single panelling was £175, double panelling adding £20 and triple panelling incorporating an additional lining of Celotex cost a further £2 10s.

Post-war the firm became M R Pascall Ltd and the first model was the 15ft Panther with coach shaped body introduced in mid-1945. By mid-1946 the price was £995 and the length had gone up to 19ft, increasing to 21ft by 1949. The firm was also producing the smaller Puma and Panda models, though these appear to have had conventionally shaped bodies, a 15ft coach shaped version of the Puma not appearing until mid-1949. A further 1949 model was the £595 15ft 8in 2 berth Python. By 1950 the 22ft Panther Mk II was selling at £1,475 and in the middle of that year the less expensive Pegasus was introduced, also 22ft long and costing £985, a price reported to be achieved by simplification, with materials, workmanship and finish remaining in the highest class. There was also a 15ft model known as the Lightweight, available in 2 and 4 berth versions in 1951-52. Towards the end of 1953, as well as the Panther and Pegasus priced at £985 and £750 respectively, a new model was the conventionally shaped £425 16ft Popular. The £1,245 Mk IX Panther exhibited at the 1957 Motor Show had equipment which included TV set, washing machine and refrigerator. A large part of the firm's business was the building to special order of vans for use as mobile offices and X-ray units, the entire production for 1958 being devoted to specials, although Mk X and XI Panther models were exhibited at the 1958 Motor Show and 1959 Caravan Show respectively. The cost in 1959 was £1,245 with an electrically heated floor available as an £18 optional extra.

It was reported in mid-1960 that the firm had been taken over by Sprite, with Roy Pascall remaining a director. It was said that this would not affect the distributing business in other makes which had operated since the Second World War. A 15ft model with a layout to the customer's choice was available in 1961, and towards the end of the year a £1,750 28ft x 8ft custom built special was introduced, the version exhibited at that year's Caravan Show having an end bedroom with double bed, bathroom, centre kitchen with fridge, and a lounge with foldaway double bed settee, treble wardrobe and TV recess. The prices of the Panther and Pegasus at this time were £1,245 and

£850 respectively. By 1962 the Pegasus had been discontinued but the 22ft Panther and 28ft Special Panther, both with layouts to customer's choice, remained in production until around 1965. By 1967 the company was owned by the Gailey Group dealer chain and in that year also built a 40ft canal cruiser.

1937 13ft 6in Pilot, whose maker, Roy Pascall, had previously worked for Ensor.

1954 Pilot Panther Mk VII, the final refinement of the coach shape.

THE CARAVAN WITH A PEDIGREE

PANTHER Mk. VII £985 EX WORKS

Combined with the unique constructional features is the thought and care taken in designing the Panther to your exact requirements.

M. R. PASCALL LTD., Pilot Works, Oakengates, Shropshire

Write for particulars or 'phone Oakengates 39

QUEST

Quest Caravans, Princess Mews, Belsize Crescent, Hampstead, London NW3, produced a three model range in 1935, an £80 9ft 2 berth, £100 13ft 6in 4 berth and £125 15ft 4 berth. These vans were also available as unfitted shells priced at £50, £55 and £70 respectively.

RAVEN

Building as an amateur for his own pleasure, Norman Wilkinson-Cox of Service Garage, Ravenscourt Square, Goldhawk Road, Hammersmith, West London, founder of Raven Caravans, first built a motor caravan on a 12cwt Ford van chassis, followed by an 8ft 2 berth trailer caravan in 1922. This 5cwt van, constructed from plywood covered with painted canvas, was fitted with a tubular axle and a belt rim brake acting on one wheel only. Offered for sale at £65, it attracted a number of enquiries and Wilkinson-Cox decided to start building these caravans for sale, following the original design with a 6ft x 4ft 6in 2 berth tent trailer weighing 2cwt.

The next model was a £125 12ft 4 berth in 1925, still of plywood but without the canvas covering,

QUEST

CARAVANS are making delighted caravanners. Built entirely by hand of the finest materials they are fully guaranteed in every respect. All steel chassis, Masonite or Insulite panelling, Raco-Epeda sprung beds, metal-framed windows and really weatherproof joints ensure a long life of reliable service. Compare our prices and quality.

De Luxe Four Berth, 15 ft. - £125
Light Four, 13 ft. 6 ins. - - - £100
Super Two, 9 ft. - - - - - - £80

All fully fitted and lavishly equipped.

Above sizes unfitted at £70, £55 and £50 respectively.

CARAVANS BUILT TO ORDER

Full particulars from :
QUEST CARAVANS
Princess Mews - Belsize Crescent
Hampstead, N.W.3 *HAMP 1122*

1935 Quest advertisement: 'Fully fitted and lavishly equipped'.

Quoth the RAVEN!!
1922
PIONEERS THEN

LOOK UPON THIS PICTURE AND UPON THAT ☞

SIXTEEN Years of Progress

SIXTEEN Years of Experience

Bring you the Up-to-date Comprehensive
Range of
RAVEN TRAILER COACHES of to-day

RAVEN CARAVANS LTD
FERRY WORKS, THAMES DITTON

The first Raven trailer caravan. Interest in it decided the maker to start building caravans for sale.

1931 15ft Raven Dominion. Available in various lengths, this popular model remained in production for several years.

followed by a £200 10ft lantern roof model in 1926, which had polished aluminium exterior panelling with plywood lining. Also introduced in 1926 was the Dominion, a box-shaped 13ft 4 berth van with cambered roof, weighing 13cwt and costing £175 with single panelling and £200 with double panelling. Offered in lengths up to 17ft, the Dominion proved a popular model and remained in production for several years.

1935 Raven Argonaut. Headroom of 6ft 4in in the centre, within an overall height of only 7ft 6in, was achieved by fixing the floor below the longitudinal timber joists.

Streamlining was adopted in 1931 with the kidney-shaped outline of the £160 15ft Argonaut. Headroom was 6ft 4in at the centre kitchen, unusually good for a van with a plain roof and an overall height of only 7ft 6in. This low height was achieved by fixing the floor below the longitudinal timber joists. The width of 6ft 8in at the axle was exceptional for that time but the body tapered slightly in plan to both ends whilst the side walls had a tumblehome. Night-time room separation by sliding doors was a novel feature. Smaller models with the new outline in 1932 were the £125 11ft Argosy and £90 Argonette, a 9ft 2 berth weighing 5½ cwt. The corner leg operated by a wheel brace was a Wilkinson-Cox invention. He had previously used DWS 'lazy tongs' car jacks as legs on some models and the new leg was probably derived from this. By 1934 this type of leg was in general use though apparently more people pirated the design than took a licence to use the patent.

In 1935 the company moved to larger premises in a former warehouse at Thames Ditton, Surrey. This building did not lend itself to being laid out for a rational progress of production and the smaller models were built on a gallery two floors up and had to be lowered by tackle down the central well, but the Thames-side site allowed the fitting out of cabin yachts and motor cruisers to be undertaken. Other products included coffee stalls, horse boxes, kennel trailers, luggage trailers and road contractors' living vans. The 1936 Viking, seen in prototype form at the

1935 Junior Car Club National Rally and exhibited at that year's Motor Show, had an oval outline with end bay windows integrated into the curve of the lantern roof. The toilet room was fitted with a wash basin, had inside and outside doors, and when not in use retracted to a width of only 16in. The larder was both insulated and ventilated, water was supplied by gravity from a wall tank detachable for filling, and a front end chest of drawers incorporating a lady's vanity fitment had sideboard wings extending over the feet of the single beds. The £295 van was fitted with a refuse chute and – reflecting growing interest in all-season use – a small coal fire and an electric fan.

The 16ft lantern roofed 1937 Yeoman, designed as a living van, was wired for mains electricity and had an exceptionally well insulated body for the period, with triple walls of Masonite, insulation board and plywood with two air cavities, although on the 1938 model insulation was by kapok blanket – under the trade name Tropal. Under the front bay window was a double bed settee, and a shallow sideboard against the nearside wall concealed a foldaway bed for an occasional visitor. The living area was also furnished with a movable table, two cane armchairs, two wardrobes, chest of drawers with dressing well, and a coal fire with mantelpiece and airing cupboard. The rear end, accommodating kitchen, toilet room and floor bath, could be shut off but when left open formed part of the living space, all work units being hidden. The Wizard was another 1937 model, a 10ft 3 berth weighing around 7cwt and with a single bed folding away vertically into a cupboard. The Arcadian was a 13ft 6in 4 berth with one single bed folding into a sideboard like the Yeoman's. An end kitchen layout in this length without sacrificing single beds had not

1937 Raven brochure

1937 Raven Yeoman.

1937 Raven Yeoman, designed as a living van and exceptionally well insulated.

way. Real industrialisation of production was prevented by the small scale of operations and whilst Raven was considered a 'big' maker, Wilkinson-Cox bought screws, hinges and other hardware items retail from Woolworths. At a period when most manufacturers did not consult women on the interior appearance and 'workability' of their caravans, Wilkinson-Cox's wife Georgie was a working director of Raven, choosing fabrics and generally supervising the interiors.

The National Caravan Council was formed in May 1939 and one of its first actions was to set up a sub-committee under the chairmanship of Wilkinson-Cox to prepare a report on the potential value of caravans in wartime. The Raven Mobile Billet, introduced in June 1940 and priced at £118, offered emergency accommodation for four people and the company also built trailer ambulances.

A 1947 advertisement referring to post-war models which would incorporate detail refinements resulting from Wilkinson-Cox's personal experience of living in a Dominion for four and a half years during the Second World War suggests that production of caravans had not restarted at that time and in the same year, although Wilkinson-Cox remained a director, Bruno Jablonski took control, the company relocated to Jablo Works, Mill Lane, Waddon, Croydon, Surrey, and the name was changed from Raven Caravans Ltd to Raven Caravans (1947) Ltd. Jablo, as Jablonski liked to be known, was an expert in synthetic resins and adhesives and through his company Moulded Components (Jablo) Ltd had first introduced Jabroc, a material from which aircraft propellers were made during the War. 1948 models were the 17ft Viceroy, 14ft Arcadian in two versions and 10ft Mignon. Wilkinson-Cox was still involved with the NCC and was a member of the interim Caravan Trade Committee which preceded the formation of an NCC Trade Division in December 1948. He was also the first chairman of the Design and Development Committee set up as one of the first acts of the Trade Division. The 14ft 6in Savoy, a 4 berth van with cavity walls, insulated roof and exterior panelling of Dura-lumin, was introduced in 1949, the same year in which Mrs Wilkinson-Cox died after a long illness.

New models seen at the 1949 Motor Show were the Duck and the 18ft 4 berth Cottage. The £490 Duck, which does not appear to have been put into production, was a 2 berth caravan body mounted on a float and, with the two-wheeled undercarriage available as a £62 extra, was both navigable and towable. The 1950 range consisted of the 22ft Viking, Cottage, 15ft 6in Savoy and Mignon. In 1951 a Viking body was fitted out for Hertfordshire County Constabulary

been achieved previously and the design was quickly copied by other makers. The £428 18ft 6in Dominion of 1939 with a bed in the kitchen for a maid was a publicity triumph for the company though this was not an original idea.

In the later 1930s, Raven along with Eccles were the leading exponents of prefabrication of furniture, reducing the delays and frustrations inevitable when furniture was built in-situ and men got in each other's

The 1939 Raven Dominion included a bed in the kitchen for a maid!

All aluminium exterior with metal window frames. Fully insulated with fibreglass. Tongued and grooved flooring. Pressed steel chassis. Brace-operated jacks and jockey wheel.

RAVEN "ASCOT"

(PRICE AS PER LIST)

Ex-works

A PERFECT "LIVING" CARAVAN

22ft. 0ins. x 7ft. 6ins.

LOUNGE with double foldaway bed, two big wardrobes, writing bureau, mirror, lockers and shelves, wheel arch seat, enamelled Tayco solid fuel stove, airing cupboard. All furniture in veneered oak.

KITCHEN with full-sized cooker, plate-rack, deep sink and draining board in metal, water pump, ample cupboards and drawers. Toilet compartment fitted with shower and pump.

SEPARATE BEDROOM with two single beds, deep wardrobe and bedside locker.

1951 Raven Ascot, a residential van with separate double bedroom and shower-equipped toilet room.

as the first mobile police station in the country. A new model in 1951 was the 14ft 4in Castle, in 2 and 4 berth versions featuring a fixed front end window set in a 57in x 32in sun flap. A canvas awning could be attached to the open flap with press studs. The roof was panelled in aluminium but wall panelling could be aluminium or hardboard at the buyer's choice. Prices for the 2 berth were £400 and £415 for hardboard and aluminium respectively, with corresponding prices of £420 and £435 for the 4 berth. Any of the vans could be purchased for £6 less without the sun flap. Wilkinson-Cox was again elected to the Committee of the NCC Trade Division in 1951.

A further new model in 1951 was the £775 22ft Ascot residential model. This van had a front end kitchen, toilet room fitted with a chemical closet and shower, and centre living room with foldaway double bed, movable settee, solid fuel stove, airing cupboard, two wardrobes and a bureau/dressing table. The rear end bedroom had two single beds, wardrobe and a chest of drawers which was movable so that the beds could be pushed together to form a double. A novel

van exhibited at the 1951 Motor Show but which may not have been put into production was the Lodge. Advertised as a complete flat on wheels, the van could be purchased without towbar, axle, wheels and corner legs, and used as a permanent home – rather an ambitious claim for a 14ft 6in van! It was supposed to be possible to buy or rent the equipment later if it was decided to move the van. Three alternatives were offered for the exterior panelling – Masonite hardboard, aluminium or Jablo resin bonded and impregnated Aero Ply. A last minute surprise exhibit at the 1952 Motor Show, again not destined for production, was the £998 Duo Cottage, comprising special versions of the Cottage with complementary layouts designed to fit together at right angles, with a sliding door providing access between the two vans.

Moulded Components (Jablo) Ltd also made Aero Jablex (later Jablon), an expanded plastic used for mattresses and upholstery as well as for sound and low temperature insulation. In 1952 it was reported that Jabroc and Jablex were also being produced in Australia, Canada and France, but whilst plastic foam mattresses had been seen in Ravens at the 1949 Motor

1953 Raven Arcadian, available as a 2 berth living or 4 berth touring van.

1933 Reade Pathfinder's front entrance door was unusual.

Show it was not adopted as standard until 1955. An innovation of 1953 was bodywork assembled from pre-fabricated shaped sections of sandwich construction, formed with a plastic honeycomb core faced externally with aluminium or hardboard and internally with plywood – a method which dispensed with much of the conventional body framing. An alternative sandwich comprising a resin impregnated corrugated cardboard core between hardboard panels was used on the £595 22ft Montrose Castle of 1953. This van was made to the design of the dealers Montrose Caravan Distributors Ltd, Cheshire and had a front end kitchen and toilet compartment, rear end bedroom with two single beds or a double, and a centre living room with a drop down section opening from the nearside wall to form an extension which housed a double bed. By day the bed converted into a settee with space behind for bedding storage.

Also in 1953 Moulded Components (Jablo) Ltd advertised that they were now in a position to supply the caravan trade with components such as window frames, tables and aluminium sinks, previously produced exclusively for Raven. A new version of the Arcadian, introduced later in 1953, had a new exterior style with front overhang and the 16ft (later 17ft) van was offered in two layouts, a 2 berth living van at £350 and 4 berth touring van at £375. The £1,100 Chateau was an exhibit at the 1954 Motor Show and this 24ft x 7ft 6in van with a Castle-type side extension was produced mainly for members of the Armed Forces at home and overseas, and for travelling showmen. In 1954 Jablonski gave evidence at the Public Enquiry into the crashes of two Comet airliners. For 1956 the Chateau and Cottage were only available to special order and the standard models, fitted with Flexitor rubber independent suspension, were the £225 Mignon and 12ft Savoy in 2 and 3 berth versions costing £190 and £199 respectively. How long Wilkinson-Cox remained actively involved with Raven is not known. As a technical expert at the 1958 British Caravan Road Rally he is described as the founder of Raven rather than as a director. Production does not in any case appear to have continued beyond 1958.

READE

Reade Caravans, Newtown Road, Eastleigh, Hampshire, produced the 10ft 3 berth Pathfinder in 1933-34. Costing 85 guineas and unusual in having a front entrance door, the van was reported to be one of the most ingeniously fitted models on the market.

RED-RICS

A Camping Trailer entered by Red-Rics won second prize in the Camping Trailer class at the Caravan Rally organised by *The Autocar* at Minehead in August 1932. The firm had showrooms in Fulham Road, London SW3, the works being in High Street, Battersea. The Camping Trailer cost £40 in 1933 and other models at that time were a £100 Caravan Bungalow, a range of 2, 3 and 4 berth trailer caravans costing from £65, and 5cwt and 10cwt luggage trailers costing £9 10s and £14 10s respectively. Caravans were also available for hire, including towing cars if required.

REGAL

A rally report in the August 1939 issue of *The Caravan* notes the attendance of two Regals.

Red Rics Camping Trailer at The Autocar Rally, Minehead, 1932. The firm also built caravan bungalows, trailer caravans and luggage trailers. (LAT Photographic)

REX

In 1939 Rex Caravans, Felpham, Bognor Regis, were advertising their 75 guinea, 9½cwt van as 'the cheapest and lightest full four berth caravan available'. There was a 65 guinea three berth model and the firm also operated a hire fleet.

REYNOLDS

Reynolds Caravans, Wickham Street, Welling, Kent, produced a 12ft 4 berth van costing £125 in 1938. 2 and 3 berth models were also available.

VALUE SUPREME

75 GNS.

9½ cwt. The Cheapest and Lightest full 4-berth Caravan obtainable

3-Berth Model

65 GNS.

Rex Caravans
NEW HIRE FLEET

FELPHAM, BOGNOR REGIS
Phone : Bognor Regis 131

1939 Rex, advertised as 'the cheapest and lightest full four berth caravan available'.

RICE

Following a wet camping holiday in the Lake District in 1925, J Cecil Rice of Gargrave, Skipton, Yorkshire, decided that what he needed was a comfortable van suitable for fast touring. A folding caravan was designed and built in a fortnight, and Rice used this himself for two years before rebuilding it, eventually going into commercial production in 1928. The basis of the design was a narrow but fairly high trailer on which the rigid roof was connected by metal stays to a hinged body section on each side. As the roof rose the body sections swung out to form seats complete with fixed backrests. Cotton duck with a rubber interleaf formed the walls between the hinged sections and the roof, the central part of the end walls being in the form of spring blinds, each complete with a celluloid window, which rolled up into cavities in the roof. Bedding could be stored under the spring interior mattresses and other equipment comprised a

The original 1925 Rice model, a folding caravan designed by its maker for his own use after enduring a wet camping holiday in the Lake District.

front end drawer and cupboard unit on which sat a two-burner cooking stove, a free-standing table containing a cupboard and drawer which had a sink built into the top, and two metal lined floor wells.

Three models were produced – 2 berth Standard, 2 berth Long Standard and 3 berth Major. Dimensions for the respective models were body length 6ft 4in, 8ft and 8ft; width closed, excluding mudguards, 3ft 8in, 3ft 8in and 4ft 7in; extended width 7ft 1in, 7ft 1in and 8ft 4in; height closed 5ft 3½in, 5ft 3½in and 5ft 8½in; headroom when extended 5ft 8in, 5ft 8in and 6ft; weight 4½cwt, 5½cwt and 7¼cwt. The bodywork had a hardwood frame panelled with treated plywood

1933 Rice advertisement. Satisfied owners took their vans as far afield as Africa, Iceland and New Zealand

finished with cellulose car fabric. Prices in 1930 were 69gns, 78gns and 88gns and the vans could be hired from the manufacturer at charges of between 2 and 4gns per week. As an option one of the single beds on the Long Standard could be converted to a double bed at an extra cost of £3, and single or double folding bunks could be supplied for any model at a cost of £1 15s or £2 10s. Rice's own design of hydraulic damping to the overrun brake mechanism was fitted to the Long Standard and Major, the housing for the sliding shaft being made as two chambers, oil passing from one to the other under pressure providing progressive damping.

The vans were well made, and satisfied owners took them to places far distant from Gargrave including Africa, Iceland and New Zealand. A Herbert Shultz left England with his wife and three children in a family car towing a Long Standard in October 1933, eventually reaching Bombay in May 1934. The Rice apparently performed excellently throughout the journey despite appalling conditions. E E Kirby, writing in *The Caravan* in March 1960, describes how in a rash moment in 1934 he wrote to Rice Caravans for details of the folding vans. Two days later the firm's representative turned up with a Major which he had opened up on the verge outside before knocking at the door. A few weeks later Mr Kirby travelled to the works to take delivery of the demonstration van at a cost of £75, eventually selling it back to Cecil Rice in about 1943 for £64. For 1934 a half length wardrobe with zip fastener opening was added, and at the 1934

A 1938 Rice still in use in 1956.

Motor show a new van was exhibited along with the established models. This was the Magna, which had rigid wooden sides when open. The vans were also fitted with a new design of ball coupling, the Rice-Edge, on which the ball was mounted on the caravan rather than the car.

Rice Caravans Ltd also built chassis, horseboxes and trailers, and by 1939 had moved to Cosby, near Leicester. In advertising after the Second World War the company claimed to have built thousands of trailers for war-time use but production of the folding vans was not resumed after the War. Since the company's horseboxes were mounted on close coupled four-wheeled chassis, the decision to retain a 20mph speed limit for vehicles towing four-wheeled trailers when the limit for private cars towing two-wheeled trailers was raised to 30 mph in April 1931 was of concern to them, and Cecil Rice campaigned for the same limit for close coupled trailers. Ironically this was conceded in 1954, the same year in which Rice and his wife died at Moutier, Switzerland, where, flying his own plane, he struck a mountain side.

RITE (CHARNWOOD)

WE Wright of the Leicester motor body builders, W Wright & Son, had built motor caravans in the 1919-25 period and in the mid-1930s produced the 16ft 4 berth Rite. This lantern roof van cost £175 in standard form including crockery and cutlery for six persons, cooking utensils and electric lighting from a 6 volt battery. A £205 de luxe version also had a fitted wireless, leaded light windows and Elsan chemical closet with tent.

By 1939 the firm was operating as a distributor for Raven caravans and also had a hire fleet as well as carrying out caravan repairs and renovations. In 1947 Wright's were offering to undertake any type of alteration, repair or repainting to any make of caravan as

A Charnwood at the 1950 Caravan Club National Rally: post-WWII came a new name and a new shape.

well as building special type caravans and trailers to customer's requirements. In 1949 they started producing vans under the Charnwood name. Models

The LAST WORD IN COMFORT

The "Rite" Model

16 ft. Long.   2 Rooms.   4 Berths.

GENERAL SPECIFICATIONS

CHASSIS. All steel chassis with twin steel tow-bar ; ball and socket hitch ; automatic brake gear with hand brake ; silico manganese steel springs ; solid square cranked axle ; fabric lined brakes ; detachable steel wheels, fitted Goodyear 4.50 × 19 tyres ; track 5 ft. 2 in.

CORNER LEGS. Patent permanent jacks with folding handle, no crawling to turn dirty screws, folds up flat when out of use.

THE BODY. Of well-seasoned selected ash and oak covered with "MASONITE" wood fibre hardboard, rot and damp-proof, and has a very high degree of insulation.

THE ROOF AND LANTERN. Framing and covering as above ; lantern sides in mahogany or pine with best double canvas, giving a perfect watertight roof.

WINDOWS. Vee Bay to front and two to each side, with birch frames and mahogany lights ; gunmetal stays and fasteners ; six opening lights in all ; one light to top door panel ; plate glass light to rear giving a direct view through Caravan ; approx. window area 30 sq. ft. ; six opening ventilating lights to lantern roof.

DOOR. Of birch and panelled as sides, fitted with locking latch and chromium pull handle, weather strip to bottom ; aluminium gutter strip fitted to front, sides and lantern roof.

FINISH. The Exterior : cream enamel to upper-part above window cills, and brown enamel to lower part. The Interior : cream enamel to roof and lantern. The grained Masonite panelling to sides and framing, polished and clear enamel. These being standard colours, can be altered to suit individual requirements.

FITMENTS. The Interior fitments in either oak or mahogany, polished and clear enamelled for easy cleaning. The Kitchen cupboards to under sink, stove and lockers under beds, of pine and brown enamelled. Inlaid futurist pattern lino. covering the floor. Wireless aerial fitted in roof. Curtains and valances fitted to all windows, the same material being used for settee covers. A ventilated food locker is let in the floor, the lighting battery being fixed under floor outside for easy access. The folding step hinges out of sight under the doorway.

at this time were the 17ft 6in coach shaped Prince Regent, 15ft 6in semi-streamlined Beau Brummell and the Beau Nash. A 1954 15ft Special had an opening rear end to allow a 12ft dinghy to be carried. In 1955 the range comprised the £260 9ft 6in 3 berth Blue Bell, £325 11ft Beacon with layout to customer's requirements, and £375 14ft 4 berth Grace-Dieu. By 1958 Wright's were building only to special order, mostly for Caravan Club members living in the East Midlands. Production seems to have ceased in the early 1960s although a 1999 advertisement for Charnwood Caravan Services of Leicestershire – 'mobile service and accident repair specialists' – may indicate a continuing involvement in the caravan business.

16ft Rite, looking somewhat dated by 1934.

RIVERS

TB Pickard's company, Associated British Caravans Ltd, Regent's Park Road, Church End, Finchley, London N3, advertised themselves as London and Home Counties Main Distributors for Country Life, Essex and Jubilee caravans in 1937, but by 1939, whilst 'agents for all caravans of repute', the firm was also producing Rivers Caravans. The range in August of 1939 was reported to comprise the 15ft double panelled Shannon with centre kitchen at £175 or end kitchen at £185, 16ft Danube with various layouts priced from £210 to £285, de luxe Danube with five alternative layouts at £285 in a 16ft length or £375 in an 18ft version. There were also 2, 3 and 4 berth versions of the Nile priced at £85, £93 and £105 respectively, with double panelled de luxe versions costing £98 10s, £116 and £130, and the Nippy sleeping trailer. Features offered on the de luxe Danube included toilet room, bath, shower, water tank and pump, radio, two doors, coal or gas fire and triple panelling, whilst special insulation for tropical climates was a listed extra. The £37 Nippy was 8ft long x 4ft 2in wide with 5ft 2in headroom. Equipment included a double bed convertible to a settee and a fold down table. For an additional £3 10s a 5ft side lean-to or a 6ft rear tent annexe could be supplied. Associated British Caravans also operated a hire fleet, sold 'every description of commercial and utility trailer' and 'everything for the amateur builder'.

An 18ft living van was built throughout the Second World War, though by 1946 the company had moved to Green Lane, London N16, and by 1947 to South Street, Epsom, Surrey. By 1948 they were also offering to design vans to suit individual requirements although their speciality was to offer many variants on a few basic models. In 1949 these variants numbered more than thirty. A 19ft 6in version of the Danube introduced early in 1949 was at that time the largest model yet produced. Insulation of walls, roof and floor was very thorough and the roof construction consisted of Holoplast plastic ceiling, glassfibre insulation between the framing members, Sundeala hardboard with sealed and taped joints, waterproof adhesive coat, heavy cotton duck, sealing coat, waterproof filling, two coats of red oxide, two undercoats and a finish of synthetic enamel or aluminium paint.

In 1951 the range, which had a three year guarantee, comprised the Danube in 16ft, 18ft and 20ft lengths priced from £890 to £1,500, Nile in lengths from 10ft to 15ft, and 15ft Shannon at £736. In a test report in *The Caravan* in October 1951, the 14ft 4in 4 berth Nile is described as sleek and smooth in both appearance and towing performance. The 17cwt van cost £383 17s with hardboard exterior panelling or £408 7s panelled in aluminium. The interior walls were panelled in Celotex insulation board covered with leathercloth, the roof was covered with canvas finished with aluminium paint, and Spencer Moulton Flexitor bonded rubber independent suspension units were fitted. 1952 models were the £414 14ft 3in Nile, £694 14ft 6in Taw de luxe, £774 15ft 6in Shannon de luxe, together with the Danube in 16ft 6in, 18ft 6in, 20ft and 22ft lengths priced at £684, £1,195, £1,450 and £1,650. Production ceased in July 1954 but B P Pickard, who was running the company at that time, retained an interest in caravanning, being one of the judges in the Concours d'Elegance at the British Caravan Road Rally in 1956.

ROAMA

The Roama Moviehome was produced by W T Rudd, Upper Ground Street, London SE1, in 1934. The 4 berth van was fitted with independent suspension and cost £125, or £140 for a de luxe version. An advertisement in *The Caravan* for February 1934 declared: 'Now in production, orders being dealt with in strict rotation'.

ROAMIO

1938 classified advertisements have been found for secondhand Roamios, a 10ft 3 berth and a 4 berth.

1939 16ft Rivers Danube. The manufacturers were originally distributors for other makes.

1953 Rivers Nile, described as sleek and smooth in both appearance and towing performance.

1934 Roama Moviehome had independent suspension, an unusual feature at the time.

ROLEAS

Happy days ..... a Roleas at a pre-war rally

IN WAR

and

PEACE

Roleas policy remains un-changed
Quality caravanning at lowest costs

Only first-class materials used
Built by first-class tradesmen
Made by a firm of over 50 years' standing

ROLEAS CARAVANS LTD

PLANT STREET, OLD HILL, STAFFS.
Telephone : Cradley 6063

Mark Round & Sons, Plant Street, Old Hill, Staffordshire, builders of lorry bodies and vans, started production of Roleas caravans in 1938. The vans were designed by T H Lewis and the initial model was a single panelled 13ft 6in 4 berth lantern roof van weighing 9¾cwt and costing £105. Models advertised in 1939 were a 9ft 6in van at 85 guineas in 2 berth form or 95 guineas as a 3 berth and a lantern roof 4 berth at £120 with single panelling or £135 double panelled. These vans were sold with a two year guarantee and were said to be made by a firm with 50 years' standing. The prototype for a new 13ft 6in lantern roof van was seen at a number of Caravan Club meets in August 1939. References in post-war advertising to 'in war and peace' suggest that production continued during the Second World War, but a 1949 advertisement carried a photograph of the 13ft 6in van 'at a pre-war rally' so presumably no new designs had been developed. Nothing is known of the make after 1949.

1949 Roleas, its design appearing unchanged from pre-war models.

ROLLALONG

1935 15ft Rollalong Standard 4 berth, advertised as 'Super-Streamlined'.

Murray Lindner of Leckhampton Road, Cheltenham, was a maker of agricultural equipment and breeder of poultry, with a worldwide sale for his patent corn bins, when he started to build Rollalong caravans in the mid-1930s. The early models were advertised as 'Super-Streamlined' and included the £165 15ft Standard 4 berth of 1935.

Models listed in a new catalogue issued in 1936 were the £110 Cotswold, £165 Olympia, £175 16ft and £190 17ft 6in vans – all single panelled 4 berths, double panelling being an extra costing between £15 and £28, and the vans could be supplied with a lantern roof at a cost of between £10 and £20. 2 and 3 berth vans were also available priced at £75 and £96 respectively. The £325 17ft Streamer exhibited at the Motor Show in 1936 was a very unusual van with a plain roof at the front and a lantern roof at the rear which continued at full height when the roof shoulders curved down, allowing double doors in the rear end in addition to the nearside door. Equipment included two movable easy chairs convertible into single beds, and a floor well in the middle of the rear end kitchen which, together with a detachable plastic curtain, provided for a shower bath with a thermostatically controlled hot water feed.

1937 vans were the £85 3 berth Star, £115 13ft 6in

ROLL-ALONG CARAVANS

Here is our new Standard 4-Berth Model. Panelled with Insulite, it is luxuriously designed and fitted with all the latest improvements. Notice the generous size of the windows. Inside there are ten roof lockers, all of ample proportions. Roominess is a feature of Roll - Along Caravans. Study them at

There are ideas and features in the Roll-Along that you will not find elsewhere

Length, 15'
Width, 6' 3"
Head Room, 6' 4"

Price
£165
ex works

Send for our Catalogue
MURRAY LINDNER
205 Leckhampton Road, Cheltenham

STAND No.
214
OLYMPIA

A 1936 Rollalong Streamer with a Ford V8. Its appearance was unusual, with twin rear doors. Two movable easy chairs converted into single beds and there was a shower in the kitchen.

4 berth Mercury, £125 15ft 4 berth Jupiter and the Streamer. The Mercury was streamlined, though markedly less so than the early vans, but the Star was a very plain model, the boxy outline only relieved by a 90° curve to front and rear edges of the roof. In 1937 Rollalong engaged a design consultant, Hugo van Wadenoyen, who was responsible for interior and exterior colour schemes. They were the only manufacturer prior to the Second World War to have such a consultant. Lindner's designs were good but in common with several other makers he did not follow a consistent policy and Rollalong did not have a clear brand image. By 1938 the firm had moved to

Seymour Road, Ringwood, Hampshire, and buyers were invited to choose from a range of furniture and devise their own layouts in the firm's standard shells. The theory was that customers would realize that they could not better Rollalong's own layouts. The Star, Mercury and Jupiter continued at increased prices but the Streamer was replaced by the £274 16ft 6in Venus. Two new models for 1939 were the £88 2 berth Eight and £115 4 berth Sunshine.

Following the Second World War, it was reported in mid-1946 that a new model would soon be in production. Vans designed by Murray's son, David Murray Lindner, exhibited at the 1948 Motor Show

Rollalong New Star, exhibited at the Motor Show in 1948.

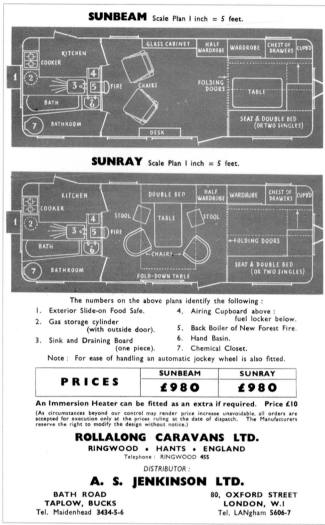

1953 Rollalong brochure. The Sunray and the Sunbeam were very similar.

were the 18ft Constellation, 13ft 6in New Star and a small export only model, the Envoy. The £798 Constellation, with coach shape body, had a lounge area that divided into two bedrooms. The solid fuel stove, surmounted by a mantelpiece, mirror and two bracket lights, was set in the middle of the partition shutting off the rear end of the van, and doors to left and right of the stove led respectively into the bathroom and kitchen. The bathroom was equipped with a 51in bath, wash basin and chemical toilet. The kitchen had a detachable larder which hung outside and there were two of the convertible easy chair beds in the lounge. At the 1949 Motor Show Rollalong exhibited the £858 22ft Sunbeam, Constellation, now costing £735, and £330 12ft New Moon, which could sleep up to six people. The Sunbeam and Constellation could both be supplied with mains wiring at an extra cost of £20, and the Sunbeam was equipped with a three-wheeled towable tank with capacity for 12 gallons each of fresh and waste water.

There were two new models at the 1952 Motor Show, the 12ft Moonray and 18ft Moonbeam. These vans had the lower parts of the body at front and rear cut away, leaving a small central floor area on a much reduced chassis frame. This sacrificed under-bed locker space but substantially reduced weight. The Moonray cost £335 plus £62 10s for an optional 8ft 6in dinghy, complete with sails, which could be carried on the roof. The Moonbeam cost £510 as a touring van or £535 for the living van version. The appearance of both vans proved too unorthodox for most buyers. Residential vans at this time were the £980 22ft Sunray and the very similar Sunbeam. The price of these two vans was reduced to £895 in mid-1953 at the same time as a new 22ft model, the £785 Meteor, was introduced. In the middle of the following year a new 15ft 9in van appeared, the £475 Shooting Star. This 2 berth, designed for permanent living or touring, had larger than normal beds – one 6ft 6in x 2ft 6in and one 6ft x 2ft 6in. Heating was by gas convector and furni-

A miniature Rollalong presented to Prince Charles and Princess Anne by The Caravan Club in 1955.

ture included a desk and dressing table. The firm also exhibited two new models at the 1954 Motor Show, the £289 12ft Nimbus and £875 22ft Stratus. Customers for the Stratus in 1955 included the concert pianist Semprini. A Mark II version of the Stratus was exhibited at the 1955 Motor Show and it was reported that this would be the only standard model produced in 1956. In the Mark III version of the Stratus, exhibited at the 1956 Motor Show, one of the lounge single beds slid into the bathroom over the full length bath during daytime. Equipment included a refrigerator and house-type water system. The 22ft Cirrus introduced in 1957 adopted an American style of open-plan layout with a waist high dining bar providing the division between lounge and kitchen. A Venetian blind could be lowered over the bar to provide further division if required. At the rear end were a bathroom and a bedroom with two bunks. Interior decoration followed the tasteful modern style

for which Rollalong had become known.

The firm also built many specials including a 22ft model for the advance manager of Chipperfield's Circus (1954), two units shipped to Marconi in Lagos (1954) and a 24ft 6in van for C J Birkmyre of Billy Smart's Circus (1955), which had oil fired heating with warm air blown through ducts under the floor to concealed grilles in each room. Lounge equipment included an elaborate cocktail cabinet, television, radio, tape recorders and reversible maps. The chassis alone was reported to weigh two tons. Perhaps the most special van was certainly the smallest Rollalong ever made, with internal dimensions of 6ft 4in long x 3ft 10in wide with 4ft 5in headroom. This miniature van, built to the order of the Caravan Club, was presented to Prince Charles and Princess Anne in 1955. Standard production ceased around 1958-59 and the firm concentrated on industrial and special purpose trailers.

ROMA

The only model known to have been produced by Roma Caravans of East Hill, London SW18, was a 15ft 4 berth van, available in 1937 at the advertised price of £185.

ROMANY

Smedley & Gray Ltd, Walsgrave Road, Coventry, produced the Romany folding caravan in 1933. When closed for towing the van had an overall height of 5ft and a length of 3ft 6½in which increased to 9ft 2in when erected on site. The body was covered in rubber-proofed fabric on an ash frame, and the price of £58 included camp beds and two lockers, the tops of which served as seats.

1937 Round Bay, whose makers persisted with railway carriage style full drop windows despite it proving impossible to completely prevent moisture entering the wall cavity.

ROUND BAY

The Round Bay was manufactured in small numbers in the period 1937-39 by Captain L E R Murray of K F M Engineering Co Ltd, Waterloo Road,

The ROUND BAY
TRAILER COACH

MOTOR EXHIBITION
STAND 173 EARLS COURT

MOTOR EXHIBITION
STAND 173 EARLS COURT

SETS A NEW STANDARD OF DESIGN & COMFORT

— ENABLES YOU TO —

Travel Anywhere in Greater Comfort than in your Car.
Enjoy the Beauty of your Surroundings Whatever the Weather.

THE LAYOUT GIVES UNUSUAL COMFORT AND PRIVACY WHEN REQUIRED.
THE DISPOSITION OF EVERYTHING ENTAILS MINIMUM MOVING ABOUT.

COACH-BUILT, DOUBLE-PANELLED BODY OF FIRST-CLASS
WORKMANSHIP AND FINISH

EXCLUSIVE FEATURES
Include special steel chassis, vacuum servo brake, giving trouble-free trailing at speed. Hydraulic jockey wheel. Dual purpose tables of novel design. Roller-bearing double-bed settee at front. Two single or one double bed at rear. Double beds can be made from both sides. Hot and cold water system without pumps and entirely frost-proof.

SPECIAL ITEMS OF EQUIPMENT
Include two wash basins and dressing tables. Electric lighting (external and internal). Gas heating, lighting and cooking. Quicktho drop windows and Birmabright casements. Larder with forced ventilation. ¼" outside panels of Sundeala. Centre partition. Airing cupboard. Staples hair-filled spring mattresses. Eight large rain-proof ventilators under the roof. Stainless steel rear bumper.

Regd. designs 819470, 819471 and Patents pending.

ROUND BAY CARAVANS
(K.F.M. ENGINEERING CO., LTD.)
'Phone : Gladstone 1050.

K.F.M. WORKS,
WATERLOO ROAD,
CRICKLEWOOD, N.W.2

Cricklewood, London NW2. The name was derived from the bull-nose front end with windows all round. There was a well-fitted dressing table in this area and a wash basin in the V-shaped tail. The 19ft vans were built to a high standard and included such expensive features as bed-settees moving on ball-bearing runners, hydraulic jacking jockey wheel and Feeny and Johnson vacuum-servo braking. The dining table was suspended from the ceiling and even when fully laid could be pushed sideways to allow diners to seat themselves. Water supply came from 2-gallon copper cans, each with a tap and a sloping bottom, so that when placed on a sloping shelf above the sink the can drained to the last drop, whilst if placed on the ground during refilling the tap was lifted clear of the dirt. Cooling of the larder was achieved by using hot air rising from the cooking recess to suck in cool air. Full drop windows were fitted, disappearing in railway carriage style into the walls, but this proved very troublesome. It was found to be impossible to completely prevent rain and condensation entering the wall cavity, so each window was provided with a hand-made metal tray to catch the drips. However when the caravan was on the move water from the trays splashed onto the inside faces of the cavity and the trays had to be replaced with complete metal pans. A further problem occurred when the small pipes draining the pans froze in cold weather and had to be replaced by larger ones.

The van was intended to carry passengers and the Murray's used to arrive at rallies with Mrs Murray in the van ready to serve a hot meal. A telephone linked her to Captain Murray in the car. The company also manufactured any part required for a caravan from 'an all steel chassis to a novel salt cellar (which keeps the salt dry)'. It was reported in 1946 that work was soon to start on a prototype lightweight caravan but nothing further is known of this van.

RUDGE

A new item which appeared in the 1927 catalogue of Rudge-Whitworth Ltd, the Coventry motorcycle manufacturers, was the Rudge caravan. This could be purchased complete with a motorcycle and semi-sports sidecar for 130 guineas. The 7ft 3in long x 4ft 10in wide x 4ft 7in high caravan was fitted out with two bed settees, a table and lockers for food,

clothing, etc. No provision was made for a wash basin or cooking stove – these had to be supplied by the purchaser and it was recommended that they be used outside the caravan. It was also recommended that when on site the towbar be lashed to the nearest hedge and the rear corners fitted with ropes and pegged down. Commercial versions were also available and,

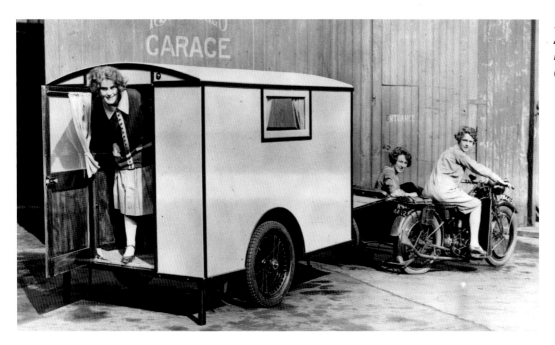

1927 Rudge. Users were advised to lash the towbar to the nearest hedge when on site! (Getty Images)

1936 Sandling, with car type wind-down windows.

together with a box sidecar, proved to be quite popular. There are reports that the Coventry Co-op was still using a commercial version for delivery of milk and bread as late as 1944. The caravan also featured in the 1928 catalogue, now including wash basin and cooking stove as part of the specification, but did not appear in subsequent editions.

SANDFORD

A 1939 advertisement by Sandford Caravans, Sandford-on-Thames, Oxford, offers 11ft 6in, 13ft 6in and 14ft 6in used 1939 Sandfords for sale.

SANDLING

Sandling caravans were manufactured by Dick Hills & Co Ltd, Union Street, Maidstone, Kent, in the 1936-39 period. A 15ft 6in 4 berth double panelled van of 1936-37 with asbestos insulated roof and car type wind-down windows cost £150. There was also a 2 berth model costing £85 in 1938, and specials were built to customer's own designs.

SAUNDERS

A rather curious classified advertisement which appeared in 1936 refers to an £85 16ft 5 berth

Something Good for the Winter

A fully-equipped 4-berth at £150

Double-panelled with an asbestos-insulated roof. Panels of Lloyd Hardboard with oak-faced ply inside. Steel chassis with Leason axle and the special SANDLING Ball Hitch. Anti-roll springing. Winding windows and Raco mattresses. Length 15 ft. 6 in. Width 6 ft. 4 in. Brace-operated jacks are fitted if preferred. Why not write for the Catalogue giving further particulars of this remarkable Caravan?

Quotations will be given for Special Models to Customers' Own Designs

Sandling Caravans
(Dick Hills & Co. Ltd.)
29, Union Street, Maidstone, Kent
(Telephone : Maidstone 2439)

van of 'Car Trailers design' made by Cecil Saunders Ltd, Works Road, Letchworth, Hertfordshire,

SCHOONER

1936 Schooner: the purpose (if any) of the large front end bulge is not known.

The interestingly styled Schooner of 1936 was manufactured by T Hodgson of Border Caravans, Carlisle. The van was single panelled and featured a table which divided longitudinally so that the two halves could hinge back to right and left to form a wide shelf against the rear wall.

SCOULAR

The only known model from this maker is the £250 4 berth 16ft Nidus of .

SHADOW

A Shadow collapsible caravan at The Autocar Rally, Minehead in 1932. Production may have ceased in the previous year. (LAT Photographic)

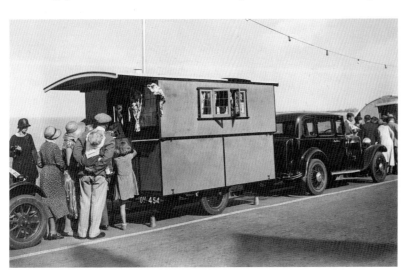

After working for Sunbeam Motor Cars, Robert Hamish Sievwright started his own coach building company in Wolverhampton in the early 1920s. He seems to have come into contact with a designer called John Lancelot Parkinson Fletcher Brewer in the mid-1920s, resulting in the appearance of the Shadow collapsible caravan. An outline patent application for the design was submitted on 29th October 1926, a full patent application following in July 1927 and being accepted on 18th August of that year. References to Shadow caravans appeared in the monthly publication *Great Highway* in June 1927 and elsewhere at about the same time. The upper half of the body lowered over and outside the lower half to close the van, raising and lowering being achieved by winding a handle which turned a worm drive running full length along the centre of the chassis and which was connected to each corner of the upper half by means of a steel rope running over three pulleys. Full details of the models available appear in the Motor Show catalogues for 1928 and 1929. The Shadow was made in two sizes, the smaller of which was 7ft 8in long x 5ft 8in wide with an overall height of 4ft 10in closed and 7ft 10in open, giving a maximum head-room of 6ft 1in. The 7cwt van slept two or three and plywood or fibreboard was used for the single panelled walls with a canvas covered fibreboard roof. The price initially seems to have been £75 10s rising eventually to £125. The larger model was 9ft 8in long x 6ft wide and originally cost £100, rising to £145, with a de luxe version costing between £188 and £215. The de luxe model is known to have been a 4 berth van with two settees converting into bunk beds. The walls were panelled with metal armoured plywood and a sliding sunshine roof was available. A Shadow was awarded first prize in the collapsible caravan class at the first trailer caravan rally in the world, organised by *The Autocar* at Minehead in August 1932 but production may have ceased around 1931. Sievwright's continued building bodies for cars and commercial vehicles for many years, probably into the 1970s.

SIDDALL

Neville Siddall worked for the Cheltenham Caravan Co. before starting production under his own name in 1932. The Siddall works were at Old Bath Road, Cheltenham, and models prior to the Second World War were straightforward, moderately priced vans which acquired a reputation for practicality and good towing.

Reflecting the revulsion with which many caravanners of the period regarded built-in toilet rooms, the 1937 Sunset had one which was only accessible from outside. The 1938 Light Four was available in two versions, single panelled with plain roof at £132 or double panelled with lantern roof at £165. Exterior panelling was Sundeala hardboard and window frames were chromium plated solid brass. Models for 1939 were the 14ft Popular Four costing £120 with single panelling or £134 double panelled, 16ft Family Four priced at £152 or £168, 11ft 3in single panelled Three Berth at £113, 16ft Sunset Junior at £189 or £209, and the 17ft lantern roof double panelled Oriel priced at £315. The first post-war models in 1946 were the Family Four and the Sunset, and from about 1947 Siddall adopted the advertising slogan 'Britain's Best Caravan'. In the early post-war years awnings were still regarded as luxury items and only a few makers fitted an awning rail as standard but, when a new version of the Family Four with a door located on each side was introduced towards the end of 1949, a rail was provided on both sides of the van. Other model names in the period up to 1955 were Grey Dawn, Morning Mist, Four Winds, Rainbow, Sundial, Oriel and Southern Breeze.

Towards the end of 1955 a completely new range of vans was introduced – the £765 14ft 4in 2-3 berth Redwing, £815 15ft 11in 4 berth Hunter's Moon and £895 17ft 4in 4 berth Southern Sun. The new models all had front and rear ends moulded in GRP and incorporating full width bays. The wheel valances were also GRP and the side walls had a tumble home, once a common feature on good class vans but Siddall's were the last maker to use it. The vans were fitted with a new 'bumped' chassis and the interiors lifted them higher into the de luxe class. GRP was also

SIDDALL CARAVANS

DELIVERY FROM STOCK

TWO-ROOM FOUR-BERTH, fully equipped, fully guaranteed; 15 ft. × 6 ft. 4 ins. × 7 ft. 6 ins. overall height. **£107**

THREE-BERTH with dividing curtain, fully equipped, fully guaranteed, 11 ft. 2 ins. × 6 ft. 3 ins. × 7 ft. 6 ins. overall height. **£78**

TWO-BERTH, fully equipped, fully guaranteed, 10 ft. × 5ft. 6 ins. × 7 ft. 6 ins. overall height. **£58**

These prices do not allow trade discount. SIDDALLS are only obtainable ex-works.

BUILT to stand out all the year round, complete with all modern refinements and fitted with high grade undergear. SIDDALLS are well known as builders of the greatest value-for-money caravans in the country.

Illustrated literature on request. Open week-ends.

Two-Room Four-Berth Model

SIDDALL CARAVANS :: OLD BATH ROAD — CHELTENHAM —

used for the roof of the £950 18ft 4 berth Torbay introduced the following year, and at the same time a cranked axle was fitted to the other models, lowering the bodies by 3½in. Neville Siddall's wife died in 1956 and although their son John worked with his father his abiding interest was in farming and in 1958 it was announced that production was to cease.

This was not the end of Siddall however, and in 1960 the designs, name and right to manufacture were bought by the Staffordshire dealers Gailey Caravan Co. Ltd. The new vans were built for Gailey by the Kelston Caravan Co. Ltd, Hambrook, Bristol, and the initial models, the Torbay and Regina, both 18ft 8in 4

1934 advertisement. Neville Siddall had previously worked for Cheltenham.

1934 3 berth Siddall. Pre-war models were straightforward, moderately priced vans which acquired a reputation for practicality and good towing.

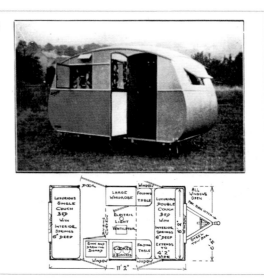

THREE - BERTH MODEL

Here is a particularly well appointed and useful size of caravan for three adults with neat dividing curtain easily towed by 9 h.p. cars. One of these was towed many hundreds of miles last year by an 8 h.p. car !

PRICE

(FULLY EQUIPPED)

£78

berths, were identical in appearance to the previous vans, but late in 1961 the radically different 16ft Delta appeared. This van was designed by Tom Karen of the Conran Design Group, with angular lines quite unlike conventional tourers. The shell had boldly coloured flat panels, a marked hipline and a ribbed unpainted window band with wrap-round rear windows. Internally, plain leathercloth wall covering contrasted with strongly coloured plain upholstery and curtains, and dark African hardwood furniture. At the 1962 Caravan Exhibition two new models were shown, the £1,950 22ft Nobleman, designed to suit the tastes of travelling showmen, and the 18ft Scotsman. By the end of 1963 the Torbay and Regina had both been discontinued, followed by the Delta late in 1964, and production ceased altogether early in 1965.

1939 Siddall Family Four. The provision of doors appears a little excessive!

1955 Redwing. Siddall's were the last maker to use tumble home for the side walls.

SILVER BALL

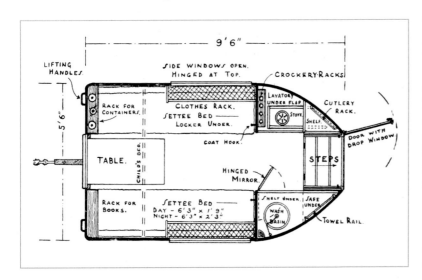

Lewis and Richards of Reed, near Royston, Hertfordshire, introduced the Silver Ball in 1933, only two examples having been produced when reported by *The Caravan* in July of that year. Costing £125, the 9ft 6in long x 5ft 6in wide van with rear entrance door had sleeping accommodation for two adults and a child. From floor to waistline the panelling was aluminium-faced plywood, the upper walls and roof being covered with stretched doped canvas. A 4 berth model was said to be planned for the 1934 season but nothing is known of it.

The 1933 Silver Ball was aerodynamically interesting, with a flat front and shaped rear!

SMITH
(VAGABOND)

D E Smith, trading as Smith Trailer Caravan Company of Tuffley Avenue, Gloucester, started production in 1925, making vans with the square ends, bowed sides and lantern roof typical of the period.

In common with a number of other makers, streamlining was adopted for the 1933 model year, and as well as fully equipped vans, unfurnished shells at prices of £45, £55, £65 and £80 for 8ft 6in, 10ft, 12ft and 14ft lengths respectively were also available.

After the Second World War, using the brand name Vagabond, production was restarted with a lantern roof model in 1946. Details are not known but this was probably the 16ft 6in Vagabond Queen living van. Later came the 4 berth Pup, priced at £279 and intended for the small car owner. This was not a particularly attractive van and nothing is known of the make after 1951.

The maker, D E Smith (left) and family with 1925 Smith caravan.

A Smith advertisement from 1933, the year streamlining was adopted.

SPEEDWELL

A 1933 Speedwell advertisement offering 'special winter prices'.

Speedwell Engineering Works, Ambleside Road, Lightwater, Surrey, produced a 9ft 6in 3 berth model in 1933. In October of that year the van was available at the 'special winter price' of £17 10s! The firm also offered to build caravans to customers' individual requirements at low rates during the winter months only. In 1937, trading as Speedwell Trailers, the firm had further special offers – the 3 berth Aero priced at £29 and the £31 Airflow. There were said to be only a limited number of these vans and that after they were sold the works were going to be rebuilt because the success of the previous few years demanded a larger output. Nothing further is known of the make however.

SPEEDWELL CAARAVANS

1934 models with improved instant coupling and jacking system will be ready shortly. Special winter prices. 9ft. 6in. model to sleep three, **£17 10s.** Caravans built to customers' individual requirements at low rates during winter months only. Terms to trade and hirers. ———— Speed with Safety.
SPEEDWELL ENGINEERING WORKS
Ambleside Road - - Lightwater - - Surrey

SPOWART

PRESDWOOD
INSIDE—AND OUT

A very fine example of interior and exterior Presdwood Panelling is this 15 ft. Super Caravan by Spowart Trailers, Glasgow. Tiling of the Kitchenette is Lacotile, the base of which is also Masonite Presdwood.

MASONITE
MADE IN SWEDEN

Masonite Ltd., Bevis Marks House, E.C.3

Spowart Trailers, Bowling, Glasgow, were offering Sedan, Sedan Cruiser, and Rainbow Cruiser caravans at prices from £50 in 1934 and there was a 15ft Super model in 1935. Despite suffering the same speed restriction noted for the Laycock the firm also produced three-wheeled vans, it being reported in 1937 that all the current Coronation models were three-wheelers. The small third wheel had a castor action and was carried by a transversely sprung auxiliary chassis. An advertisement in October 1937 announced that all 1938 three-wheeled models would have full width lantern roofs, oak interiors and Godins windows at no extra cost.

1935 Spowart Super. Some models featured a third wheel despite the handicap of a 20mph speed limit for such vans.

SUMMERFIELD *See* CHELTENHAM

SUNRAY

SUNRAY CARAVANS
FOR TIP-TOP VALUE

"Kent" Light 2 berth, 2 wheel model £80
"Devon" 2 berth, 2 wheel model .. £85
"Gloucester" 3 berth, 2 wheel model £105
"Surrey" 4 berth, 2 wheel model .. £130
"Bedford" 3 berth, 3 wheel model .. £110
"Sussex" 4 berth, 3 wheel model .. £135

4 Berth, 2 Wheel Surrey Model

All models are framed with ash and panelled with Masonite Presdwood, mounted on strong steel chassis with Brockhouse Chromium Plated Easy-clean Wheels. Two wheel models are fitted with Leason brace-operated jacks. All models have ample locker and wardrobe space and are fitted with Milbro double cooker, large porcelain enamelled wash basin, good quality lino, carpets, crockery and cutlery and numerous other refinements. Rice Edge Ball Hitch.

Manufactured by
SUNRAY CARAVANS BALLARD'S JOINERY WORKS
Rainham, Kent
Phone Rainham 81446

The Sunray "Surrey."
4 Berth Double Lined.   Suitable for 12 H.P. Car

The Sunray Surrey is framed with Ash, panelled with Masonite, lined with Limba and the furniture is of Oak. The roof is fully insulated of 4-ply construction including ½" Insulating board. Mounted on a strong steel Leason chassis fitted with easy-clean Chromium Plated wheels, complete with brakes including parking brake, brace operated legs and ball hitch.

The length is 14' 3", height 6' 5", width 6' 3", weight 14¼ cwts. The furniture consists of 1 Pullman Bed Settee and 1 Double Bed Settee each 6' × 4' by night.

There is 1 large Wardrobe and one large cupboard the doors opening to make two rooms, roof lockers on either side, 1 chest of 3 Drawers, 1 food cupboard, roof vent, 1 china cupboard, 1 large enamelled porcelain wash basin, Milbro double cooker, Chromium Plated Lamp, good quality Lino, Carpet, Crockery, Clock, Mirror and numerous other refinements. Beautifully finished in shades to approval. Subject to our usual guarantee.

(Terms—1/3rd with order, balance on delivery.)

Delivery 14/18 days.

Price   -   -   **£135** or Terms.

1938 Sunray Surrey. Here was another maker who produced three-wheeled models.

Introduced in 1938, Sunray Caravans were manufactured by Ballards Joinery Works, Rainham, Kent. There were six models – the £80 2 berth Kent, £85 10ft 3in 2 berth Devon, £105 12ft 3 berth Gloucester, £130 14ft 6in 4 berth Surrey, £110 12ft 3 berth Bedford and £135 14ft 6in 4 berth Sussex. The latter

1939 Sunray Surrey, its outline considerably more attractive that the 1938 model on the left.

two were three-wheeled vans with a sprung castor wheel at the front and a 'floating drawbar', pivoted to allow vertical movement.

SURREY

M I H Winder of Milner Road, Ravensbury Park, Morden, Surrey, built Surrey caravans from 1934. The 7½cwt 10ft x 5ft 6in 2 berth model cost £87 10s in 1935. Sides and roof were single panelled in standard Masonite Presdwood on ash framing, painted with six coats of white lead paint and finished in turquoise, blue and cream, but the roof panelling does not appear to have been canvas covered as was the normal practice. There was an ash-framed inward opening louvred window in each side with an oval metal-framed window at the front. The front end kitchen included an enamelled basin, aluminium draining board and two Valor oil stoves in an aluminium lined recess. A single light powered from the towing car battery provided night time illumination. As was common practice at the time, standard equipment included crockery, cutlery and cooking utensils, even extending to a dish cloth and duster. The dealers Welfords of Warninglid had a fleet of Surreys for hire. Astonishingly, considering the low price, Surrey offered a trade discount of 20% to dealers, which begs the question whether manufacture was financially viable, and production probably only continued for a short period.

1935 Surrey. With a 20% trade discount to dealers, manufacture of the £87 10s van can hardly have been financially viable.

SWALLOW

The makers of the 12ft 4 berth 'super-streamlined' Swallow had premises at Leslie Grove, East Croydon, and in 1934 were trading as Caravan Buildings, though by the beginning of 1935, when the price of the 10½cwt van was £110, the name had changed to Cara-Constructions. In October 1935 the firm was offering 1934 and 1935 models at prices between £70 and £80 as the last of their stock of caravans which 'must be cleared regardless of cost'. Whether this was because production had ceased or was simply the disposal of ex-hire vans is not clear. They were also offering Cara-Bungalows, which were 21ft x 7ft converted saloon coaches with solid rubber tyres, costing £35 each, fittings and furniture being available at extra cost.

1935 Swallow. The makers also offered 21ft x 7ft converted saloon coaches with solid tyres as cara-bungalows.

TAYLOR

John Taylor was head of an old-established coach-building company based at Foundry Street, Barnsley, who began building caravans in the early 1930s to maintain full employment for his workforce. The vans were mounted on Dixon-Bate chassis and the range included 2 and 4 berth models at prices ranging from £35 to £60. The vans are thought to have been of high quality and therefore no doubt uneconomic to produce at these prices. The business appears to have eventually passed into the hands of the local co-operative society, who used the premises for maintaining their own transport.

THOMSON

1922 Thomson. Prior to this the firm had built horse drawn caravans.

Daniel Thomson was a Scottish joiner and cartwright who started building horse drawn caravans in 1908. The early vans were the bow top gypsy type, followed after the First World War by showmen's vans with elaborate carving and decoration. Horse drawn caravans continued to be built until 1926 but trailer caravan manufacture started about 1922. For a time both trailer caravans and bodies for motor caravans were made, and a hire fleet of trailer caravans was also operated. The early trailer vans had the square ends, bowed sides and lantern roofs typical of a number of contemporary makes but by 1930 streamlining had been adopted, and early 1930s models had a shallow projecting tail which served as an outside locker to house a latrine tent, spade and other loose equipment. The 16ft 4 berth of 1934 cost

£175 including Dunlopillo mattresses and chromium-plated steel window frames with a choice of oak or mahogany for the interior woodwork.

Caravan manufacturers in the 1930s did not generally consider aerodynamic drag to be an important factor in design, the purpose of streamlining being regarded as primarily aesthetic. However, wind tunnel tests carried out at the Royal Technical College, Glasgow, by Daniel's son David, using models of caravans bodies behind a 12/4 Austin, a popular towing car at the time, indicated significant drag at speeds of 35mph upwards, and although the speed limit for cars towing two wheeled trailers was then only 30mph, the 1936 Almond was the first in a long line of models with a V roof and carefully sloped end walls set at the precise angle indicated by the tests. Thomson's also built the Everyman caravan for the camping equipment supplier's, Black's of Greenock. The factory, at Carron, Falkirk, was extended during the Second World War and the firm also invested in new machinery. War work included the manufacture of trailers, ambulances and ammunition boxes.

A range of caravans was in production again by 1946, including the £495 14ft 6in Endrick, and in 1947 Thomson's were advertising Avon, Endrick, Kelvin, Carron, Forth and Don models. Vans exhibited at the 1948 Earl's Court Motor Show were the £175 8ft 2 berth Dart camping trailer, £395 12ft 4 berth Avon and £750 17ft 6in 4 berth Kelvin Star.

1947 Thomson Endrick. Caravan production had restarted by 1946, following war work which included the manufacture of trailers, ambulances and ammunition boxes.

The Dart was actually a mini-caravan which, whilst not having full headroom, had a rigid body and was equipped with double bed, dining table, clothes storage and cooking and washing facilities. Writing in *The Caravan* in August/September 1949, Norris Bridgens describes a West Country trip with a Thomson camping trailer towed by a two-cylinder Jowett Bradford van. The 1 in 6 climb out of Gunnislake was accomplished at 6mph in bottom gear and, having stalled on the 1 in 4 Porlock Hill due to 'the driver of the Morgan in front muffing his gear change', Bridgens received a 15 minute telling off from an AA Scout on the foolishness of attempting the climb with such an outfit.

1948 Thomson Kelvin Star, one of three models exhibited at the 1948 Motor Show.

Thomson camping trailer with two-cylinder Jowett Bradford van in 1949. Norris Bridgens received a 15-minute telling off from an AA Scout for attempting to climb the 1 in 4 Porlock Hill with such an outfit.

1952 Thomson Braemar. The open fireplace was very questionable on safety grounds.

1952 Thomson Almond. Introduced in 1949, 2,200 had been produced by 1954.

The Avon was sold by Black's as the Good Companion and Thomson also acted as distributors for Raven caravans. The 1949 Motor Show saw two new models, the £650 20ft Deveron living van, which had a choice of gas or solid fuel heating, and the Almond tourer. Almond models featured in the range for some years and in 1954 it was reported that 2,200 had been produced. The £750 22ft coach shaped

Braemar introduced at the beginning of 1951 had the unusual feature of an open grate fireplace – very questionable on safety grounds. As well as the 14ft Almond at £298, three new models were exhibited at the 1952 Motor Show, the £185 9ft Carron, £450 17ft Annan and £675 22ft Solway. Furniture in the centre lounge of the Solway included a Put-U-Up bed settee and matching fireside chairs. In 1955 Thomson were also distributing vans made by Carrson of Fife, and David Thomson, managing director of Thomson's, was a board member of Africaravans Ltd, Natal, South Africa, a company established in 1956 for the production and sale of Thomson caravans throughout Africa, later sold to Caravans International.

The range for 1956 comprised 14ft 6in Almond models in £335 Mark V (without toilet compartment) and £355 Mark VII (with toilet compartment) versions, £275 11ft Leven, £435 16ft Forth and £675 22ft Mark III Solway. Towards the end of 1956 a completely new range of vans was introduced, all with 'Glen' names - the £295 11ft Glendale, £375 14ft Glenalmond and £480 16ft 3in Gleneagle. New shaping included a shallow V roof rounded at the ends and bow windows front and rear on the two larger

vans. New models shown at the 1958 Motor Show were the 10ft Glen and the Glenrosa. Although initially for export only, the Glen became available on the home market in 1960. The Glenrosa was advertised as an 18ft van although in a road and site test in the February 1959 issue of *The Caravan* the body length over the bays was said to be 19ft 9in, with an overall width of 7ft 9½in – 3½in over the legal limit! There was also a 22ft Glenlyon model at that time and later in 1959 Thomson's announced the £850 30ft x 8ft Great Glen mobile home, although this does not appear to have been put into production and certainly by 1962 only tourers were being produced, the largest model being the 18ft 6in Glenrosa. Towards the end of 1962 the vans were restyled again, with a distinctive profile to be known as the T-line. The 'Glen' names were retained, the new models being the 10ft Glen, 11ft 6in Glendale, 13ft Glenelg, 15ft Glenalmond and 16ft 6in Gleneagle. At that time approximately one third of the vans being produced was exported, one third sold in England, and the remaining third sold in Scotland.

By 1965 the floor area of the factory had been extended to 97,000sq ft with up to 15 acres of parking area for finished vans. Thomson's became a public company in 1967 and group profit for that year was £207,592, rising to £280,508 in 1968, with caravan production for the first three months of 1969 being 21% higher by value than for the corresponding period of 1968. In 1969 Thomson's registered a new company, Thomson T-line (Homes) Ltd, with the intention of manufacturing mobile homes, chalets and special units. Only a range of holiday caravans was actually produced but in 1973 fifty 26ft Strathallan holiday vans, extensively modified for residential use, were supplied to house British Aluminium Corporation workers and their families at Invergordon, Cromarty Firth in the Scottish Highlands. The holiday vans in 1974 comprised the 21ft Strathblane, 21ft Strathclyde, Strathallan and 30ft Strathdee. By 1976, with sales falling, budget Clan and River models joined the Glen vans, but production finally ended in 1982 following four years of continuous losses.

THORN

R L Thorn is known to have been building caravans in the East Midlands before the Second World War. In 1950 he went out to Canada and became a substantial caravan manufacturer there.

TIMMIS

W F Timmis manufactured caravans at some time prior to the Second World War.

TRAVEL TRAILERS

1937 Travel Trailers Short 4. The makers had previously specialised in high grade sectional buildings.

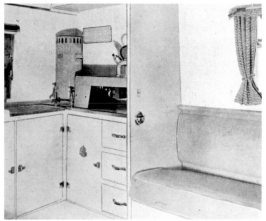

Vivians (Hounslow) Ltd, Staines Road, Hounslow, Middlesex, had specialised in high grade sectional buildings for 17 years before introducing the £298 22cwt 16ft 6in Travel Trailers Short 4, designed by A H Bull, in 1937. The rear end kitchen, equipped with three-burner Vac stove and Vac water heater, was lined with stipple-glazed asbestos sheeting and separated from the rest of the van by a roller blind. The furniture and partitions were built from Venesta blockboard, the interior was finished in Glossex hard semi-gloss paint and the floor, apart from the kitchen, was covered with Karvel carpeting. An Economy

Model was available at £260. Production resumed for a few years after the Second World War, a 1949 advertisement describing the model S4 as having 'a distinctive "quiet" interior design with more room than you would think.' The advertisement features a drawing of a van which appears little different from the 1937 van although length and price are not stated.

TRAVELWEL

Travelwel Caravan Co, Alveston, Gloucestershire, claimed in their advertising to have been making caravans since 1928, but no details of their activities prior to the Second World War are known. The claim is made in a 1953 advertisement which appears to be the first indication of post-war activity, although since the firm did very little advertising it is difficult to be sure. The model range in 1953 was quite extensive for what seems to have been a small company and comprised the 'new' £495 22ft x 7ft 6in Residential, £395 17ft 6in x 6ft 6in Maisonette, £295 13ft 6in x 6ft 6in Family Four and the 'famous touring vans', the £150 8½cwt 2 berth, £185 9½cwt 3 berth and £245 14cwt 4 berth.

Late in 1956 it was reported that the business of Premier Caravans Ltd, Newton Abbot, Devon, was being wound up, but that the name would be retained by Mr L Kerkut, a director of the company, who was to make Premiers at Bristol, where he had acquired the old established business of Travelwell (sic) Caravan & Trailer Co. It appears that initially both Premier and Travelwel caravans were built – dealers were still advertising Travelwel to the beginning of 1958, although confusingly one dealer referred to the Travelwel Marquis, which is listed elsewhere as a Premier model. One report of November 1957 even speaks of two new Travelwel vans, so perhaps there was some indecision about which name to use.

UNIVERSAL

Universal Trailer Industries Ltd, Delrow, Aldenham, near Watford, Hertfordshire, manufactured a range of utility trailers and in 1938 introduced a £45 2 berth sleeping trailer. Equipment

included a lean-to tent, air beds, Demon stoves, five gallon water tank, crockery, and electric lighting powered from the towing car battery.

1938 Universal sleeping trailer. A range of utility trailers was also manufactured.

'UNIVERSAL' THE TRAILER BUILDERS TO THE WORLD

OFFER THE FINEST TRAILER VALUE

ON THE ONE HAND — AND ON THE OTHER

The New Sleeping Trailer

EVERY TYPE OF TWO-WHEEL TRAILER and Chassis FOR PRIVATE USE and every trade. Leaflets are available for many special types of TRAILERS FOR TRADES AND BUSINESSES. OUR STANDARD LIST describes all our Standard Models. PROMPT DELIVERY IN FIVE SERVICEABLE COLOURS.

- END KITCHEN
- HARDBOARD PANELS
- LOW CENTRE OF GRAVITY
- NO SWAY
- NO SWING

Well tested during the past season this Model Two Berth Sleeping Trailer is ideal, particularly for the owner of a light car. Equipped with everything required for two persons, including air beds, a 5-gal. water tank, tap, sink, two oil stoves, etc., and A LARGE WHITE SIDE TENT, it is complete and ready for the road.

VAGABOND *See* SMITH

VAGABOND VAN

HW Greenwood, trading as St Leonards Motor and Caravan Works at St Leonards, near Ringwood, Hampshire, produced Vagabond Van caravans in 1934. He claimed to have over 25 years' practical engineering, joinery and aircraft experience.

The 10ft long x 5ft 10in wide 2 berth model cost 95 guineas and had ash/pine framing finished internally with stain and varnish. The single panelling was canvas covered plywood below the waistline, with proofed canvas above.

Furnishing was basic with camp-type beds and mattresses folding to store in narrow seat lockers during the day, a cupboard across the V front end and a two-burner stove. Since the beds/bedding must have fully occupied the seat lockers, the front end cupboard appears to have been the only storage for clothing and personal effects. Equipment included saucepans, cutlery and crockery.

The van could also be hired, with charges varying between £2 17s 6d and £3 per week depending on the season.

There was a 3 berth model and the hire fleet was said to include various makes of caravan as well as tent trailers and goods trailers.

The 1934 brochure included a poem extolling the virtues of caravanning, the first verse of which read:

I'm a vagabond man with a Vagabond Van,
If but for a few short weeks;
My clothes are patched, there's a bank overdraft –
But the roof has got no leaks!

I know not where the white road runs,
    Nor what the blue hills are,
But a man can have the Sun for friend
    And for his guide a Star.

And there's no end of voyaging,
    When once the call is heard—
For the river calls, and the road calls,
    And oh! the call of a bird!

1934 Vagabond Van. The maker's brochure included a poem about 'a vagabond man with a Vagabond van'.

VANCRAFT *See* VANMASTER

VANMASTER & VANCRAFT

The early history of this make is rather confusing. R G Sparrow of Ongar Road, Dunmow, Essex, was advertising Vancraft caravans from around 1948 and in a 1949 advertisement claimed 15 years of caravan building experience, although no details are known of any models before the Second World War and in 1953 Sparrow was only claiming to have been building caravans since 1939. Around 1949, P H Sparrow of West End Avenue, Leyton, London, E10, was also advertising Vancraft caravans. After advertising both Vancraft and Vanmaster caravans in mid-1949, R G Sparrow was only using the Vanmaster name by 1950, although P H Sparrow continued to advertise Vancraft caravans into 1954 when the range comprised £295 14ft, £305 15ft, £395 16ft, £495 17ft and £495 18ft vans. R G Sparrow's 1949 Vancraft Standard was a 17ft 6in x 6ft 8in 3 or 4 berth with end kitchen and two entrance doors, priced at £495. The van was fitted with a Pither's stove and insulated with Fibreglass. The 1951 Vanmaster range comprised a 22ft van in Special, Standard and Economy versions priced at £695, £620 and £490 respectively. There were also 17ft 6in and 15ft vans at £360 and £295, and holiday caravans were available for hire. 'Early

1951 Vanmaster Special, also available in less expensive standard and economy versions.

1967 Vanmaster, with a moulded GRP body and produced by various firms.

delivery' was offered in 1951, an improvement on 1950 when delivery on the Special was quoted at three to four months. The Special was also available as an unfurnished shell costing £360 in 1950. In 1951 P H Sparrow's Vancrafts were offered in 15ft, 16ft and 17ft 6in lengths with prices ranging between £295 and £445. The 1952 Vanmaster Standard cost £650 and was advertised as 'the only caravan to customer's layout at fixed price (over 100 different layouts built)'. Production ceased around 1955, although R G Sparrow was still advertising Vanmaster touring caravans for hire in 1957.

In 1967 R G Sparrow, then located at Holly Hill, Basset, Southampton, and producing Ocean Queen yachts, re-entered the caravan market with a 12ft 6in Vanmaster tourer. The body was moulded in GRP and featured bays at both ends and a 4ft x 2ft roof hatch.

This van was available as an unfitted shell costing £185, or could be fitted out to the buyer's requirements costing from £395. Sparrows were not able to produce the van in sufficient quantities and General Caravan Services of Hampshire took over manufacture and marketing. They too found difficulty in meeting demand and for around two years from 1968 had the shells fitted out by Chas. Mitchell & Sons Ltd of Downton, near Salisbury, makers of Avon caravans. In 1971 production was taken over by W & J Tod Ltd, boat builders, of Weymouth, Dorset, who produced unfitted shells only, adding a 15ft model. Production ended later in the 1970s as the number of people prepared to fit out a shell for themselves declined.

VICKERS

Although it appears that Harry Vickers was in business before the Second World War, nothing is known of the vans from this period, and whilst postwar vans were in production before 1951, an advertisement in May of that year only refers to the Vickers holiday camp at Westgate, Morecambe, and to being 'agents for leading makes of caravans'. The caravan factory was at White Lund Road, Morecambe, and the furniture was produced by cabinet makers, most of whom had previously been employed by Waring and Gillow's at Lancaster. Until around 1952 the vans were fairly plain in appearance and had chipboard floors carried on 3in x 2in timber bearers mounted on Leason chassis. The resin bonded plywood roofs were covered with linen bonded on with high oil base paint and finished with undercoat and gloss paint. Production numbers were very small – around one van every two weeks – and most of them were sold for siting at the Westgate camp. Around 1952 the floor construction was changed to a box section with 3in x 1in timber, skinned top and bottom with ½in resin bonded ply. This permitted a lighter steel chassis, which Vickers manufactured themselves. Front and rear bays were fitted after 1952 and shapely, high quality touring vans of various lengths were made until about 1963. The £555 16ft Lunedale of 1959 was available in six different layouts and had exterior panelling of 18 gauge aluminium, oak lining and leaded light windows designed by a local man, Malcolm Gudgeon, with a tulip design in the centre surrounded by 6in square panels.

The firm became increasingly involved in building vans to special order for travellers and after production of tourers ceased this became their sole occupation until going into liquidation in 1977. The bodies on vans built for travellers gradually acquired embellishment in the form of stainless steel panels, polished aluminium mouldings with coloured trim inserts, and engraved windows featuring a basket of flowers and a bunch of grapes in each corner, coloured to the customer's choice. Internally the vans came to have engraved mirrors on all doors and to the interior of the roof lockers. From 1975 the single axle was replaced with close coupled twin axles to cope with the increasing weight resulting from all these additions. Harry Vickers died aged around 80 shortly before the firm closed down.

1961 Vickers 14ft model. Shapely high quality tourers were built until c.1963 but the firm later specialised in building vans to special order for travellers.

WALFORD

A mid-1930s make of which no details are known.

WALPOLE

The Walpole Caravan Co, Brasenose Driftway, Horspath Road, Cowley, Oxford, were producing a £95 4 berth sectional van, which could be taken apart for storage, in 1934. 1935 models were a £65 2 berth, £85 Light 4 berth and £105 14ft 6in 4 berth.

1934 Walpole was a sectional van. It could be taken apart for storage.

By 1936 the price of the Light 4 berth had increased to £95 and the 14ft 6in van, now named the Oxford, cost £120.

WANDERLUST

A NEW STANDARD IN CARAVAN TRAVEL COMFORT

The Finest Value Double Panelled Four Berth Two Room Caravan on The Market

Complete **£125** Ex Works

or by deferred payments

Specifications of the "WANDERLUST" STANDARD Model.

Length 14ft. 6in. Width 6ft. 5in. Height 7ft. 10in.
Double-panelled frame-work of seasoned ash.
Exterior—Sundeala or other hard board walls.
Interior panelled in mahogany.
All-steel chassis. Brace operated legs.
Five windows, four ventilators, in addition to double door.
Two full-size double bed settees.
22in. wardrobe.
2 burner Milbro wickless oil cooker.
Deep wash basin and draining board.
Well ventilated Larder (away from Cooker).
Airing cupboard.
Specially constructed Bottle Cupboard.
Cutlery Box.
Exceptional locker space.
2 Electric Lights with independent switches.
Curtains fitted to match upholstery.

You can obtain *some* good features in every Caravan—but you can get them *all* in a "Wanderlust"—the real modern Caravan that will give you home comforts.

The layout has been planned by an experienced Caravanner for practical caravanning, and the spaciousness of the interior, the utilisation of every possible space for lockers, cupboards, etc., must be seen to be appreciated. Furthermore, the cost—we invite intending purchasers of a Caravan to compare the "Wanderlust" item by item, specification by specification, with any other caravan on the market. We have no hesitation in stating that the "Wanderlust" will compare favourably with many at double the price.

Send to-day for illustrated booklet.

BARRATT & ROBINSON LTD.
Established 1877
288-310, YORK WAY, KING'S CROSS, LONDON, N.7
Telegrams: KASTOREN HOLWAY, LONDON ● TELEPHONE NORTH 4021

The Wanderlust of 1938-39 was made by Barratt & Robinson Ltd, York Way, King's Cross, London N7. Advertised in March of that year as a 13ft 6in x 6ft 5in 4 berth costing £125, by August the length had increased to 14ft 6in although the price was unchanged. Said to be designed by an experienced caravanner, the Wanderlust was double panelled on an ash frame and equipped with a two burner oil stove for cooking. A 2 berth de luxe version was offered as a living van at £198 10s, a particular feature being a double bed which folded against the rear wall during the day, leaving more clear floor space than could usually be found in a van of this size. Seating was provided by two movable chairs, and heating by a Smith & Wellstood coal fire. Cooking and lighting were by gas and the toilet room was fitted with a Sanutrene chemical closet, shower and wash basin. Other furniture included a wardrobe, writing bureau, chest of lockers, airing cupboard and table.

1939 4 berth Wanderlust. The 2 berth living van version offered foldaway double bed, movable chairs, coal fire and toilet room equipped with chemical closet, shower and wash basin.

WAYSIDE (1)

W B Stubbs & Son, of Progress Works, Hawksworth, Nottinghamshire, was originally established in the early nineteenth century and is listed in White's directory for 1885 as William Blount Stubbs, agricultural engineer and implement maker, machinist, blacksmith, wheelwright and farmer. In the depression of the late 1920s W H Stubbs, who owned the business at that time, decided that he would design a caravan for his workmen to build instead of laying them off. The 1929 Wayside collapsible trailer caravan was the result, named after Wayside Cottage in Hawksworth where Stubbs was born. The van was well built with ash chassis, steel towbar, automatic brakes, semi-elliptic springs and adjustable legs. The body was constructed on an ash frame with whitewood panels and fitted out with lockers, cooker, sink and electric light. The wood roof, covered with painted canvas, was raised and lowered by a winding mechanism. Infills between roof and body were made of rubber impregnated khaki twill with a window on each side, and there was an entrance at each end,

secured by turnbuckles. Open for use the caravan measured 7ft square with 6ft headroom. The spring mattress berths were each 2ft wide and the closed height of the £67 10s 4cwt caravan was 5ft. Alternative layouts were available at extra cost and optional extras included a folding table for £1 10s and a folding lavatory seat for £1 5s. The cost of supplying and fitting a towing bracket to the purchaser's car was £1 10s. Two models were available in 1933, costing £60 and £70, with a lean-to tent for either van costing an additional £10. An extra berth or two children's berths could also be ordered. The caravans were guaranteed for six months and a total of 30-40 were built.

1929 Wayside, built by an agricultural engineer to avoid laying off men in the Depression.

WAYSIDE (2)

A 1938 advertisement by J Brockhouse & Co Ltd lists a number of caravan makers using Brockhouse Chassis including one called Wayside, but no other reference to this manufacturer has been found.

WEATHERSHIELDS

Weathershields Ltd, Moor Road, Birmingham, produced the Cara-Bed folding sleeping box in 1934. Designed to be carried on the rear luggage rack of a car and sleeping two, the cost was £20.

1934 Weathershields Cara-bed: sleeping accommodation only, carried on the rear luggage rack.

Folds compactly for carrying on luggage grid, and does not interfere with normal driving.

Opened out in a few minutes, it is made absolutely rigid by strong supports and is rattleproof, waterproof and windproof at all points.

Completely equipped with mattress in sections, all self-contained, yet full weight is only equal to one extra passenger.

Ample sleeping accommodation for two adults and hammock provided at end for child or clothing, etc.

Internal electric light; spring-type ventilator in roof; efficient "lift-the-dot" fasteners.

A coachbuilt job designed by Craftsmen for lasting service.

Convenient for storing when not in use—ground space taken up only 4' 2" × 1' 8"

£20 OR ON DEFERRED TERMS

Write to-day for fully descriptive folder

WEATHERSHIELDS, LTD.
48 MOOR ST., BIRMINGHAM

WEATHERSHIELDS'
CARA·BED
for Carefree Touring!

WEL-FOUR *See* FREEMAN

WILTON

R E Wiltshire of The Wilton Curb Company Ltd, Percy Street, Newcastle-on-Tyne, was the designer of a new collapsible caravan reported in *The Caravan* in August 1933. Weighing 5cwt and claimed to take 15 seconds to erect or make ready for towing, no canvas was used in the construction of the 7ft long x 5ft wide van – all panels being made from coach painted plywood. By 1934 the firm was trading as The Wilton Caravan Company, and in production form, named The Whippet, the van cost 59 guineas. The weight had increased to 5½cwt but the erection time had gone down to 10 seconds! The Chalet was a larger model, fitted with a two-burner petrol stove and washing cabinet, which cost 75 guineas. By 1935 the prices had reduced to £59 and £75 and the vans were fitted with Wilton's 'unique patent lavatory'.

1934 Wilton Whippet, whose claimed erection time was 15 seconds, later reduced to 10 seconds!

1934 Wilton Chalet. By 1935 both Whippet and Chalet were fitted with Wilton's 'unique patent lavatory'.

WINCHESTER

Bertram Hutchings and his wife, of Winchester, were both followers of the 'simple life' and proprietors of a food reform shop. Newly married in 1911, they decided to live in a tent, moving for the winter into an 18ft caravan which they had used for their summer holiday. Whilst very comfortable this was cumbersome and heavy, requiring two horses to draw it, and after living in the van for some months the couple decided that a 14ft van could provide almost equal accommodation but be light enough to be drawn by a single horse. This van was built early in 1912 with assistance from relatives in the coach building business. A similar van followed and the two were so well received that Hutchings decided to go into serious production. By the summer of 1912 a small fleet of these lightweight 14ft vans had been built and were hired out at £5 per week plus £1 for a horse.

Prior to the First World War, hiring appears to have been the most important part of the business and, interviewed in 1936, Hutchings only referred to the 14ft hire vans although other sources refer to the first van produced being an 8cwt 6ft 4in long x 4ft 6in wide pony caravan for personal use and that a 10ft van weighing 12¾cwt was built in 1912. Whilst in produc-

tion form the 10ft van weighed 15cwt, this was still little more than half the weight of a gypsy caravan of equivalent size. Larger vans were also made under the model names of Concord and Voyager. With his own van Hutchings used a light gig which trailed behind to act as the caravan 'dinghy' or tender. A pony for the gig ran alongside and for steep hills could be harnessed next to the horse. The idea was not taken up at the time but an obvious present day parallel is the trend for large motorhomes to tow a small car.

The Hutchings continued to live in caravans until the outbreak of war in 1914, by which time they had a hire fleet of 15 vans together with 12 horses. The horses were quickly commandeered by the War Office and it appeared that production would have to cease but it soon became apparent that caravans had many uses for war purposes and several were sent overseas to be used by Red Cross detachments and for officers' quarters. Hutchings was not accepted for war service on medical grounds but was proud of his contribution to the war effort in building caravans on motor chassis for various uses, the first in 1915 being a mobile recruiting office for the Royal Navy.

Hutchings built his first trailer caravan in 1920, but motor caravans proved more popular in the first

1920 Hutchings and Model T Ford. The first trailer caravans were very similar in appearance to the earlier horse drawn vans.

few years of the decade and a number were built until buyers came to see that the imposition of taxation by horsepower made them a less attractive proposition than a car and caravan combination. Building of four-wheeled Concord models in lengths up to 21ft continued after the War – intended for semi-static use and being delivered by lorry or by rail to the nearest station and on to the site pulled by two horses. Occasional orders for these vans were still being received as late as 1936. The first trailer caravans were very similar in appearance to the horse drawn vans but by 1924 the Voyageur had evolved. Selling at between £200 and £250, usually 12ft long with straight ends, bowed sides, lantern roof, nearside door and real leaded windows – a bay one at the rear – the Voyageur combined romantic appeal with a practical interior, retaining a traditional look but better suited to motor towing, and remained in demand until 1932.

In the late 1920s, along with other makers, Hutchings was trying to attract users of the new models of small cars which were expanding the motoring community. The Austin Seven was the best known although the Jowett was probably more popular with caravanners, and the Tom Thumb, priced at about £87, was aimed at this market. This 7ft 6in long van had a plain roof and the side walls were slightly bowed from end to end to reduce drag. The overall height was only 5ft 10in but on site headroom of 5ft 8in was achieved by lowering the caravan floor to the ground and closing the ensuing gap with canvas brailing. Hutchings himself was short, and the relatively low headroom was probably decided on the basis of what suited his own height! This type of construction did not allow a conventional axle and the Tom Thumb appears to have been the first successful model with independent suspension, using pairs of leaf springs.

Other small vans were the Nimblette of 1929, originally with a roof more or less semi-circular in cross section but reverting to a more conventional plain roof for 1930-31, and the Lady Nimble, exhibited at the 1929 Motor Show. This van had a lantern roof, cavity walls and an emergency toilet, a proprietary closet called the Vantour.

At the 1930 Motor Show Hutchings introduced a streamlined van with the roof curving down to all four body corners. This was the Winchester and it acquired such fame that the model name was adopted as the brand name. In 1931 the range comprised the 8ft 3in 7cwt 2 berth Nimblette, 9ft 10½cwt 2-4 berth Lady Nimble, 12ft 15cwt 3-4 berth Voyageur and two versions of the Winchester, a 12ft 6in 3-4 berth weighing 8¾cwt and 14ft 6in 4 berth weighing 11½cwt. Dorothy Una Ratcliffe (Mrs McGrigor Phillips) described a 5,000 mile tour in 1931 from Cape Town to Durban in her book *South African Summer*. Her 14ft 6in Winchester was painted crocus yellow and brown with a vivid belt of marigold dividing the two colours, and was fitted with grids fore and aft to carry tents. The name 'African Marigold' was painted in black and orange letters above one of the windows. An indication of the variety of special order vans being produced is given by some of the vans in the yard when Mrs Phillips collected hers, including one painted a sober grey and inscribed 'Prepare Ye the Way of the Lord', and a finely decorated model built to the order of one of the Cholcotes, the hop picking Romanies.

The fact that streamlining had become the dominant factor in caravan design was amply demonstrated at the first trailer caravan rally in history, held at Minehead on 27th August 1932. Five out of six awards for 2, 3 and 4 berth vans were won by streamlined models, four of them Winchesters. In May of the following year the RAC held a rally at Cheltenham at which Bertram Hutchings competed in the driving tests towing a much admired 16ft 8in Winchester with streamlined lantern roof. An 18ft lantern roof living van won four prizes at the 1935 Junior Car Club National Rally and was a star exhibit at the following Motor Show. It divided into three rooms, the centre one incorporating the toilet and bath. Floor, walls and roof all had cavities, there was a coal fire with hot water tank and airing cupboard above, refrigerator, cold tank and electric water pump, six electric lights and a fan run from a battery chargeable from the car, a large tent locker and vacuum-servo brakes – all contributing to the price of £435. This van led on to a series of large luxury models under the name Royal, reaching a length of 20ft in 1938. Another model of the late 1930s was the Winchester Wagon, which had an American-influenced coach shaped body but only sold in small numbers. Chemical closets in Winchesters of this period were specially made with a rubber-lined lid clamping down at three points to prevent splashing out whilst the van was on the move. Specials built for Bertram Hutchings' own use were the 11ft Dumpy of 1933 and a 14ft 6in model in 1937. Originally located at Southgate Street,

Winchester, by 1931 the firm had moved to Elm Street and by 1939 to Stockbridge Road.

Caravan building gave way to other work during the Second World War and as late as August 1946 it was reported that whilst caravan production would resume as soon as possible, war work was still preventing this. In 1948 the 14ft Winchester cost £975 and the 20ft Royal £1,800 including a toilet and shower compartment with hot and cold running water. At the 1949 Motor Show, as well as the Royal, now priced at £1,750, were 2 and 4 berth versions of the 14ft Winchester Earl's Court, the latter costing £1,025. Bertram Hutchings' son, Lionel, spent his honeymoon in a Winchester caravan on a tour of

1931 14ft 6in Winchester. When this streamlined van was introduced in 1930 it acquired such fame that the model name was adopted as the brand name.

Interior of the 1931 Winchester.

Late 1930s Winchester Wagon, whose American-influenced coach shaped body did not prove popular with British buyers.

1953 Winchester Royal. The make was renowned for elegance, superb workmanship and completeness of equipment.

Devon following his marriage to Margaret Samways on 4th April 1949.

By 1951 the Royal was available in 18ft and 21 ft versions. New models exhibited at the 1953 Motor Show were the 12ft 6in 2 berth Pipit and, reviving a pre-war name, the 15ft 6in 4 berth Voyageur, together with an 18ft Royal. The 1954 show saw the Pipit, a new 16ft 6in van, the Widgeon, and an 18ft 6in Royal, whilst in 1955 as well as the £850 Pipit and £1,700 Royal, a new £1,150 Voyageur was exhibited, 16ft 6in long with the same layout as the Widgeon but having a full width lantern roof with six perspex lights on each side at the top of the walls. In the British Caravan Road Rallies Lionel Hutchings won the Class C award in 1954, the *Caravan* Trophy in 1956 when Winchesters also won the Team Prize, and the Brighton Trophy in 1958.

Winchesters were called the Rolls-Royce of caravans, testament to their elegance, superb

workmanship and completeness of equipment. This quality was achieved in premises unsuited to efficient production – the Stockbridge Road works consisted of a row of sheds behind a red brick Victorian crescent and some vans had to be lowered to the ground from a shop floor about 9ft higher. In the early post-war years when caravan manufacturers had to switch to aluminium for exterior panelling due to a shortage of hardboard, sheet as thick as 16 gauge was used to ensure flat wall panels.

Some idea of the practical features built into the vans can be gained from a report on the Pipit appearing in *The Caravan* for May 1954. A rubber pad on the metal drawbar cover protected the paintwork from damage when the throw-over type jockey wheel rested on it, and without getting into the van it was possible to open a cupboard just inside the door containing two water cans, wheel brace and gas locker key, all held in place by spring clips. Recessed into the floor was a doormat which when lifted out revealed a ventilated panel allowing the van to be kept aired when not in use. The panel lifted out in turn to reveal a framework with large gaps so that when the van floor was swept the dirt could be easily deposited outside, and because the mat was surrounded by a capping, raised to protect the Hardura floor covering from scraping shoes, a small part of the floor to one side was gently sloped to make it flush with the capping for a few inches so that dirt could be brushed over the capping. Holes in the bottom of the roof lockers allowed dust or spillages to be brushed out, and beading around the top of the gas locker in the wardrobe included a gap in one corner for easy cleaning. The table was hinged so that it could be turned up to the ceiling for better access to the chest of drawers between the berths, and in a drawer under the drainer was a loose metal tray for soap, dish mop, etc. Fittings included a book rack, fitted crockery cupboard, cutlery tray, magazine rack and shaving mirror.

Production ceased in 1959 but this was not quite the end of Winchesters because in 1961 it was reported that, with the full co-operation of Bertram and Lionel Hutchings, Stephens & West Ltd, manufacturers of Stirling Caravans, were to make a new version of the Pipit, and Winchester models were included in the Stirling Range until 1963. Bertram Hutchings died in 1967 at the age of 81.

WINDSOR

The only model known to have been produced is a 12cwt 4 berth van of 1936.

WINSOME

Nothing is known of the activities of L Mellor (Hartshill) Ltd, Victoria Street, Hartshill, Stoke-on-Trent, prior to the Second World War but in advertising in 1949 they claimed to have been in the caravan trade for 20 years. The first post-war model appears to have been a 16ft 4 berth lantern roof van of 1947, later known as the Majestic. In 1948 L Mellor, at that time trading as Winsome Caravans, Stubbs Gate, Newcastle, Stafffordshire, offered one of his recently introduced Winsome Wizards as a prize in a competition to find out what the caravan public wanted. The Wizard was a coach shaped van 16ft 3in long x 6ft 10in wide, priced at £550. The layout provided two double beds with a front end kitchen, and Isoflex insulation was a £20 extra. There were two new coach shaped 4 berth vans in 1949, the 18ft 6in Craftmaster and 18ft 3in Pioneer. Prices in 1950 were £565 for the Craftmaster, with a Pither's stove available as an extra, and £450 for the Pioneer, with a full oven cooker as an extra. For 1951 the Pioneer became the Pioneer II, there was a new 20ft van, the Champion, and at the end of the year two versions of the Whirlwind were introduced, the conventionally shaped 20ft, later 22ft Mark I and the coach shaped 22ft Mark II, both 4 berths vans with a separate end bedroom.

It was reported in 1953 that the company had extended their factory by 5,000 square feet. Models at

1951 Winsome Whirlwind Mk I. A Mk II version with coach shaped body was available at the same time.

1947 Winsome. The makers claimed to have been in the caravan trade since 1929.

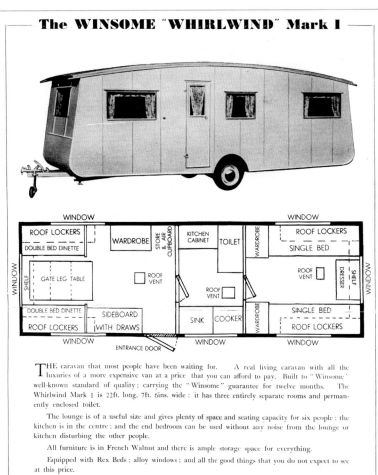

WINSOME "PERFECTION"
A Maximum Sized Van with a charm all its own

1955 Winsome Perfection – the firm was at pains to point out the high standard to which the furniture was constructed.

this time were the £360 Whirlwind Sixteen, £430 Whirlwind Eighteen and the Whirlwind Mark I. For 1954 the Whirlwind went into a Mark III version, the Mark IV being introduced later that year. This £515 van had kitchen and toilet room at the front end, the remainder of the van being occupied by a lounge which could be divided by sliding doors into two double bedrooms at night. A completely new 22ft model, the Perfection, was introduced towards the end of 1955. In its advertising the company was at pains to point out the high standard to which the furniture was constructed, all being veneered in Mellor's own works. The edges of all the doors were bevelled and edge banded in walnut, the front surrounds of all units were in walnut with cross banded recess panelled tops, the sideboard and drawer unit had a two-stepped bow fronted top and the roof lockers were also bow

fronted. The furniture was jig-built and resin bonded with no pins or screws used in the construction. All this was reflected in the price of £795 excluding a solid fuel stove which was available as an extra.

Production ceased around 1957 when L Mellor exchanged caravan manufacture for horticulture and became managing director of a nursery specialising in chrysanthemums, but early in 1962, with H F Wilshaw, he resuscitated the old company and production recommenced at City Road, Fenton, Stoke-on-Trent. The first model was the 22ft Winsome Mark I, joined later in the year by the Mark II and the Winsome Majestic in 26ft and 28 ft versions. The 24ft Winsome Classic followed in 1963 and touring caravans were added to the range in 1964 with 10ft, 12ft and 14ft Wizard models. Production finally ceased around 1966.

WORTH

R Worth & Sons, St Thomas Hill, Launceston, Cornwall, built caravans to customers' designs at prices ranging from £50 to £700 in 1938. The firm supplied anything 'from a screw to a complete job' and also undertook renovations, reconstructions and gas installations.

YORKSHIRE

In a 1938 advertisement, the dealers Yorkshire Caravan and Trailer Co, of Bawtry, near Doncaster, refer to 'our 19ft Bungalow Caravan'. This £105 model featured two rooms, an end kitchen and double panelling. A classified advertisement has also been found for a second hand 1947 16ft Bawtry special built by Yorkshire Caravan Co.

FOREIGN IMPORTS

COVERED WAGON

A coach shaped American van imported in small numbers by Clive Scarff of the Surrey dealers, The Nomad Caravan Co, in 1937. Equipment included Warner electric brakes, safety chains, mosquito screens, ice box, twenty gallon water tank and step-down transformer to run low voltage lighting, fan etc from a mains supply. British buyers however were deterred by the 19 and 20ft lengths and high weight. The imports ceased when the price in America rose sharply.

1937 Covered Wagon, imported from America in small numbers.

SCHULT

In a 1938 advertisement Schult Trailers Inc, Elkhart, Indiana, USA, invited enquiries from potential British manufacturers or distributors for their cara- vans, but as far as is known Schult models were never made or sold in this country.

SPORT NIETER

The 67 guinea Roamanee tent trailer was marketed by Sport Nieter Ltd, Mill Ridge, Edgware, Middlesex, in 1938-39. Closed dimensions were 7ft 6in long x 4ft 6in wide x 3ft high opening to 15ft long and 7ft high on site. A 1938 report states that brakes were extra for the British market, suggesting that the Roamanee was an imported model.

1938 Sport Nieter Roamanee – this tent trailer appears to have been an imported model, but the country of origin is not known.

SUPREMUS

The Nottingham dealers Midland Counties Caravan Co, imported Supremus models in 1938. The vans were made in Brussels by a Yorkshireman, Colonel A Wilson, whose caravan building experience was said to date back to 1921.

In total there were seven models – three trailer coaches and four streamlined vans. The trailer coaches were the 12ft Captain costing 148 guineas, 12ft 6in Major at 165 guineas and 16ft 6in Brigadier at 295 guineas, and the streamlined vans were the 175 guinea 11ft Peter Pan, 180 guinea 12ft Lady Kitty, 200 guinea 15ft Lady Sonia and 214 guinea 15ft 6in Lady Nancy. All except the Captain were double panelled with glass silk insulation and all the streamlined models had lantern roofs. The vans were steady enough on tow for passengers to travel in and were noteworthy for the high quality of their furniture. The Manchester dealers, The Times Service Stations Ltd, sold a 15ft Supremus as the Lancastrian and this van cost between £210 and £250 in 1939.

"SUPREMUS"
The WORLD'S BEST-BUILT CARAVANS & TRAILER COACHES
Supreme Examples of the Coach-Builder's Art

Glorious Balance

Perfect Towing

Weight **where it** ought to be

The strongest chassis and under-gear of ANY Caravan

Four-berthed, fully equipped, double-panelled, glass-silk insulated, Models from 165 guineas

They Challenge The World

The magnificent "BRIGADIER" (weight 25 cwt.), at 295 gns.
BUILT BY MESSRS. A. WILSON & SON, BRUSSELS
BRITISH CONCESSIONAIRES:
MIDLAND COUNTIES CARAVAN CO., SAWLEY CROSS ROADS, SHARDLOW, DERBY
(Nr. Donnington Motor Race Track) Phone: SHARDLOW 205

1938 Supremus Brigadier, made in Brussels by a Yorkshireman.

NON-PROPRIETARY CARAVANS

The term 'non-proprietary' or 'non-prop' is used to identify caravans of no known make. It covers amateur-built vans and the products of very small makers with only a local trade, no reputation and often no brand name. Some examples of advertisements for this type of van which appeared in the August 1939 issue of *The Caravan* are given below:

FOR SALE, new 2/3-berth coach-built Caravan, completely fitted out, oak finish inside, £75. B. Walker, 28, Chiltern Avenue, Bushey, Watford, Herts. Phone Watford 3636.

FOR SALE. New Trailer Caravan; 15ft. long, steel chassis, double panelled, 4-berth, 2 rooms, price £115. Terry, 23, Clarendon Road, Norwich.

Another van in this category appeared in the *Bolton Journal and Guardian* for 28th June 1935 under the headline 'Vicar's plan to help unemployed'. The 13ft 5in 4 berth was designed and built by the Vicar of Westhoughton and an unemployed man, Mr R Mayor, with the idea of getting unemployed men to take up caravan building, although whether any did is not known.

In his book *The History of the Caravan* W M Whiteman, formerly editor of *The Caravan*, describes how the housing shortage in the years immediately following the Second World War led to huge demand for any sort of caravan, however unsuitable, to live in. Despite a scarcity of almost every kind of material, component and accessory needed for building caravans, many new manufacturers started business. Some sincerely wanted to join the growing industry, some were looking to make a quick profit and then get out of the business and a great many were just unqualified and over-optimistic. Whiteman mentions finding one self-styled manufacturer in north-east London

Amateur built van and Hillman on tour in 1932. The appearance is similar to the Winchester Nimblette of 1930-31.

building a caravan in the street outside his house – having no other premises – and two young men in Surrey, trading under a dignified company name, who were building a large residential caravan in a stable with a door so low that it was doubtful whether the van could be got out when complete, even with the wheels removed.

Replying to a reader's letter about inferior quality caravans in the June 1949 issue of *The Caravan*, Whiteman stated that the magazine did not accept any make for the advertisement pages or allow it to be mentioned in the editorial pages until they had investigated it. This presumably did not extend to the magazine's classified advertisements where numerous new vans of unknown make were offered for sale – some claiming to be 'professionally built'. A few examples are given below:

February 1949
JUST COMPLETED. 16ft. equipped caravan for four persons. Would accept easy terms. Caravan Gables, Saunderton, High Wycombe.

June 1949
JUST COMPLETED. Coach-built caravan, 18ft. 4in. x 7ft. 0in. Suitable for luxury letting or private use. Three compartment, 5-berth. Dunlopillo, end kitchen, two draining boards, Calor gas, kitchen, heating, lighting. Ladies vanity dressing table drawers. Two hanging one convertible airing cupboard, many drawers. Separate lavatory with Elsan. Good headroom. Price £595, easy terms available. Seen Leigh-on-Sea, Phone 77205. Box No. 4580 c/o THE CARAVAN.

BRAND NEW CARAVAN 4-berth. Makers price £450 – my price £395. Stone, 112, Northfield Avenue, London, W.13. Phone EAL 3528.

August 1949
JUST COMPLETED. Two door 18ft. 6in. x 7ft. double panelled professionally built caravan. 4-berth, end kitchen, built in Elsan toilet. All gas fittings. Boden-Davis chassis. Ultra radio. Not yet used. Owner bought cruiser. Ideal permanent home, £625. 26, Church Road, New Mills, Derbyshire. Telephone New Mills 2173.

A BEAUTIFUL HOME on wheels, with a difference. One only, the unique design of an expert in built-in-furniture, carried out in first class craftsmanship. Double lined, ample cupboards and storage, end kitchen. Calor gas lighting and cooker, wired for electricity from the main, Pither heating stove. 16ft. long, 3 berth. Brand new, a real bargain at £650. Hemmings Joinery Works Ltd., Wiggenhall Road, Watford, Herts. 'Phone 4870.

Caravan under construction on a bomb site, Chumleigh Street, London SE5, post-WWII – possibly destined to feature in a classified advertisement in The Caravan.

INDEX OF MANUFACTURERS AND PERSONALITIES CONNECTED TO MAKES LISTED IN THE MAIN A-Z SECTION